ZIMBABWE

MOZAMBI

Gaborone

TRANSVAAL

Mafeking

VOORTREKKER
MONUMENT   ■ Pretoria
Johannesburg
Roodepoort
Soweto
Vereeniging

SWAZILAND

Potchefstroom
VAAL DAM
VAAL
RIVER   Parys   Heilbron
Kroonstad   Newcastle
Harrismith   Dundee   BLOOD RIVER
ORANGE FREE STATE   Ladysmith
imberley   PAARDEBURG   BLOUKRANS   Richard's Bay
Bloemfontein   Pietermaritzburg   TUGELA RIVER
uckhoff   LESOTHO   Durban

MOUNTAINS

NATAL

DRAKENSBERG

Port St Johns

aaff Reinet

S NEK

East London

Grahamstown

Port Elizabeth

THE REPUBLIC
OF SOUTH AFRICA

PERSPECTIVES ON SOUTHERN AFRICA

1. The Autobiography of an Unknown South African, by Naboth Mokgatle (1971)
2. Modernizing Racial Domination: *South Africa's Political Dynamics*, by Heribert Adam (1971)
3. The Rise of African Nationalism in South Africa: *The African National Congress, 1912–1952*, by Peter Walshe (1971)
4. Tales from Southern Africa, by A. C. Jordan (1973)
5. Lesotho 1970: *An African Coup Under the Microscope*, by B. M. Khaketla (1972)
6. Towards an African Literature: *The Emergence of Literary Form in Xhosa*, by A. C. Jordan (1972)
7. Law, Order, and Liberty in South Africa, by A. S. Mathews (1972)
8. Swaziland: *The Dynamics of Political Modernization*, by Christian P. Potholm (1972)
9. The South West Africa/Namibia Dispute: *Documents and Scholarly Writings on the Controversy Between South Africa and the United Nations*, by John Dugard (1973)
10. Confrontation and Accommodation in Southern Africa: *The Limits of Independence*, by Kenneth W. Grundy (1973)
11. The Rise of Afrikanerdom: *Power, Apartheid, and the Afrikaner Civil Religion*, by T. Dunbar Moodie (1975)
12. Justice in South Africa, by Albie Sachs (1973)
13. Afrikaner Politics in South Africa, 1934–1948, by Newell M. Stultz (1974)
14. Crown and Charter: *The Early Years of the British South Africa Company*, by John S. Galbraith (1975)
15. Politics of Zambia, edited by William Tordoff (1975)
16. Corporate Power in an African State: *The Political Impact of Multinational Mining Companies in Zambia*, by Richard Sklar (1975)
17. Change in Contemporary South Africa, edited by Leonard Thompson and Jeffrey Butler (1975)
18. The Tradition of Resistance in Mozambique: *The Zambesi Valley, 1850–1921*, by Allen F. Isaacman (1976)
19. Black Power in South Africa: *The Evolution of an Ideology*, by Gail Gerhart (1978)
20. Black Heart: *Gore-Brown and the Politics of Multiracial Zambia*, by Robert I. Rotberg (1977)
21. The Black Homelands of South Africa: *The Political and Economic Development of Bophuthatswana and KwaZulu*, by Jeffrey Butler, Robert I. Rotberg, and John Adams (1977)
22. Afrikaner Political Thought: *Analysis and Documents* (3 vols.), by André du Toit and Hermann Giliomee (*Volume I: 1780–1850*, 1983)

23. Angola Under the Portuguese: *The Myth and the Reality*, by Gerald Bender (1978)
24. Land and Racial Domination in Rhodesia, by Robin Palmer (1977)
25. The Roots of Rural Poverty in Central and Southern Africa, edited by Robin Palmer and Neil Parsons (1977)
26. The Soul of Mbira: *Music and Traditions of the Shona People of Zimbabwe*, by Paul Berliner (1978)
27. The Darker Reaches of Government: *Access to Information About Public Administration in England, the United States, and South Africa*, by Anthony S. Mathews (1979)
28. The Rise and Fall of the South African Peasantry, by Colin Bundy (1979)
29. South Africa: *Time Running Out*. The Report of the Study Commission on U.S. Policy Toward Southern Africa (1981)
30. The Revolt of the Hereros, by Jon M. Bridgman (1981)
31. The White Tribe of Africa: *South Africa in Perspective*, by David Harrison (1982)
32. The House of Phalo: *A History of the Xhosa People in the Days of Their Independence*, by J. B. Peires (1982)
33. Soldiers Without Politics: *Blacks in the South African Armed Forces*, by Kenneth W. Grundy (1983)
34. Education, Race, and Social Change in South Africa, by John A. Marcum (1982)
35. The Land Belongs to Us: *The Pedi Polity, the Boers and the British in the Nineteenth-century Transvaal*, by Peter Delius (1984)
36. Sol Plaatje, South African Nationalist, 1876–1932, by Brian Willan (1984)
37. Peasant Consciousness and Guerilla War in Zimbabwe: *A Comparative Study*, by Terence Ranger (1985)
38. Guns and Rain: *Guerillas and Spirit Mediums in Zimbabwe*, by David Lan (1985)
39. South Africa without Apartheid: *Dismantling Racial Domination*, by Heribert Adam and Kogila Moodley (1986)

South Africa without Apartheid

SOUTH AFRICA
WITHOUT APARTHEID
Dismantling Racial Domination

Heribert Adam

Kogila Moodley

UNIVERSITY OF CALIFORNIA PRESS

BERKELEY · LOS ANGELES · LONDON

University of California Press
Berkeley and Los Angeles, California

University of California Press, Ltd.
London, England

© 1986 by
The Regents of the University of California

Library of Congress
Cataloging-in-Publication Data

Adam, Heribert.
South Africa without apartheid.

Bibliography: p.
Includes index.
1. Apartheid—South Africa. 2. South Africa—
Race relations. I. Moodley, Kogila. II. Title.
DT763.A6248 1986   305.8'00968   86–1473
ISBN 0–520–05769–4 (alk. paper)
ISBN 0–520–05770–8 (pbk. : alk. paper)

Map of the Republic of South Africa
courtesy of the British Broadcasting Corporation,
copyrighted by David Harrison, 1981.

Printed in the United States of America
1 2 3 4 5 6 7 8 9

Contents

PREFACE   ix

INTRODUCTION   1

1. THE CONTRADICTIONS OF APARTHEID   9
   Group Formation 13, Group Boundaries 15,
   Race and Class 16, Politics and Market 17,
   Business and Apartheid 22

2. ETHNICITY, NATIONALISM, AND THE STATE   27
   Politicized Ethnicity 27, Five Types of Ethnic
   Dominance 36, Variations of Ethnicity: Afrika-
   ner and Black Nationalism 43

3. CONFLICTS IN WHITE POLITICS   58
   The Labor Racists 58, The Orthodox Ideologues
   62, The Ruling Technocrats 67, The Critical
   Moralists 73

4. CONFLICTS IN BLACK POLITICS   77
   Political Alliances 77, Explaining Political Vio-
   lence 103, Prospects for Negotiations: The
   ANC and Pretoria 117

5. COMPLIANCE WITHOUT CONSENT   129
   Legitimacy, Hegemony, and Ideology in the Eth-
   nic State 129, Compliance through Coercion
   134, Dependency and Co-Optation 142, Con-
   sumerism as a Substitute for Legitimacy 154,
   Legitimacy Reconsidered 166

6. INDUSTRIAL RELATIONS, UNIONS, AND EMPLOYMENT 170
   The Welfare State 170, Embourgeoisement and Labor Stratification 174, Trade Unions and Arbitration 179

7. A PLURAL OR A COMMON SOCIETY? 196
   Religion and Resistance 197, Economic Interdependence 203

8. POLICY IMPLICATIONS 215
   Constitutional Alternatives 215, Implications of the Group Areas Act 222, Security and Group Rights 227, Addressing Economic and Status Grievances 230, Addressing Educational Grievances 233, The Style of Accommodation 238, Reeducating the White Constituency 244

   CONCLUSION: PROSPECTS FOR AN EVOLUTIONARY TRANSITION 248

   APPENDIX: CHRONOLOGY OF EVENTS IN SOUTH AFRICA 265

   NOTES 269

   BIBLIOGRAPHY 283

   INDEX 293

   ABOUT THE AUTHORS 317

Preface

SOUTH AFRICA EVOKES A MORBID fascination. A vast literature of condemnation wallows in moral predicaments. Ambivalent friends of Pretoria respond with ever more sophisticated justifications of the unjustifiable. Foreigners cherish the easy accessibility to an English-speaking police state, where the press is critical, intellectuals are tolerated, and the repression occurs out of sight. The apartheid issue allows even diehard conservatives to look radical in a unique laboratory for social engineers. A worthy cause attracts causeless entrepreneurs. Instant experts pontificate about ready options for a creeping revolution. Some claim to seek "moral clarity" that derives from the "scale of the land and its antagonisms."[1] Many more, one suspects, secretly enjoy what Gordimer calls "the last colonial extravaganza."[2]

In which category do we fall, after a lifelong relationship with a vexed problem that defies solution? For a full answer it seems necessary to trace our concerns and biases back to our own intellectual history and to acknowledge our background, beliefs, and the friends to whom we owe a debt. At the risk of sounding narcissistic, we include brief autobiographies which may help to ground our conclusions.

Kogila Moodley spent the first twenty-five years as a member of the Indian community in colonial English Natal. Although my immediate family is relatively secular and unorthodox, we were nonetheless part of an intact traditional Hindu Tamil-speaking clan. Culture maintenance and politicization nurtured one another. Several Congress activists, among them

Monty Naicker, were regular visitors to an extended family in a Durban city home. As Congress sympathizers, members of our family engaged in civil disobedience and courted arrest during passive-resistance campaigns. We shared detailed accounts of the numerous harassments to which they were subject. At the temple, women relatives would tell in hushed voices about the latest police raid at their home in the early hours of the morning.

A cultural renaissance and a spirit of noncooperation prevailed among Indians, carried over from the colonial experience in India. It expressed itself in a resistance to Western consumption patterns and dress codes, after-school vernacular-language education, satirical political cabaret entertainments recounting the experiences of indentured laborers on the sugar plantations, and the reading of rousing revolutionary Tamil poetry. This cultural revivalism strengthened an alternative self-definition for an oppressed community. As children we attended political rallies and marched in defiance campaigns. At high school, we participated in rallies against the Group Areas Act and joined in fund-raising for the Treason trial.

Later, I was among the last generation of the few "non-White" students to attend an "open" university, where the policy of the National Union of South African Students (NUSAS), at its progressive height, supported academic integration and social segregation. At the University of Natal, social science courses were taught by a varied faculty, including C. P. Jooste, Hamish Dickie-Clark, and Fatima Meer. Two individuals exerted a profound influence on me in these formative years. Leo Kuper, one of the most intellectually demanding, principled, politically uncompromising, and committed sociologists, was one of the few who insisted on teaching only to racially integrated classes in the otherwise White section of the university campus, at Howard College. Pierre van den Berghe's comparative race relations research refreshed and addressed our political commitment.

Upon returning from two years of graduate studies in

Michigan, I had the opportunity to examine the operation of "tribal academia." The only academic employment available for a person in my racial category was as a lecturer at the then newly founded all-Indian university, staffed mostly by paternalistic Afrikaners, arrogant English colonials, and a few cowering Indians. The contrast between the non-authoritarian, casual American campus life and the stiff racial hierarchy at home proved mind-boggling. The Rector's secretary unabashedly warned against using the White women's toilet; Indians were asked to refrain from playing tennis in interracial company and to restrict Indian use of the tennis courts to Mondays and Wednesdays. Well-intentioned White colleagues made a point of inviting me alone to tea on the day when they entertained their White colleagues to dinner in the evening. It would have been difficult to reciprocate a dinner invitation in any case, since our family home was being expropriated under the Group Areas Act. The Durban City Council sold the property, at a handsome profit, to a Portuguese immigrant.

My interest in the sociology of knowledge and in the work of Max Weber led me to participate in an academic exchange program in West Germany, under the aegis of the Deutsche Akademischer Austauschdienst. This afforded me the opportunity to spend time in West Berlin and at the Max Weber archives in Munich. My subsequent marriage to a foreigner, the co-author of this book, not only improved my German but extended my social science perspectives from Weberian sociology to the Frankfurt School. My earlier work dealt mainly with issues in colonial education and the political behavior of minorities; in recent years it has broadened to include Canadian ethnic relations and educational policy analysis. Throughout, I have sustained contact with South African developments through frequent research and family visits.

Vancouver, our home for the past twenty years—initially an opportunistic compromise by two cultural emigrants—has proven to be a valuable base for international research and academic mobility. At the edge of a faded empire, the city has welcomed immigrants from all over the world (including 10,000 South Africans) who have added cosmopolitan vitality to an Anglo cultural hierarchy.

The other author, Heribert Adam, remembers an elementary school teacher in Nazi uniform giving us nine-year-olds patriotic lectures that conflicted with the values taught in a strict Catholic home. The daily Allied air raids, the years of chaos and hunger after the collapse of fascism, and the official reeducation in democracy at all German high schools inevitably politicized. When I refused the predetermined career in the celibate priesthood, the ground was laid for a less conformist and more autonomous life. In this endeavor to transcend and comprehend the narrow confines of a traditional middle-class German upbringing, I owe much to my teacher and thesis advisor Theodor W. Adorno, called "Doktorvater" in the patriarchal German tradition. With exposure to Jürgen Habermas, Ludwig von Friedeburg, Max Horkheimer, Helge Pross, and Manfred Teschner at the Frankfurt School, I was steeped in an unorthodox radical political tradition at an impressionable stage. From 1961 to 1965 I formally joined this illustrious group as an associate at the Institute and later had occasional contact with two permanent Frankfurt emigrants, Leo Loewenthal and Herbert Marcuse, during a year-long Berkeley scholarship. The Frankfurt Institute in the early sixties was an extraordinary mixture of encyclopedic knowledge and socialist commitment, intellectual arrogance and esoteric speculation. Compared with the vast eclectic imagination of Adorno, many of my North American colleagues later seemed like pedestrian social engineers with their economistic reductionism, positivistic reformism or, worse, apolitical empiricism.

Later, by chance I spent almost two years in Southern Africa, teaching full-time at Natal University in 1967. It did not endear me to the authorities, who were doubly suspicious because of my illegal courtship of my future wife at that time. Subsequent visa applications were refused. The experience of apartheid had taught me the limits of critical theory. Amazingly, none of the Frankfurt School members had ever been to any Third World country. In the Eurocentric philosophical tradition of German Marxism, issues such as racism, colonialism, and underdevelopment existed only as abstract aspects of grand theory. An attempt to apply familiar theories of fascism and psychoanalytic explanations of anti-Semitism to racial discrimination in South Africa soon made it obvious that the conceptualizations did not fit settler societies in which democratically organized ethnic minorities had entrenched their dominance over excluded indigenous subordinates. The settlers had themselves become indigenous. Nor could the more orthodox Marxist theories of imperialism, dependency, or internal colonialism easily come to grips with the peculiar subjectivity of dominators and dominated alike.

The result of this experiential challenge was a book published first in German under a title that translates as *South Africa: Sociology of a Race Society*[3] and later expanded in English as *Modernizing Racial Domination.*[4] The study argued both against the then prevailing liberal emphasis on an irrational, intransigent South African racism in conflict with a nonracial capitalism, and against the popular prophecies of imminent revolution. South Africa is often seen as the last outpost of an outdated colonialism; instead, Afrikaner minority rule should be understood as the flexible, adaptable domination of a pragmatic oligarchy, perhaps the future model of efficient political policing. This controversial thesis encountered many vocal critics across the entire political spectrum; nevertheless, *Modernizing Racial Domination* became something of a classic, with four reprints in subsequent years. The basic argument has been proven remarkably correct by events. What were mere rumblings from a few technocrats in the late sixties have become the ruling tendencies one and a half decades later.

In a book, *Ethnic Power Mobilized,*[5] co-authored with an Afrikaner friend, Hermann Giliomee, during a year together at Yale, the reasons for the cleavages within Afrikanerdom were traced and the reactions assessed in the light of the rising costs of traditional domination. The present study takes this theme further by evaluating the demise of apartheid and by a much closer focus on Black politics.

The new analysis departs from Frankfurt School theorizing by giving much greater weight to conscious political action. Where critical theory emphasized the constraints on human agency, to the extent of near-determinism, here policy choices by conscious actors are stressed as equally decisive in shaping historical outcomes. Within constraints, both resisters and the agents of control can choose among several strategies. Neither side is a mere prisoner of circumstances. It is within these parameters that South African power relations are probed in their many nuances.

This study is based on data from a great range of sources: (1) regular reading during the past five years of most of the essential primary sources published in and on South Africa—editorials, leaflets, daily commentaries by the South African Broadcasting Corporation (SABC), lively activist literature, measured academic journals.

(2) Participant observation—election campaigns, sessions of Parliament, day-long Indian weddings, formal conferences. We went with van Zyl Slabbert on the hustings in Cape Town, watched Jerry Coovadia chair crowded United Democratic Front (UDF) boycott meetings, and observed Mahmoud Rajab, our brother-in-law and a former member of the President's Council, drum up support for his candidacy.

(3) Formal and informal interviews—separately or together—with about 140 opinion leaders on South Africa, from African National Congress (ANC) representatives in New York, London, and Lusaka to senior civil servants and generals in Pretoria, M. G. Buthelezi in Ulundi and N. Motlana in Soweto, half a dozen Black managers of Anglo in Johannesburg and sugar barons in Natal, editors in Cape Town and diplomats in Windhoek, Africa experts in the U.S. State Department and their counterparts in Ottawa and Bonn. During 1983–1985 we engaged in exhaustive discussions with spokespersons of all Black political tendencies and with union officials. We visited resettlement camps in the Ciskei and talked to our beleaguered sociology colleagues at Fort Hare; we were escorted around decentralized growth points in Zu-

luland and found ourselves in the midst of a student protest
against a conference at the university in Ngoye.

(4) Week-long systematic group discussions with ten classes
in African high schools in Umlazi and Kwa Mashu and with
their Indian counterparts in other Durban suburbs, an exercise we repeated with groups of African students from the
Natal Medical School and student teachers at the training colleges at Ntuzuma and Springfield. The focused group discussions—some lasting one and a half hours, others three—involved 180 students who also filled out questionnaires at the
end. The answers of this sample as well as two similar commercial pilot surveys with selected workers in Johannesburg
enter this study as background information. The responses
are not presented explicitly because the relatively small sam-
ples were not representative.

In this context we owe special thanks to Oscar Dhlomo and
Pat Samuels, who introduced us to the school principals, who
then allowed us unhindered access to their students and staff.
They understood that the group discussions could not be in-
hibited by the presence of even well-meaning authority figures, and they introduced us most graciously to an initially
suspicious audience. We are particularly grateful to Mr. Ma-
sondo, the principal of Menzi High, to Mr. Mthembu, the vice-
principal of Umbumbulo College of Education in Umlazi, to
Mr. Nhlapo, the principal of Isibonelo High School in Kwa
Mashu, and to Mrs. Msimang, the forceful rector of Ntuzuma
College of Education. We only hope that their students
learned as much from us as we did from them; if so, the time
off from regular instruction was surely not wasted. If there is
any realm where more privileged outsiders and particularly
foreigners can have a marked and welcome impact it is in as-
sisting as teachers or with other contributions to an education-
ally deprived environment, in which the students are so motivated to absorb relevant information that only their lack of
exposure limits them at present.

We are also grateful to Pat Nthembu for organizing a most
informative session with her friends from the Natal Medical

School, and to Bobby Godsell and Mark Nigel for facilitating discussions with workers and management at the Elandsrand Mine.

During our two decades of active involvement with South Africa, service on the Buthelezi Commission by Adam, numerous conferences in South Africa and elsewhere, and dozens of lectures from Stellenbosch to Harare, many colleagues have become personal friends. Among the South Africans with whom we had the most intellectual interaction, the following stand out. Hermann Giliomee's energy in night-long debates, in journalistic education, and on the tennis court never fails to impress. He, his wife Annette, and their children are for us the epitome of hospitality and Afrikaner authenticity without its "master symbols." Few people in Cape Town have more savvy, and more public hopes resting on their shoulders, than F. Van Zyl Slabbert. Although he is constantly on show, even when we were jogging along Kirstenbosch mountain, he manifests a relaxed warmth, particularly in the company of his wife, Jane. We shared frequent meals and ideas with many other pillars of the critical establishment in the Cape, among whom were André and Mareta du Toit, Tony Heard, Wilmot James, Jairam Reddy, Pieter le Roux, Mike Savage, H. W. van der Merwe, David and Virginia Welsh, Johan Degenaar, and Francis Wilson.

In Natal, our "home territory," the extended family always absorbs us first. Devi and Mahmoud Rajab bring us up to date on local developments. The little time left we spend discussing politics with Tony and Libby Ardington, Jerry Coovadia, Dushane Grice, Gavin Maasdorp, Tony Mathews, Fatima Meer, Pat Poovalingham, the Rustomjees, Lawrence Schlemmer, Dennys Schreiner, and Chris and Pam Saunders. On a beautiful Sunday afternoon we once walked along a deserted South Coast beach with the family of Oscar Dhlomo, whose quiet dignity and political sagacity we learned to appreciate. With "the chief" we had several more formal encounters. Knowing the sincere commitment of the persons involved on both sides in a growing rift between liberation strategies, we find their antagonism tragic. As outside insiders, we can only

attempt to be particularly fair in explaining their political positions. This is no easy task when applied, for instance, to Rowley Arenstein, a gentle human puzzle whom no label fits. The
Durban seventy-five-year-old advocate is one of the eleven
persons still banned since the 1960s for being a communist.
Although he would not deny the label, one could hardly find
a more sober critic of Moscow, and of all correct party lines.
Simply ignoring his banning order, he now champions Inkatha's cause but gives legal advice to any victim or political or-
ganizer who wishes to benefit from his vast experience. Over
the years we have spent days with him arguing, and tape-re-
cording his memories about struggles long past. There are
other shrewd, undogmatic observers in Southern Africa
whom we can count among our candid sources: John Kane-
Berman, the astute and articulate director of the Institute of
Race Relations; Henni Serfontein, a genuine investigative and
imaginative journalist; John Dugard, a liberal legal pillar in
Johannesburg; and Don Mothobi, top civil servant in Harare.

Among the South African experts closer to home we could
always count on creative dialogue with four old friends: Theo
Hanf in Freiburg, Stanley Uys in London, Pierre van den
Berghe in Seattle, and Arend Lijphart in La Jolla. All four
read an earlier version of this manuscript and made valuable
suggestions.

Among our friends in Vancouver, Hamish Dickie-Clark, a
nostalgic South African emigrant, let himself be used as a constant sounding board. With his thorough grasp of theory, he
clarified many ambiguous issues and reinforced our perspectives. Other associates—Maurice Halperin, Kasval Chetty,
Monte Bryer, Tissa Fernando, Yuwa Wong—willingly allowed
themselves to be drawn into discussions on South Africa.

The book would not be in its present readable format without the skillful editing of Jane-Ellen Long and the professional advice of William McClung, the editorial director of the
University of California Press. What made us apprehensive at
first turned out to be a vast improvement. Anita Mahoney at
Simon Fraser University contributed to the result by typing
the manuscript with unfailing accuracy under the pressure of

deadlines. The flexible assistance by Jean Jordan in the Sociology Department and the unbureaucratic arrangements by a supportive Dean of Arts, Bob Brown at Simon Fraser, were greatly appreciated. At the University of British Columbia, Dan Birch, Acting Vice-President, and congenial colleagues provided an environment conducive to writing.

We owe gratitude to a generous research grant (410–81–0456) from the Social Science Research Council of Canada, that above all defrayed the high travel costs during a three-year period. We hope that the book will pay its debt by contributing to a more informed debate in North America about South Africa. It is our contention, nonetheless, that events in South Africa are little influenced by America, but they increasingly influence United States policy. Therefore our study does not primarily hope to affect the foreign policy discussion in the United States but aims much more at contributing to the domestic debate in the post-apartheid state.

Finally, the book is dedicated to Percy and Amartham Moodley. They belong to the previous generation of apartheid victims, whose guiding philosophy was never to complain. Instead, they made their niche despite forced relocation, and managed to educate four children at universities abroad at great personal sacrifice, to compensate for the insularity of South African Black education. They—our parents and in-laws—have retained their pride and dignity despite the abuses of discrimination. We stand in awe of such achievement and at the same time hope that our children, and those rebelling in South Africa now, never need to emulate their extraordinary example.

Introduction

SOUTH AFRICA WITHOUT APARTHEID explores a
society and state in rapid transition. It addresses three fundamental questions: How has the morally reprehensible
apartheid order in South Africa survived so long? What will
bring about its demise and how will it vanish? What kind of
society, state, and racial relations can be expected beyond
apartheid?

Our analysis synthesizes a vast array of data in a wide-rang-
ing academic debate. It is not a travel report, an impression-
istic account, or a running commentary on fast-moving events.
It is an interpretative, historically oriented study that employs
empirical data as a means for understanding and modifying
qualitative reasoning. The political theorizing at the core of
our analysis, though it may initially seem daunting, should
leave the reader with deeper insights into the problems of the
political economy of race relations in South Africa.

We have, however, attempted to minimize social science jar-
gon to address politically interested general readers and those
in a position to influence the course of events in South Africa.
For the same reason we have given only a selected critique of
the extensive literature. Our major focus is on current, controversial issues. To the probable charge of "presentism" we
can only respond that the historical dimension underlies our
analysis throughout.

Our study departs from standard textbooks on South Africa, which largely confine themselves to institutional analysis.[1] Much of the political dynamics now takes place outside

formal institutions. This extra-legal and extra-parliamentary activity beneath the visible political terrain increasingly shapes the fate of the institutions, from the value of the currency to the prophylactic reactions of the state. We try to capture the sentiments that will prevail after the curfew hour has arrived. We let the major actors speak for themselves but also probe beyond their public resolutions. Their cognitive maps are tested against reality as we evaluate it on the basis of manifold other evidence.

Readers seeking confirmation of strongly held views may be disappointed. Our eclectic approach denies us the comforting certainty of predetermined answers. No social analysis, however, can claim objectivity; *pace* Max Weber, our biases and political preferences inevitably color even our most academic reasoning. We cannot, therefore, claim "to avoid commitment to any political viewpoint or ideology."[2] We can nevertheless attempt, as politically inactive but politically aware social scientists, to achieve a scrupulously realistic assessment of evidence reaching beyond the propaganda of activists. No one can claim value-free scholarship, especially in a conflict where a stance of neutrality can only be interpreted as moral indifference. In any attempt to sketch a solution to the problems of South Africa, however, moral indignation must be balanced with political pragmatism; that is, existing prejudices, vested interests, and power relations must be taken into account. Analysts must guard against projecting their own good intentions onto political actors.

In this sense the study comprises a much more specific and politically oriented explanation than the partisan accounts of activists. Such an exercise is only worthwhile if one believes, *contra* theories of economic determinism or historical inevitability, that wise political leadership and rational choices can affect final outcomes. At the same time we attempt not to lose sight of a central assumption in critical theory, namely, the extraordinary manipulability of people in technologically advanced capitalistic societies. Chapter 5 focuses on the changing techniques of sophisticated control when most attention is focused on the recurrent use of primitive coercion. The questions of whether and how capitalism can save itself and of what kind of socialist alternative is available in this unprecedented legitimation crisis serves as the guiding thread of our study.

We believe, however, that a critical explanation of the major contradictions in current policy is a precondition for pragmatic policy recommendations. The recommendations themselves are more implicit than explicit; a firm grasp of the issues will inevitably lead readers to draw their own conclusions. Thus, the study is a "think-piece" rather than a detailed prescription. Toward this end, we scrutinize the nature of resistance as well as specific obstacles faced by the opposition movements. Instead of falling into the common error of romanticizing the forces of emancipation and overestimating their powers, we analyze their weaknesses, cleavages, and strategic mistakes. Although this attempt lays us open to the charge of giving comfort to the oppressor and belittling the heroic efforts of the victims, we feel that a thorough understanding of the constraints on resistance ultimately serves liberation goals better than self-deception can. Such understanding can at least prevent some martyrdoms and perhaps make opposition more efficient. We would prefer to be judged right for the "wrong" reasons—detachment, realism— than be proven wrong for the "right" reasons—identification, commitment.

On the other hand, we are conscious of the danger of a post-moral mentality that has grown numb. We do not wish to turn victims into statistics, into "people with tears wiped off." The daily exercise in moral indifference that is life in South Africa is epitomized in the technocratic cynicism that experiments with societies in the name of control. We try to balance this public discourse with the undercurrents of unreported, private sentiments that always inform our abstract, analytical reasoning. For this reason we have included some eyewitness accounts of typical events.

Our emphasis on the strength of the state forces must not be taken as a denial of the significance of opposition. The time is long past when the South African state held the reins and the oppressed majority merely reacted. Blacks are not pawns; they shape their lives according to their own designs and opportunities, ubiquitous regulations notwithstanding. Even in the most regimented setting the acquiescence of the servants has proved to be a myth perpetuated by the masters: suffering is rarely tolerated passively, though the hidden striving for release or the simple struggle to maintain dignity and identity may seldom be recognized. However, good intentions or the justness of the cause does not exempt the academic analyst from attempting an honest assessment of the balance of power. The continuous crisis of an intolerable system has been diagnosed, and bemoaned, for decades. The system's downfall has been predicted many times, and undoubtedly the vulnerability of racial minority rule has increased, yet decades of brave opposition efforts have failed. Perhaps, we argue, liberation must be reconceived as a far less spectacular affair than both its proponents and its detractors would like to admit.

Political activists cannot afford to entertain such skepticism: it might well paralyze liberation efforts. Submerged in the day-to-day struggle, the activist clings to all signs of progress to sustain the mobilization, just as powerholders tend to underestimate the smoldering fire in the confidence that they can control the flames. Dispassionate evaluation seems the task of the noncombatant. And such evaluation is essential, for though devout commitments act as a powerful catalyst for action, wishful thinking is no substitute for sober analysis.

With the aim of providing such an analysis, our study focuses on ethnicity and the state with a special emphasis on the problems of legitimacy of "ethnic states." Thus we devote considerable attention to ethnic conflicts outside South Africa. We illustrate the meaning of ethnicity and race relations in other divided societies to afford a comparison with South Africa—not, however, in order to lend an air of respectability and normality to apartheid. Contrary to the conservative claim that South Africa represents just another example of a universal racial or cultural incompatibility of meaning, the comparison highlights the unique outrages committed by Pretoria, unmatched in worse repression elsewhere. In addition, from other conflicts we can draw practical lessons that an exclusive focus on South Africa might cause us to overlook.

Many studies grapple with similar issues in the South African context. A vast Marxist literature assumes that, for the most part, capital accumulation accounts for the dynamics of change. Labor requirements determine racial policies. State coercion varies in response to changing modes of production. According to the Poulantzan tradition, these factions align themselves—not without difficulty. Dominant power blocs are able to press their conflicting priorities according to historical hegemonies: in the initial period of capital accumulation in South Africa, the mining houses set up compounds and were responsible for the development of a migrant labor force; in their competition for the cheap labor of Black workers, the farmers created labor tenancy and squatting; in turn, a threatened White working class demanded state protection, through job reservations and wage differentials, from this cheap labor force. A collaborating ethnic-state coalition solved these conflicting demands, first in its segregation policy, later through coercive apartheid.

This school came to be (falsely) labeled *revisionist* because it was supposed to have revised the dominant liberal doctrine of incompatibility between expanding capitalism and apartheid. (In the classical European-Marxist tradition, *revisionsim* refers to a denial of the role of the proletariat and the Soviet Union as leaders of historical change.) Apartheid, far from being irrational, serves the interests of the dominant class, the revisionists argued; apartheid and capitalism are inseparable, the collapse of one inevitably leading to the demise of the other. The unique alliance of capitalism and racism in South Africa facilitates the ascendancy of a nonracial socialism, surmise the more optimistic proponents of the school.

In standard Marxian terms, the state merely reacts to, coordinates, or manages crises in the interests of maintaining the overall system. An implicit economic reductionism denies political autonomy. Less orthodox writers in the 1980s, therefore, stress the "symbiotic" relationship between state and capital.[3] In the Gramscian tradition the institutional independence of state bureaucracies was rediscovered. Stanley Greenberg contends that in establishing the machinery of control the state has overextended itself and eroded its coherence.[4] Unlike the governments of other Western societies, where state and market are perceived as separate, in the racial South African (and the Israeli) state, according to Greenberg, the government cannot act as an effective neutral economic arbiter because of its involvement with the private economic sphere. Moreover, the politically unincorporated cannot identify with the ethnic state; hence all labor relations, as well as other conflicts, are inevitably politicized. Paradoxically, it was precisely this contradiction between ideology and economic imperative on which the earlier liberal writers pinned their hopes for the downfall of apartheid.

These reformulations open the state institutions to empirical inquiry rather than treating them as mere appendices to capital interests.[5] However, to extend the concept of conflicting reactions from the private realm to the now equally autonomous public arena involves further fallacies. It overestimates the implications of political conflict within the bureaucracy and prematurely hypothesizes a "debilitating vulnerability" for the embattled state. It also overestimates the importance of the state's loss of legitimacy, disregarding the value of intact coercive means. Independent interests of bureaucratic actors alone do not unravel a state on whose existence the competing bureaucracies depend in the first place.

While the focus on the uneven institutional development of relatively autonomous bureaucracies amounts to an advance over the previous neglect or monolithic treatment of the state in Marxist theory, such a focus still adheres to a reductionist paradigm, albeit this time a bureaucratic one, by failing to treat ideologies and issues of political culture as independent variables rather than as derivatives of underlying interests. Individuals are not mere carriers of attitudes, qualifications, or institutional interests; they experience the world, interpret and mediate social reality, and act on their perceptions. Historical processes do not occur outside individuals but through them and are thereby circumscribed by subjective possibilities as well as objective constraints.

In this study we emphasize the cultures and ideologies that determine how changing interests are perceived, redefined, and negotiated. While not discounting the valuable insights of neo-Marxist class and more recent institutional analysis, we are suspicious of the neat, compartmentalized paradigms of class or state actors who always know what their real interests are and act accordingly. We give equal weight to the idiosyncratic, the manipulated consciousness. Such subjectivity, shaped by multifaceted, distinct life histories, of course runs the risk of drawing contradictory or at least confusing conclusions. But the distinct individual and collective histories ("identity") that account for social behavior can be ignored only at the peril of developing unanchored, abstract insights.

Frederick Johnstone, in reviewing the burgeoning literature with a class approach, writes of the "paradigmatic prominence" that these focuses on the cheap-labor system and on capitalist exploitation, coercion, and resistance have acquired in studies of South Africa.[6] They do answer some questions convincingly; however, the class approach, as Johnstone admits, has yet to prove its insightfulness on issues of meaning, religion, or identity. These "ideal interests" (in the Weberian sense) are as real as material ones. To relegate them to the realm of epiphenomena imperils political action. It is our hope that the present study will illuminate the interplay of material and ideal interests.

Unfortunately, in the critical writing on capitalist exploitation in South Africa little realistic analysis exists concerning appropriate political strategies and tactics. Merely denouncing the system by reciting its atrocities in turgid and repetitive tracts remains an apolitical exercise. The rediscovery of the relative autonomy of the state in neo-Marxist literature has yet to lead to a concomitant appreciation of the potential for change afforded by the inevitable contradictions. The common tendency to think in absolutes—increased repression versus revolutionary liberation, cosmetic reforms versus fundamental change—absolves the writers from attempting to imagine how to exploit the state's contradictions and to utilize the new openings for the opposition. Another major goal of this book, then, is policy analysis with some pragmatic validity (i.e., a determination of what can actually be done), as well as inquiry into what kind of liberation is likely to occur.

Finally, we unashamedly confess a reformist bias: the minimization of suffering here and now seems to us a worthy goal even though it may occur at the expense of a more noble dream; to postpone small-scale reform in the hope that present misery will accelerate a more fundamental transformation to us smacks not only of cynicism but of immorality. Indeed, it is true that apartheid cannot be reformed but must be eradicated. Yet this dismantling of a political system does not necessarily require the destruction of a society. It is an illusion that the alternative can only emerge from the ashes. If this were so, it would hardly be worth the price. At the same time, real reform must be rescued from its present proponents in Pretoria. The demystification of reform rhetoric must be high on the agenda of anyone interested in speedy evolution.

I

The Contradictions
of Apartheid

ON THE TWENTY-FIFTH ANNIVERSARY of the infamous Sharpeville incident of 21 March 1960, South African police, without provocation or warning, killed twenty unarmed Black marchers at Langa township in the Eastern Cape. Most were shot in the back. The outnumbered contingent of White and Black police with two armored vehicles felt that the Blacks, on their way to a funeral, would threaten the White township.

The repetition of this crudest form of state violence against politicized youngsters and workers threatened by recession after two and a half decades of anti-apartheid opposition suggests that little has changed in the repression by a minority regime. The rulers command the guns, and the subordinates are left with no alternatives but to submit or perish.

Yet this simplistic conclusion overlooks a decisive change that has come about in the 1980s. In the early 1960s, apartheid laws were tightened; today racial policies are disintegrating and are decisively challenged on various fronts. Momentum has been building to alter the social face of South Africa. A conjunction of forces has emerged that is proving far more powerful than the fledgling resistance of the 1960s. Its force results both from the increased politicization of the oppressed and from the abandonment, by important ruling-class elements, of past policies. Minority domination, no longer standing on a solid base, finds itself in a state of ideological and strategic fragmentation. Gone are the confident dogmatism and ideological solidarity of the Verwoerdian era. Contradictory policies rather than consistent repression characterize state behavior. A deeply split ruling class now makes concessions forced by the anticipation of worse alternatives and searches for legitimacy alternately with insisting on upholding past practices. This fluctuation opens new avenues for the forces of emancipation, both through unanticipated consequences of new policies and as a result of formerly excluded groups being drawn into the ruling sector.

The South African state is in the process of a fundamental reorganization. Its constituent groups have formed new alliances that transcend the monolithic conception of Black/White antagonism. It would therefore be misleading to see these developments as a White capitulation and a Black victory. The scenario is far more complex and includes many actors with a number of different interests and goals.

In the significant restructuring of domination, White control is only being revised, not abolished. Exclusive apartheid ideology has been modified to allow political co-optation of the Colored and Indian middle groups, who control substantial administrative areas of their "own affairs." African collaborating elites are cultivated at the regional and municipal levels. The previously rigid social distance has given way, permitting some integration. In order to facilitate labor negotiations, Black unions have been recognized and bargaining procedures institutionalized. In the process, White unions and Afrikaner farmers have been dropped from state protection. In an informal political realignment, English business interests have initially moved closer to the government camp, which shed its most extreme right-wing ideologues in a formal split of the National Party in 1982.

This reorganization of central political institutions occurs at the behest of the ruling party and is aimed at strengthening Nationalist Party hegemony. Political power-sharing in the sense of diminished Afrikaner control has not taken place. However, the constituency of the dominant section has been extended to include conservatives from other racial groups. This move amounts to a symbolic deracialization of domination, while the racial order was simultaneously entrenched in constitutional reforms. Although some changes were made out of economic necessity, the major aim of the restructuring is to forestall revolution: controlled change is promoted in order to avert fundamental change. This counter-revolutionary intent, above all, accounts for the "revolution from above." It could be called technocratic liberation.

It is wrong to dismiss this policy as simply cosmetic and devoid of significant consequences. Neither designed according to a grand blueprint nor able to control its (unintended) consequences, the technocratic process bungles along, shaped by many pressures and unanticipated constraints. A government is not a monolithic administration, and it is often out of the interstices of bureaucratic planning and contradictory policies that real change emerges.

Neoapartheid, as the new trends have been labeled by many skeptics, is above all reflected in a new terminology and administrative style. Reform has replaced maintenance of traditional racial discrimination. The expressed ideal is that consensus politics be substituted for racial coercion. The promise of cooperation is dangled and harmony is assured. Stability and economic progress have become priorities. Prosperity is no longer defined solely in terms of White interests but is seen as interdependent with Black improvements. The new South African nationalism includes, in theory, all people living in the country.

For the first time the permanence of the Black urban population has been formally acknowledged. Leasehold, even freehold, rights for this group outside "homelands" have been recognized. In the Cape, the Colored labor preference policy that discriminated against Africans has been abolished and the legal position of township dwellers equalized with those who live in the rest of the country. The program of relocations has been held in abeyance.[1] "Orderly urbanization" is supposed to replace discriminatory influx control. The policy of denationalization has been reviewed and the question of Black citizenship has been reopened.[2] It is officially admitted that urban Blacks at present have no adequate channels through which to exercise political influence. "Negotiations" with all representative leaders inside *and* outside existing institutions are to guide the constitutional development of Blacks. Interracial politics in common parties, previously banned, has been allowed again. Sex across the color line has also been legalized, although members of mixed marriages are not exempt from myriads of other racial regulations. At present no changes of the Group Areas Act are envisaged, although Blacks are allowed to trade (but not to live) in the central business districts of cities.

This reform program emphasizes efficiency and merit at the expense of ideology, promising compromises instead of intransigent insistence on past policy. Leading policymakers portray themselves as technocrats, insisting that all disputes can be solved by applying rational criteria. Depoliticization of contentious decision-making is flaunted. Commissions and scientific inquiries into controversial problems abound. The technocratic vision amounts to a messianic scientism: all problems are seen as solvable by the proper application of superior knowledge. This new technocracy is in its own way as arrogant as its racist predecessor, although it is no longer blind to the threat posed to its power.

In its corporate, technocratic self-image the South African polity emulates most Western industrialized states. The government parts company with liberal democracies, however, in its vision of communalism. Instead of individual enfranchisement, South Africa insists on a group democracy: group rights are institutionalized to insure self-determination in a multination state. Minorities, policymakers claim, will be protected from the permanent domination of the majority. Because a one-person one-vote system in a divided society is assumed merely to reaffirm existing group divisions, a very large majority of Whites object to the institution of universal franchise, equating a Westminster system of "winner takes all" with political suicide and as a threat to group survival.

Internationally, oligarchic rule and authoritarian corporatism are not considered illegitimate per se. Almost three-quarters of the world's 160 independent states are pseudo-democratic and dictatorial entities with sham elections in which the ruling oligarchy cannot be challenged. In many states ethnic minorities permanently rule over ethnic majorities or exclude effective political participation by ethnic outgroups. The South African state, however, differs from authoritarian governments elsewhere in fundamental respects that make it an illegitimate polity and an outcast among the nations of the world. The essence of South Africa's illegitimacy lies in three aspects of its corporatism: (1) imposed group membership; (2) legalized racial-group boundaries; and (3) the convergence of race and class. Each decisive feature needs to be reviewed in turn and the implications for intergroup relations drawn.

Group Formation

Unlike any other country with ethnic conflict, South Africa imposes group membership from without. In divided societies elsewhere, individuals voluntarily align themselves with their ethnic groups. In South Africa, in contrast, self-identification is not permitted. If a group identity is not self-chosen, why should its members want to preserve it? The imposition of an identity on subordinates by the superordinate groups inevitably leads to its rejection. An imposed identity is a stigma, not a source of pride. Any system that imposes identities, therefore, cannot expect approval even if it guarantees equal rights. If the formation of the group is itself considered an affront to its alleged members, the principle of group rights becomes meaningless. There is little evidence that in South Africa, apart from the ruling sector and perhaps some rural segments of the Black population, the people have internalized their official labels. In addition, the official policy of collective denationalization of those South African citizens who are deemed to belong to a separate state clearly violates international law.

Imposed group membership represents a particularly invidious distinction if the group does not differ culturally from those who decide on the label. This is the case with the so-called Coloreds. For "brown Afrikaners" with a history, language, and religion identical to those of White Afrikaners, no discernible different ethnic criteria exist. And yet even American race-relations experts fall into the apartheid trap by differentiating South African Coloreds from the similar case of American Blacks: "The Cape Colored of South Africa, in contrast to American Negroes, do constitute a separate subnation that was brought into being by race crossing."[3]

It is of course true that a long history of discrimination and stigmatization can in itself create a group identity. However, only the victims can legitimately decide to perpetuate the consciousness of persecution. This crucial problem of *assigned* group identities is unrecognized by the propagandists who declare South Africa to be a society of minorities. "In political terms," pontificates the SABC, "there is no real dispute about the two defining characteristics of the South African situation. They are, first, the existence of a variety of groups with a strong sense of their identity and, second, the inextricable interdependence of all those groups."[4] The government assumes that these categories of people "demand guarantees on their future and insist on control over their own affairs."[5] But the low percentage of participation in the Colored, Indian, and urban Black elections clearly demonstrates that these people have little interest in their artificially defined group affairs. Since political participation is only allowed on an assigned group basis it is rejected altogether.

In short, any future South African constitutional system of group rights that is not based on self-association will have a built-in illegitimacy, even if the group members enjoy equal franchise, equal state allocations, and equal power and rights. If, however, the basis is self-identification, communalism, consociationalism, or group democracy may well be considered forms of political representation as legitimate in a divided society as is individual political incorporation.

An extension of the present political system to include Blacks is thus unlikely to bestow lasting legitimacy upon the system. Even if Pretoria succeeded in attracting Black so-called real leaders into the administration of the country at the executive level, they still would hold their position as Blacks. Representatives of an invidious category would be challenged for perpetuating an offensive system. It is not

Blacks as Blacks in the cabinet that can make the difference, but who delegated them, how they were elected, and why they were chosen.

Group Boundaries

Racial and biological criteria for group membership are institutionalized in South Africa. As has often been pointed out, it is the only country in the world that has legalized racial stratification. While all societies with a multiracial population practice racialism to some degree, they do not officially endorse racial distinctions as criteria for differential rights. In fact most such societies have adopted policies of increasing integration. Where racial distinctions are upheld, as in affirmative action programs, it is for the purpose of eradicating racial injustice rather than perpetuating it. In the wake of the reaction to German fascism and of the strong anti-racist currents in the anti-colonial movement, South Africa remains the sole bastion of a White minority ruling over a disfranchised majority defined by racial criteria.

From this perspective, the South African case is more than a conflict between a local oligarchy and its disfranchised subjects. White South Africans rarely understand the revulsion other people feel toward their racial system. South Africa lends itself to ideological identifications. Apathy here is difficult to sustain; neutrality becomes immoral. Black Americans relive the civil rights struggle in Soweto. Progressive Germans fight fascism in Pretoria because their parents supported Hitler at home. White liberals in South Africa expunge their country's colonial record. South Africa allows purity.

But could not the dominant racial group also claim rights as a conscious ethnic entity? Why should a "White nation" be considered illegitimate? Samuel Huntington has supported the Nationalist Afrikaner view that South Africa represents a society of racial communities rather than a society of individuals. He has allied himself with the assertion that "racial communities also have moral claims and rights" that should be recognized in law and practice.[6] However, as has been argued, such a claim can only be upheld when the members of the racial communities identify with their categorizations. Such identification is lacking among all spokespersons of the non-White population, who, on the contrary, reject racial labeling. The very need for legislation for four racial groups testifies to the non-voluntary nature of the groupings. Ironically, in South Africa the official racial categorization has contributed to the rejection of ethnic boundaries that perhaps would otherwise have been supported voluntarily.

Three and a half decades of formal apartheid preceded by a long period of informal segregation have, however, created their own group consciousness. Contrary to the liberal hope, it may well take a long time to eradicate the traces of apartheid from the minds of the populace. Indeed, apartheid itself could endure long after all apartheid laws have been repealed. Unity in political opposition alone, unsupported by basic cultural similarities, provides a fragile base for solidarity.

However, the important difference between ethnicity and race must not be obscured. The preservation of ethnicity for maintenance of a cultural heritage is of course worthwhile. To base distinctions on race, on the other hand, is invidious. Not multiracialism, but the nonracialism of genuine colorblindness, is the liberal ideal of Western democracies. Ethnic and race relations are therefore not identical in their policy implications. As Banton has aphorized: "Good racial relations would be ethnic relations."[7]

Race and Class

The concentration of wealth in White hands and the poverty widespread among Blacks supply the third ground for the South African state's illegitimacy. The close relationship between income level and race underlies the charge that the essence of apartheid is exploitation and labor control. Race and class overlap to a high degree in South Africa. The small Black middle class is comprised mostly of professional people, but few of its members possess substantial independent wealth. An emerging Black bureaucratic bourgeoisie is achieving salary parity but is still frustrated by indignities of status. The few Black businessmen operate under so many severe restrictions that to all intents and purposes a free-enterprise system does not exist for them.

Likewise, the Black labor market is constrained by influx control and bureaucratic tyranny. Black education suffers from gross comparative underfunding and is undermined by the general culture of poverty. Historically, shortages in the local labor market have been filled by immigration from Europe rather than by training of the indigenous subordinate population. With such a history of inequality, discrimination, and neglect, it is not surprising that few cross-cutting ties and interests between the same strata in the different groups have developed to blunt the collective perceptions of one another. In the absence of shared perceptions and normal contact, intraclass solidarity can hardly assert itself, despite common interests in an integrated, interdependent economy.

Technocratic reformers now aim at deracializing White domination as far as possible, by substituting class for race as the main criterion of stratification. But if income inequality and educational inequality continue to overlap to a large extent, deracialization will be only nominal. Formal class privileges in reality continue to be racial advantages. Illegitimate racial distinctions are continued, although they are masked by the allegedly color-blind material markers.

Politics and Market

The substitution of class distinctions for racial ones is paralleled by a liberal distinction between political and economic democracy. This assertive neoclassical theory is aimed at diminishing state interference in society. Color-blind market forces are to be given a free hand and political intervention is to be curtailed. Among the freedoms to be constitutionally protected are not only the rules of the market but also the identity of minorities. However, a theoretical acceptance of political democracy is not to be taken as insuring economic equality. Democracy means economic *freedom*, but not the use of state power to guarantee that a formal equality of opportunity also produces some equality of results. In the rhetoric of academic technocrats, exclusion of Blacks from the central political institution is justified no longer in ideological terms such as identity or self-determination, but as a matter of costs. Sampie Terreblanche, for example, stresses "the economic costs of Black representation in Parliament," which he considers "will be astronomically high and therefore unpayable."[8] The ruling class is worried not about existential obliteration but about the redistribution of the accumulated wealth that could take place following real political incorporation.

The South African oligarchy, then, faces the problem of finding a legitimate formula to avert the economic consequences of formal Black political incorporation. The mechanism they have chosen to block eventual political equality from achieving its economic ends is that of decentralization. By regionalizing political power as far as possible, they deflect Black economic ambitions from the whole pie to its pieces. Decentralization minimizes the danger of an all-out conflict. Jan Lombard argues for "the geographic decentralization of both fiscal powers and fiscal responsibilities with respect to welfare functions."[9] His concern is that "class conflict is institutionalized in the parliamentary system" when racial parliaments compete for a share of the state budget. Lombard therefore advocates separation of the "order functions" of the state (on which political consensus may be achieved) from "interventionist economic welfare functions," which are better left to the market. In addition he suggests that two unusual principles be entrenched as basic tenets of common law: maintenance of a sound national currency, and the setting of limits to taxation. These principles are designed to protect private property from inflation and confiscatory taxation in a post-apartheid state.

Such advice on restriction of state intervention is now particularly popular in South Africa's business circles as a result of the past government history of interference on behalf of Afrikaner sectional interests. The propagated liberal dogma, however, overlooks the fact that the bargaining units are hardly equal. Unchecked market forces could result in greater inequities if there were no potentially equalizing state protection of the weaker party. The issue is not that of greater or lesser state interference per se (which takes place anyway at all times), but on whose behalf political and judicial power intercedes. This political question is obscured by the glorification of free enterprise and the condemnation of state regulations as undue interference. Such a stance reflects the confidence of a more mature capitalism that no longer needs to rely on state assistance, but it can also contribute to the erosion of capitalism if it fails to recognize that it may exacerbate existing inequalities. Under the principles of profit maximization and cut-throat competition even the most well-meaning enterprise is limited in its welfare functions. The private sector is unable adequately to assume most public duties, from the provision of education to housing, health care, and environmental and consumer protection. The more a free market heightens existing inequities rather than contributes to the formation of a broad-based middle class, the more will the mass of the excluded have to seek the political kingdom for relief. This inevitable politicization spells the death sentence to an unchecked free-market system.

Whether a genuine federalism can counter these politicizing trends remains an open question. Regional homogeneity together with greater political involvement of larger numbers of people in decentralized decision-making may also heighten awareness of the frustrating limits of local power. Decentralizing economic decisions can shield opponents in legitimate institutions and bring out novel forms of regional resistance. After all, genuine federalism implies a devolution of power from the center to a formerly less powerful periphery.

The Nationalist Party technocrats and the classical liberals of the Progressive Federal Party now find a common ground in their advocacy of greater regionalism. Political decentralization still has to address regional economic disparities. With the decline of subsistence agriculture and increasing structural unemployment, only a uniform welfare scheme can guarantee stability. Otherwise, the poorer sections of the population will still move into the more affluent regions. The present funding of up to 75 percent of budgets of "independent" Bantustans by Pretoria will seem trivial compared to the amounts required to absorb a flood of work-seekers in decentralized growth points or, alternatively, to finance vast welfare schemes in the cities at the expense of a small, privileged productive sector.

This anticipated predicament led to a significant shift of state policy under the Botha administration. In the boom of the 1960s and early 1970s, the consolidating Afrikaner state felt strong enough to impose its ideology on a reluctant business community. Now it needs the assistance of national and international capital to make decentralization work. Despite the sense of *déjà vu* conjured up by the false promises and leaky arguments, the economic neoapartheid of the 1980s includes decisive shifts in causes and priorities.

Under Prime Ministers Hendrik Verwoerd and John Vorster, priority was given to the *political* development of the Bantustans. Partly as a response to external criticisms and partly as a means of diffusing internal pressures for political inclusion, independent homeland states were supposed to develop self-governing political structures. Bantustan administrations relieved the strained White bureaucracy by enticing rural Blacks to administer their own poverty and to police themselves. The grand apartheid scheme of independent states also provided the legal framework for denationalizing the citizens in the central area.

These governments neglected the *economic* development of the Bantustans. What few economic incentives the state provided concentrated on improving subsistence farming or creating cottage industries of the handicraft or furniture-manufacturing type as examples of successful Black entrepreneurship. Initially, Bantustan investment was closed to private (White) capital. Later a scheme of border industries was pushed but, on the whole, because of lack of infrastructure and insufficient government subsidies, failed to attract sufficient investment. Consequently, deterioration of the countryside accelerated, paralleled by an increase in the number of illegal work-seekers in squatter camps ringing the few metropoles.

Workers on White-owned farms whose jobs were eliminated by the introduction of mechanization, together with people relocated from century-old Black areas in places declared White, were dumped on the already overcrowded Bantustans regardless of whether they could earn a living, thus exacerbating the already severe rural poverty. Infant mortality, malnutrition, alcoholism, corrupt officials, a prolonged drought, and soil erosion from overstocking plagued rural life, leading to comparisons between the rural ghettoes and gulags and concentration camps. To be sure, for those stranded and unable to find work, body and spirit were killed by circumstance rather than by deliberate state design. But had it not been for remittances from clan members employed in the urban areas, and a remarkable spiritual stamina derived from ancestral and religious traditions of cohesive communalism, the society in some of the rural slums would have disintegrated completely. Clearly, any government interested in overall stability could not ignore these conditions of destitution for long. An astute observer summarized the shift in the meaning of *grand apartheid*: "Ethnic partition today has come to mean not the solution to the national question, but a short-term camouflage of the unemployment crisis."[10]

As a result of these pressures and failed promises of apartheid, in the 1980s the Botha administration began to shift its emphasis to the economic development of the impoverished rural regions. Subsistence farming now provides a livelihood for an ever-smaller number of migrant workers and their dependents. In response to massive unemployment, Pretoria has begun to promote Bantustan capitalism. Eight development regions with forty-eight strategically chosen industrial growth points, aided by a newly created Southern African Development Bank, are intended to slow down the Black urbanization rate. The state has provided massive subsidies as a bait to draw not only local but also foreign investors to the cheap-labor areas. These subsidies include a 40 percent rebate on railage costs, a 95 percent subsidy on the local workers' wage bill up to R 110 a month per worker, a 70 percent subsidy on factory and rentals, and equally high subsidies on housing and interest rates, as well as a 10 percent tender preference for government contracts. Foreign capital and know-how are indeed vital to the growth points. Areas such as Isithebe in Zululand now attract substantial European, Japanese, and Taiwanese capital; not only are the state subsidies and the labor surplus attractive, but the production costs are cheaper than in parts of Asia. While Isithebe will never resemble the planners' models, the ever-expanding amount of acreage claimed by modern factories testifies to the success of such large-scale social engineering. Rather than allowing the economically logical gradual integration of rural work-seekers into the urban centers and the emergence of an informal economy, as has occurred the world over, the South African government has substantially slowed down urbanization and has shaped new patterns of industrialization.

This South African capitalism, which instituted mining, industrial development, commercial agriculture, and a generally modern society equal to its counterparts in North America and Europe, also produced the greatest problem for that society: a Black proletariat that remains unincorporated and stigmatized. No other work force in the history of industrialization has been so excluded for so long from the system it made possible.

Business and Apartheid

While workers in the early phases of industrialization enjoyed few rights anywhere, a stage has now been reached in South Africa at which for important sectors of local capital the costs of apartheid exclusion outweigh the benefits. For the first time capitalists are rebelling against the high taxes resulting from creation of employment in decentralized growth areas; they worry about calm labor relations; and they dislike operating in a siege economy, cut off from technological innovation, easy capital inflows, and access to markets abroad. Conservative South African business, unable to transfer the costs of ethnic exclusiveness to other groups, "doesn't want to end up in bed with government as part of a political system."[11] Anglo-American Corporation, South Africa's largest company, sees "no future for any of us aside from an African quagmire unless we . . . seek to have the government realise the deep concern we feel about conditions as we find them today."[12] South African capitalists now repeat a truism learned long ago by their counterparts elsewhere: unless this outside force is politically incorporated and given a share in the fruits of its labor, those who monopolize the goods will not be able to enjoy them either. During the first half of this century, the outsiders of Afrikaner origin mobilized to win state power in order to wrest their share from British imperialism. Now Anglo-Afrikaner monopoly capitalism faces a similar choice: to initiate genuine power-sharing, or to have that power wrested from it bit by bit, in the name of democratic socialism. If it can engineer reform through successful liberalization, it can to a large extent control the outcome. If it continues to refuse meaningful structural and symbolic concessions, the result of the conflict is much less certain.

To be sure, democratic socialism, wherever its proponents have claimed to realize it, has thus far failed, if to varying degrees. The unique circumstances in South Africa may counteract this trend, however. South African–style capitalism has been thoroughly discredited through its association with racialism. When the apartheid state officially adopted a free-enterprise ideology in the early 1980s, it removed the last doubt about the existence of a "symbiotic relationship"[13] between state and business. Before that move, capital could at least claim that its optimal profits were also hampered by apartheid ideology. A unionized work force no longer believes that the Chamber of Mines and other employers' organizations are on their side, fighting a common political enemy. In a 1984 representative survey of 551 Black production workers, 91 percent agreed that employers "work with and support the government."[14] "It is also obvious to us that management will always support the government," declared Chris Dhlamini, the president of the Federation of South African Trade

Unions (FOSATU), the country's largest emerging union federation.[15] Because the state has become closely identified with business interests, both will be targets for liberation. But perhaps nowhere in South Africa is the cognitive gulf as wide as in the role-perceptions of workers and employers. In the first joint statement of the six South African employer organizations, during the visit of Edward Kennedy in February 1985, employers presented themselves as being "in the forefront in successfully urging the South African government to make meaningful policy changes." The progressive image projected as a reply to the disinvestment lobby portrayed the factory as a paradise of racial harmony: "The business community is in the front line in developing and maintaining harmonious relations between Black and White in South Africa, especially on the shopfloor."[16]

Much of this self-praise can be dismissed as propaganda. The numerous strikes—particularly those over union recognition—unjustified dismissals, and unfair labor practices, as well the silent suffering of millions of workers who are underpaid despite above-average profits, form a long history of exploitation, although vast differences among employment practices can of course be encountered. In some ways, however, the argument may be made that it was the state, guarding the system as a whole, that had to force employers into progressive labor policies, not vice versa.

On the other hand, the same joint statement revealed more clearly than ever before contradictions between the attitudes of business and the state bureaucracy concerning the political incorporation of the work force and the management of labor control. For the first time, too, Afrikaner business, in the form of Die Afrikaanse Handelsinstituut, set aside ethnic loyalties to join their English and Black colleagues in openly criticizing the government. Capital's need for stability and productivity now transcends ethnic boundaries.

In addition to the business-government squabbles usual in Western societies—over level of taxation and degree of market interference on behalf of the public—in South Africa arises the unique contentious issue of apartheid funding. Organized business, exaggeratedly described by its leading mouthpiece as being "on the verge of mutiny," increasingly objects to profit erosion by high inflation. In this view, the state "is engaged in massively inflationary experiments in social engineering which require equally massive bureaucracies to police."[17] More than in other Western societies, the private sector in South Africa constantly denounces public services as "state socialism." However, the civil service forms the main constituency of the National Party, in competition with the extreme right wing, and the government cannot afford to implement a policy of salary freezes and attrition that would alienate the members of its overexpanded bureaucracy. In fact, at the beginning of the major recession in 1983–1984, the cabinet had to buy Afrikaner referendum votes by a 30 percent raise in civil servants' salaries. Organized business and the White middle class, annoyed by new taxes on fringe benefits to finance political luxuries, now, ironically, blame apartheid controls— from which they were supposed to benefit—for the stagnation of their real income. This reflects the growing confidence of a capitalism that no longer needs to have labor supplies guaranteed by state regulations. In fact, given the vast quantity of surplus labor and the growing influence of the unions, an "orderly urbanization policy" that would relax influx control is seen both as having a dampening effect on unrealistic wage demands and as serving to maintain overall stability.

For the state the crucial conflict in the second half of the 1980s will be over the costs of past ideological blueprints. To what extent can the South African state afford both a vast apartheid bureaucracy and massive subsidies for decentralized growth points at the expense of urban areas? Will state expenditures be allocated according to the differential revenue-generating capacities of the various "population groups" (the new euphemism for *race*) or according to nonracial financial formulas? Will the economic recession finally force Pretoria to abandon political priorities for economic necessities? Can the ruling technocrats reeducate their own constituency, particularly the police and Afrikaner civil service, to accept deracialization?

To find answers to these questions we must turn to a comparative evaluation of ethnicity and nationalism. Is it true that "when people were forced to choose between ethnic and class interests, ethnicity did not invariably prevail," as Merle Lipton asserts for South Africa?[18]

2

Ethnicity, Nationalism, and the State

Politicized Ethnicity

ETHNIC CONSCIOUSNESS always exists within some specific sociopolitical context. How ethnicity asserts itself—when it rises, declines, or disappears—depends primarily on the policies of the dominant group. Grievances of excluded groups and threats to the status or security of the dominant group result in ethnic mobilization. Ethnicity lays claim to rightful entitlement, attempts to thwart intrusion into monopolized realms, and inspires collective action in the name of cultural self-determination.

In these endeavors ethnicity can be manipulated. Elites use, and even create, ethnic symbols; the intellectual leaders of a group define situations in ethnic terms, and these portrayals and explanations then often become a living reality for followers who in turn perceive and interpret their own experiences in terms of the dominant values of their reference group.

Nationalism is the political expression of shared ethnic consciousness, or politized ethnicity. Modern nationalism began with the French Revolution, a secular mobilization of the populace to create an identity as a nation, defined linguistically, rather than as members of an empire, defined by religion. In the name of self-determination the Central European middle classes reacted against Napoleonic subjugation: the aristocratic corporatism of an estate-ordered polity was challenged by emancipated citizens under the banner of Republican patriotism. Similarly, colonial dependency and foreign rule in the Americas and later in Asia and Africa were opposed by nationalist independence movements.

The demand for political power expressed in the nationalist movements for independence was based on two separate justifications. In the French and English tradition of political theory, national affiliation was viewed as resting on individual decisions to join a national community. This view established a subjective, voluntaristic concept of a nation, regardless of the individuals' origins. According to the Central and Eastern European tradition, on the other hand, all people born into a distinct linguistic/cultural group formed a nation. This deterministic notion of nationality therefore advocated unifying common cultures in a single state and breaking up multinational empires such as that of Habsburg.

The few early socialist theorists of nationalism such as the Austro-Marxists Otto Bauer and Karl Renner adopted a deterministic, objective notion of nationality. In 1907 Bauer defined the nation as "the totality of men [sic] bound together through a common destiny into a community of character." That common destiny sets the nation apart "from the international character groupings, such as an occupation, a class, or the members of a state, which rest upon a similarity, not a community, of destiny."[1]

This difference between the voluntaristic (French/English) and the objective (German) notion epitomizes the split between African and Afrikaner visions of nationalism in South Africa. The Congress alliance always stressed that everyone who wanted citizenship should be admitted regardless of origin, race, or creed. In the Afrikaner definition of nationality, on the other hand, South Africa is made up of many cultures and nations. The self-determination or "inner sovereignty" of objectively defined groups is considered sacred, independently of the group members' perception of themselves. It is out of this background, and not only because of a Machiavellian policy of fragmentation, that South Africa imposes nationalities on people who may not want them.

In order to seek common ground between the two definitions and clarify the theoretical impasse it may be useful to

sort politicized ethnicity (nationalism) into its major components: cultural ethnicity, economic ethnicity, and political/le-
gal ethnicity.

Cultural ethnicity denotes a feeling of commonality based on
language, religion, or regional particularities. Sharing values
and customs results in a similarity of outlook. Language in
particular serves as a decisive identity-forming device that distinguishes groups beyond the ability to communicate. Religious beliefs, which frequently include rules of endogamy and
exclusion, perpetuate group boundaries. Regional particularities (music, food, customs, accent) can function as markers of
nationalism even in the absence of religious and linguistic distinctions, as the example of Scotland shows. Origin and ancestry are, obviously, the criteria for descent groups. The unique
collective history of groups shapes the individual identities of
its members.

Because cultural ethnicity is inextricably intertwined with
individual identity, a good case can be made for its perpetuation and cultivation if group members so desire. Heritage
maintenance in the face of the pressure for conformity imposed by imperialist cultures forms a worthy goal in itself as
well as serving to further self-determination. Cultural autonomy of distinct subgroups instead of amalgamation into a
common national culture can be defended on grounds of
moral justice as well as administrative feasibility. At the very
least, denominational schools and/or separate language education are, rightly, available as alternatives to a public school
system in most democratic societies.

Economic ethnicity denotes the situation of economic inequities or privileges coinciding with ethnic group boundaries.
Unlike cultural ethnicity, ethnic economic differentiation violates generally held notions of equity. To ascribe status based
on descent contradicts the principle of individual merit as the
sole criterion for the allocation of scarce resources. If economic privilege or disadvantage is made to depend on ethnic
membership, then equality of opportunity ceases to exist even
as an ideal. Identification of groups based on economic ethnicity—be it in a split labor market or in a cultural division of

labor—must be distinguished from cultural identification even though in a wider sense a cultural identity reflects the economic position of a group.

Because the ruling Afrikaner Nationalists have used state power massively in aid of members of their ethnic groups and to restrict market access by competitors from the disfranchised groups, ethnicity in South Africa has become synonymous with economic discrimination. Unless at least formal legal economic equality for all South Africans is established, including abolition of differential state expenditures per capita for different ethnic groups, ethnicity in *all* its aspects will inevitably be associated with unfair advantage and degradation. The state policy of enforced ethnicity has discredited the concept almost beyond repair.

Political ethnicity denotes ethnic privilege or exclusion institutionalized in the practice or law of the state. Political power relations differentially incorporate ethnically defined groups, who use ethnic symbols to defend or challenge the status quo. In the special cases of *ethnic states*—South Africa and Israel— the public realm is defined exclusively in terms of insiders and outsiders.[2]

In an ethnic state, cultural or racial outsiders are not merely excluded from the rewards of power, but their very existence is ignored; the state defines itself solely in terms of the ideology of the dominant section. Subordinate ethnics do not form part of the polity, however differentially incorporated, but are considered noncitizens or, at best, second-class citizens. Even if equality is guaranteed in theory, as it is in the Israeli constitution, the legal practices of an ethnic state are shaped by the values and interests of the dominant group. The raison d'être of an ethnic state is the preservation of ethnic hegemony. State symbols and institutions reflect this ethnic hierarchy. Laws reinforce religious preferences or racial privileges. The ethnic individual derives his identity through his group membership.

In South Africa and Israel, the public institutions express the national aspirations of a single subgroup. The national anthem and history textbooks, immigration laws and land sales, the state bureaucracy and the boardrooms of the private sector all clearly state the same message of dominance. These de facto plural or multinational states do not reflect this reality in the public realm: the outsiders remain invisible, objects of administration and control whose destiny is decided for them. The subordinate ethnics are foreigners in their own country.

Whether politized ethnicity leads to an ethnic state or merely to conflicts in a plural multination state, cultural, economic, and political ethnicities are usually intertwined. For example, cultural ethnicity can seldom be completely a matter for the private sector. Public education in itself makes cultural ethnicity a political issue. Whether and how a language is taught in school or recognized as an official means of communication affect the career opportunities of linguistic groups. Ethnic groups in power have often used educational policies and language prerequisites to deprive outsiders of equal access to status and power, particularly civil service positions; Malaya is a case in point. The still vastly differential allocation of educational resources to the various groups in South Africa (despite some equalization) proves the obvious point that educational advantage reinforces economic and political dominance. If there is one consistent result of the vast research on strife in multination states, it is that competition, not ignorance or lack of contact, is the main cause of ethnic antagonism.[3]

Nationalist Afrikanerdom has defined this competition in racial terms. A "White nation" made up of all elements of the diverse European cultures will not accept loss of political control. Instead of being satisfied with cultural autonomy within South Africa, Afrikaner nationalists view a separate political identity as a precondition for cultural survival. Willem de Klerk, the editor of the most progressive Afrikaans paper, which extols a "new identity," nonetheless insists that "the Afrikaners as a group dare not diminish to a small minority which makes its cultural contribution by giving up its political power bases."[4] This is a clear expression of the priority of instrumental political ethnicity over the expressive aspects of primordialism, although the two are complementary.

To primordialists, kin solidarity is intrinsically valuable.[5] Group solidarity endures mainly because it bestows a sense of belonging and worth. It is a psychic gratification that all humans share, an intuitive bond, recognition of a unique history as members of a distinct group. In these formulations ethnicity easily becomes a static, deterministic, and reified concept. However, "primal needs" never assert themselves in a political vacuum; they rise and wane in response to situational factors. The focus on the emotive power of primary group membership can nonetheless explain the success of ethnic entrepreneurs who tap the reservoirs of shared experience. When there is competition with other interest groups, effective bonds can be formed by an appeal to ethnic solidarity. An emphasis solely on class and material interests overlooks the ideal interests and concerns about status that are also part of human nature. In fact, ethnicity may well strengthen the expression of class-based frustrations and at the same time defeat intra-class unity.[6] In fostering a sense of collective self-esteem, ethnic pride is not false consciousness, as orthodox Marxists suggest, but often a precondition for the articulation of class grievances. Class analysis and a close attention to ethnic dynamics are interrelated.

A more interesting question concerns what happens when ideal and material interests come into conflict. For example, Afrikaner nationalism at present negotiates its supremacist identity by a process of deracialization associated with economic necessity and political stability. It manages, redefines, and manipulates its ethnic boundaries according to various influences and exigencies.

Such a political interpretation of ethnicity differs, even more than primordialism does, from the sociobiological focus on preferential kin selection. Ethnicity as nepotism does not explain policies. State policies toward subordinate groups do not follow kin boundaries. According to sociobiologists such as P. van den Berghe, Afrikaner nationalists should have given preferential treatment to genetically related kin-groups such as the Coloreds rather than to non-related English-speaking

Whites or European immigrants. Policy contrary to this indicates that differential treatment depends on concrete historical circumstances and not on kin preferences.

Neo-Marxist economic generalizations prove as unhelpful for the understanding of contemporary ethnic conflicts as the universalistic notions of genetic-evolutionary priorities espoused by sociobiologists or the psychological reductionism of primordialists. Any attempt to determine why governments adopted certain policies when they clearly had other options and why opponents responded as they did must take into account the specifics of the situation. This historical approach throws doubt on such popular models as Edna Bonacich's "split labor-market" and Michael Hechter's "cultural division of labor" as generally applicable concepts of ethnic group formation.[7] Conflict between higher-priced, politically powerful labor on one side and cheaper, "foreign" migrants on the other may be found in both South Africa and the United States. No differentially paid subproletariat exists in the migrant labor system of West Germany or among the ascendant immigrant groups of Canada. Likewise, the postulated "ethnic solidarity" of occupational diversity as "a function of overall patterns of intergroup stratification and interaction" (Hechter) remains problematic in situations where selected immigrants are dispersed throughout the occupational hierarchy and strive for individual achievement rather than relying on a collective shelter.

All Western industrial countries report a marked increase in ethnic hostility and expressions of dogmatism and authoritarianism during periods of economic recession. The most common explanation for such right-wing sentiment is that the heightened level of economic anxiety generates a need for scapegoats, so recent immigrants or visible minorities are frequently singled out. Widespread working-class racism in particular is explained by economic factors. The fear of being replaced by members of formerly excluded subordinate groups is cited as the main reason for the racial hostility of relatively privileged workers. Thus, attitudes of supremacy

are ascribed a realistic economic base. Cheaper and more docile (alien) workers are said to be rightly perceived as a real
threat to the achievements of an established working class.

A close examination of historical cases reveals a far more
complex picture. In South Africa the White resistance to non-
White colleagues being employed in the same occupation continued despite iron-clad guarantees of job security, based on
the political power of the White working class. The reason for
this attitude lies, then, not in the fear of replacement but in a
feeling of *status reduction*. To have to do devalued labor is the
ultimate degradation for the White supremacist in South Africa. He would rather avoid employing any Black labor than
make concessions by sharing the same work. In South Africa,
the ultra-right advocates a self-sufficient, exclusive White
mini-state in which the dominant group would free itself from
its dependency on subordinate labor by doing all the manual
tasks itself. To be sure, like the Zionist dreams for Palestine,
such labor exclusiveness proves ultimately unworkable, since
great profit is derived from exploiting cheap labor. Nevertheless, the widespread appeal of occupational exclusiveness
needs to be explained.

An individual's occupation provides much of the person's
sense of identity. To share this occupation with outgroups de-
grades it and thus lowers the individual's sense of self-worth.
Once a racial division of labor has been established, those in
the higher-status categories are hostile to sharing their work
roles with outsiders, no matter how sure the continuity in rewards and career prospects. In Western Europe indigenous
workers have been known to opt for wage reduction or unemployment rather than agree to do "demeaning" work that
is considered the monopoly of foreign migrants. Hence, psychological rather than purely economic factors must be
viewed as decisive in shaping responses to demands for economic integration.

This perspective can also explain why, contrary to Marxist
notions of working-class solidarity, politically conservative
professional groups and other members of the middle and
upper classes usually show the least ethnic hostility. This is

frequently attributed to their better education or their greater wealth. A more plausible explanation focuses on professionals' satisfaction of *status needs*, which makes feelings of racial superiority superfluous. In contrast, the average industrial worker or office clerk is often alienated from his job, so he may choose to base his identity on the denigration of other lower-class workers. This reaction can be called *occupational ethnocentrism*, namely, the glorification, because genuine identification with a meaningless activity has become difficult, of alienated work as particularly skillful and superior.

When even these psychological crutches for ego-weakness are no longer available, extreme cases of ethnic hostility emerge. Recent surveys in West Germany showed that antagonism toward foreigners is greatest among retired and older people. Here economic competition in a split labor market cannot explain ethnic antagonism. Instead, psychological status needs, arising out of the centrality of occupation to individual identity, seems to account for the sense of racial superiority. Neither the alleged rigidity of old age nor the socialization of this age group in the Nazi period could alone cause this marked shift. Similar data have been reported from Britain. It therefore seems that the sudden *status insecurity* generated by retirement best explains the higher incidence of outgroup rejection. Although no data are available, it may be hypothesized that a similar syndrome can be found among unemployed persons regardless of age.

It may appear that a purely psychological explanation has been suggested as a substitute for economic accounts of ethnic antagonism. However, these psychological motivations are always mediated by the objective conditions of the work situation as the most important determinant of status needs. If, on the whole, individual outlooks depend on work conditions, then crucial conclusions regarding the reduction of ethnic hostility can be drawn. Naive preaching of multicultural understanding and evocation of sympathy with the victims will not achieve results as long as the root causes of hostility exist. It is only when people are allowed to lead lives they perceive as meaningful (particularly in their most important activity) that they can be expected to react to outsiders in a humane rather than a hostile fashion.

Five Types of Ethnic Dominance

In an attempt to make sense out of all this and to draw insights from a comparative analysis, we distinguish five distinct types of contemporary state policies toward subordinate ethnics: state violence toward scapegoat minorities; state competition with self-reliant ethnic groups; state tutelage of stigmatized subordinates; state provision of foreign labor supplies; and state incorporation of ascendant immigrant minorities. Each context requires different conceptualizations but allows for obvious cross-national comparisons within the same type. A comparative overview of ethnic conflicts elsewhere can best place the South African situation in perspective.

State Violence against Scapegoat Minorities

The obvious example of extreme state violence is the industrialized genocide in Nazi Germany of Jews and other stigmatized minorities. None of these minorities were objective threats to the dominant group. "The average Jew," writes Gordon Graig, "baptized or unbaptized, was German in his virtues and vices, his dress and manners, and his deeply felt patriotism."[8]

Without visibility and self-identification, records of ancestry became the selection criteria for this scapegoat minority. The victims were set up as villains, independent of their behavior. To be sure, a convenient tradition of historical anti-Semitism was used to whip up hostility, but Jews were basically interchangeable. The height of anti-Semitism occurred in a society that was, as Horkheimer remarked, the least anti-Semitic in Western Europe.

The fate of the victims has to be explained in conjunction with a movement in which the scapegoat minority fulfilled the indispensable function of a common cause welding together its heterogeneous elements. In order to achieve total mobilization, an enemy had to be overcome, a morale and esprit de corps created. Jews were defined as the obstacle in the path of the chosen goals—a formidable impediment, yet easy to overcome with proper determination. Dehumanizing Jews as vermin and parasites served to portray the enemy as both weak and dangerous.[9]

While Nazi fascism was certainly not a unique historical accident or an exclusively German phenomenon, its reappearance in other situations occurs in quite different guises. From a sociological viewpoint what are decisive are the specific historical and sociopolitical conditions that allowed the fascist movement to sweep into power and then to use, unhindered, the state machinery of coercion for the extermination of a scapegoat minority.

When scapegoat minorities come to occupy specialized economic positions, they serve as ready targets for the less fortunate majority population. Like Jews, Asians in East and South Africa, Armenians in Turkey, Chinese in Malaysia or Vietnam, and Lebanese in West Africa form so-called middlemen minorities on the basis of their dominant role in distinct economic activities. Without the political power and the network of social connections of the culturally different majority, these trading minorities find themselves in a tenuous position, despite common citizenship and attempts at political identification with the majority. Their insecurity also leads to frequent alternative life planning (children's education abroad, foreign accounts, bribery), which in turn gives rise to accusations of disloyalty from the dominant group. It is the weakness of middlemen minorities that has led to the worst state atrocities against these tenuously placed ethnic outsiders.

In light of this structural ambiguity, scapegoat/middlemen minorities have tended to cultivate cultural narcissism when faced with hostility. Exclusivism, endogamy, self-help, and cultural revivalism become the armor that permits them to survive in a hostile environment. These communities have acquired few psychological scars. They have immunized themselves, so to speak, from the outside stigmatization by withdrawing into their own psychological and material world. The success stories of Indians in South Africa, of Palestinians in the Gulf states, and of Chinese migrants in South Asia bear testimony to a remarkable adaptation despite racism and intense discrimination. In short, it is not so much the cultural tradition of a group as the social environment, epitomized in state policies, that activates or lays to rest cultural heritage.

Scapegoated middlemen minorities have, through their cultural strength, partially succeeded in overcoming discrimination, despite a hostile social environment.

State Competition with Self-Reliant Ethnic Groups

Different from state violence against insignificant minorities is ethnic competition among relatively self-sufficient groups. Self-reliance refers to the "institutional completeness," the spatial concentration, the population ratios, and the sociopolitical clout that such powerful, ethnically mobilized entities wield. They often form mini-nations in multination states.[10]

As recent events in Northern Ireland, Lebanon, and Cyprus have vividly demonstrated, precipitants for ethnic mass violence exist when sizable ethnically organized groups with different cultural traditions compete in the same state for more rights under unequal institutional conditions. What these situations have in common are that, first, the dominant group has restricted institutionalized competition in its monopoly over state power and so has reduced the subordinate group to second-class citizenship; second, the dominant group has translated its culture into national values that it is said would be threatened by the ascendancy of the excluded group; and, finally, the competing groups foster members' allegiance through separate institutions, particularly education, and label intergroup links of individuals as traitorous.

Where self-reliant ethnic groups compete, the disadvantaged section faces two options: secession, or overthrow of the dominant group. When the dominant section is also numerically stronger (Canada/Quebec, Nigeria/Biafra, Spain/Basques, Sri Lanka/Tamil), it resists secession at all costs. Such states usually employ co-optation policies. Numerous formulae of ethnic engineering, from an enhanced federalism to multilingualism to the elite-cartel of consociationalism,[11] have been advanced to preserve national unity. What ultimately binds the disparate segments together and militates against secession, however, is economic interdependency of the two groups. Formal partition has occurred only in predominantly agricultural societies (India, Pakistan/Bangladesh, Palestine). Political independence in an industrial setting is thwarted by economic interdependence.

Where seizure of power exists as a real possibility, dominant minorities actively pursue political partition. In South Africa, Blacks are denationalized and are made foreigners in their own country. By setting up pseudo-states, the ruling minority hopes to shed moral responsibility for Black citizens. It pronounces their civic death. This policy makes the subgroups administer their own poverty and police themselves. Since the subgroups remain dependent economically, their political independence, even if hostile, poses no threat to the center.

The outcome of such contests depends in the final analysis on the resources—particularly of military hardware and trained activists—each side can muster. Third-party interference often becomes necessary to contain conflicts (e.g., Lebanon, the United Kingdom in Northern Ireland, United Nations peace-keeping forces in Cyprus). If the dominant group lacks a constraining ideology it seeks early political compromise rather than a more costly victory in a civil war. Where the ruling group commands large economic resources, as in South Africa, that leverage is extensively used for co-optation as well as coercion. In this way an unjust regime may experience apparent stability for a long time. True stability based on legitimacy in multination states, however, can only be guaranteed by shared mechanisms of conflict regulations in polities with a basic moral consensus.[12]

State Tutelage of Stigmatized Subordinates
From these ethnic group competitions and nascent nationalist conflicts must be distinguished situations where a stigmatized minority has no hope of successfully challenging the group in power. What distinguishes such stigmatized groups from scapegoat/middlemen minorities (which are also stigmatized,

but in a different way) is that the stigmatization affects its victims psychologically although they do not endorse it. Their cultural background and social deprivation usually prevent collective ethnic resistance, permitting, at the most, only achievement-oriented individual escapes from discrimination.

Unlike scapegoat minorities, who are stereotyped as economically cunning and superior, stigmatized groups are considered inherently inferior. They are, if employed at all, assigned the least desirable, most demeaning, and lowest-paying jobs, which are said to fit their character. This economic powerlessness reinforces their sociopolitical subordination.

Because these racial outcasts have had their cultural identity destroyed, they cannot fall back on cultural narcissism for self-defense. In the two situations characterized earlier, the subordinates had their own reference group. For the stigmatized minority, on the other hand, the significant others are the members of the dominant group. Degree of acceptance in the mainstream becomes the yardstick of success, in spite of any rhetoric of separatism. Among self-reliant ethnics, on the other hand, assimilation is frowned upon.

India provides the clearest case of a culturally integrated yet stigmatized minority. Among all systems of inequality, the Indian caste ranking comes closest to being accepted by most of its victims. In this respect it is unlike racial discrimination, which generally lacks a religious foundation. The politicization arising from racial indignities in an industrial urban setting such as South Africa can therefore be expected to be much more intense than the outrage about century-old status ascription in Indian villages. In this respect the frequently drawn analogies between the South African racial order and caste structures are misleading. Conscious resistance on one side and compliance without consent on the other characterize the South African scene. Fatalistic loyalty, if not compliance resulting from religious consent, marks the caste order.

The dominant group's attitude toward stigmatized minorities is one of paternalistic benevolence. As in feudal slave societies or colonialism, the status differences and rigidly stratified roles make state demonstrations of hostility superfluous.

The assumed childlike inferiority of the outcasts triggers condescension on the part of the dominant group. An attitude of pseudo-tolerance and benevolence toward those who "know their place" is common. Individuals who are perceived as "stepping out of line" are targets of swift retaliations, culminating in lynchings or other forms of vigilante fascism. Mass rebellions of these subordinates are rare. Resistance expresses itself in seemingly apolitical riots, individual deviance, drug abuse, and other disguised forms of protest, particularly among the demoralized youth.

The stigmatized ethnic group members verge on perennial unemployment in advanced industrial societies. As surplus labor they depend heavily on subsidies—with which the state secures their acquiescence. The politically articulate leadership and upper stratum of the stigmatized group are co-opted with affirmative action policies. Such quotas do not threaten the privileges of the dominant section; on the contrary, they greatly enhance the legitimacy of the system and in fact may perpetuate these invidious distinctions, as some perceptive observers have stressed.

State Provision of Foreign Labor Supplies

Two sets of immigrant minorities evoke two distinct types of state policies. One set is temporary labor, so-called guestworkers as in Western Europe. The second set is made up of immigrants who settle permanently in the host country. The first type may best be considered by examining the policies of the foremost labor importer, West Germany.

Germany has specified as official state policy that it is not a country of immigration. Very few labor migrants ever acquire citizenship rights.[13] As non-citizens or second-class citizens, the migrants are denied all political rights, including voting rights. These groups are treated as sojourners. If the conservative party (CDU) had its way, certain categories of family members, including children over six years of age, would be barred from joining the breadwinner. State policy encourages maintenance of social ties with the country of origin with the view of eventual returning.

The de jure status of sojourners proves, however, to be a de facto myth. To all intents and purposes the temporary migrants have become permanent immigrants. Refused the right of participation in politics, made unwelcome by the general population, they form a stigmatized outgroup. The state cannot use violence against them, however, because they constitute a vital part of the economy. The migrants show no effects of castelike stigmatization. Although they are treated as pariahs, their response is significantly different from the outcast minorities in nation states. Legal sojourners are not part of the local status system: denigration hardly affects them, because their reference group lies at home and among their fellow migrants. If they wished, they could return to their country of origin, an option former slaves and native minorities do not have. Therefore the migrants remain free of the self-denigration that demoralizes and paralyzes caste minorities.

State Incorporation of Ascendant Immigrant Minorities

States that have traditionally accepted large numbers of immigrants (e.g., the United States, Canada, Australia, New Zealand) have attracted significantly different immigrant populations since they began to use qualifications rather than cultural affinity as their major selection criteria. The earlier immigrants were primarily from the surplus rural population of Europe; now more immigrants tend to be urbanized professionals from Third World countries who do not rely on ethnicity as a psychic shelter for adaptation. In the past, ethnic gatekeepers in the immigrant neighborhoods of North America provided employment, translations, and information. This extended patronage network has now largely been subsumed by the welfare state, in which individuals can become successful without recourse to ethnic brokers. The demise of traditional immigrant ethnicity is evinced in the high proportion of interethnic marriages and in the decline of ethnic schools, the ethnic press, and ethnic politics.[14]

Instead, a system of "symbolic ethnicity" has developed. This is characterized by voluntary associations, and frequent oscillation between identities. Whereas caste minorities are eager to shed their stigma, ascendant immigrants display pride in their ethnic origins. A recent analysis of the United States concluded that pride in origin has reached such heights that lack of an ethnic background is perceived as a cultural disadvantage.[15] Under these circumstances ethnic identity is only one of many alternate identities that can be developed, displayed, manipulated, or ignored according to the situation of the moment.

This overview of five types of ethnic interaction should not be taken as a static picture. Scapegoat minorities may evolve into self-reliant, competitive groups; stigmatized subordinates may shed their psychological handicap; and foreign migrant laborers can become successful immigrants. In many societies the types overlap or exist side by side.

The review of state policies toward subordinate ethnic groups reveals that no single formula or general conceptualization can be meaningfully applied. The main lesson that can be drawn is that resistance to reductionist dogmatism, combined with a heightened sensitivity for historical uniqueness without foregoing attempts at meaningful comparisons, may best serve a critical social science interested in demystification of conventional wisdom.

Variations of Ethnicity: Afrikaner and Black Nationalism

Among all recent nationalist movements, the success of Afrikanerdom stands out as an example of effective and enduring ethnic mobilization. Against the odds, a severely disadvantaged farming group managed to capture exclusive state power in 1948 and has been tightening its grip on an expanding military-industrial complex ever since.

In the Boer War at the turn of the century, the Afrikaners were defeated and their population decimated. In the country as a whole, they were outnumbered approximately 10 to 1. The cheap Black labor streaming into the new industrial centers put the Afrikaners at a competitive disadvantage, and they were not much better educated than the Blacks. Above all, Afrikaners commanded far less wealth and resources than the economically dominant English section of the population, on whose trade and merchandise the *hinterlanders* were dependent. And yet, despite or because of these handicaps, the ethnic movement turned the tables. It succeeded where, for example, Quebec nationalism, fighting against a similar enemy with much the same cultural imagery, has so far failed.

Afrikaner nationalism achieved its goal of securing control of the South African state through an initial skillful use of the group's symbolic resources rather than by use of any material advantages. Ethnic entrepreneurs manipulated language and religion and manufactured historical myth until a relatively strong sense of unity was forged. After this gradual, cumbersome process of identity formation under the influence of a few professionals and clerics, in the 1920s and 1930s the movement laid economic foundations for a prosperous ethnic bourgeoisie. This ethnic prosperity was greatly expanded once the state could be used to further Afrikaner occupational opportunities in the public service and in a spreading state capitalism.[16] The nationalist movement channeled the displaced and impoverished urban peasants away from socialism into the ethnic fold by providing protective employment and status in a racial caste system. The extensive use of cultural symbols and the manufactured meaning attached to new collective self-definitions gave the class of poor Whites the emotional potential for an ethnicity that transcended mere economic interests.

The obvious question arises: can Blacks in the 1980s emulate their dominators? Can a Black cultural revivalism expect to turn the tables on Afrikaner nationalism as that movement did on British imperialism half a century earlier? The answer to this question turns out to be a guarded no, for the foreseeable future. The structural impediments need to be highlighted, to offset the optimism generated by the efforts of Black nationalism along the Afrikaner model. The economic climate now is very different from that of the 1930s and 1940s and the role of the state in any conflict will be far greater.

During the period of Afrikaner mobilization—the last

quarter of the nineteenth and the first half of the twentieth
century—South Africa typified an expanding colonial economy. With its mineral wealth, mild climate, and high proportion of permanent settlers with European know-how and resources, South Africa faced economic prospects equal to those
of its colonial counterparts in Canada and Australia. The labor market depended on new skills, and newcomers could be
absorbed relatively easily. The two world wars further stimulated the economy. The Afrikaner economic advances were
directly linked to the expanding prosperity in South Africa.

Half a century later, the prospects for capitalism in the region are far more gloomy. South Africa has not escaped the
global recessions. The sharp increase in worldwide competition cannot be entirely offset by South Africa's relatively cheap
labor costs. Structural unemployment looms on the horizon,
although technical skills are currently in high demand. The
rapid monopolization of the market by South Africa's giant
conglomerates has diminished the chances of new small-scale
(Black) entrants to the market.[17] Only a growing Black bureaucratic, rather than entrepreneurial, bourgeoisie can be
realistically envisaged. The careers of this group, however, are
blocked by the racial control of the central civil service.

When Afrikanerdom developed its ideological underpinnings it faced a relatively weak central state. The atrocities of
the Boer War notwithstanding, Afrikaner nationalists could
rely on some measure of fair play and understanding by the
authorities, who were often descendants of the same ethnic
group in coalition with English interests. The mobilizers did
not encounter the severe restrictions on their political activity
that Black nationalists face today. Not only have the techniques of state surveillance and repression been improved, so
have the mechanisms for manipulation and co-optation. Access to the state-controlled television can make or break political movements. In short, while the mobilizers of Afrikanerdom could to a large extent rely on their efforts, Black leaders
today are much more subject to external constraints. Many
political activists have effectively been silenced; censorship
stops intellectuals from propagating radical unifying alterna-

tives; moreover, the audience for such alternatives is often preempted by a host of state-tolerated or state-supported competing elites in the Black community.

The all-pervasive state control makes it unlikely that African nationalism will succeed in an organized war effort. For the army to serve as the tool to inspire militancy and forge nationalist unity, as has happened in European nations and in wars of liberation around the world, seems unlikely in South Africa at present. Conditions in industrialized South Africa do not resemble those in underdeveloped Nicaragua, Cuba, or Zimbawbe, or those faced by the Boer commandos at the turn of the century. While the underground armed resistance is unlikely to cease, the efforts of a few thousand committed guerrillas will not change the lives of the dependent majority, apart from boosting their morale. Given the certainty of response from a well-armed state, the military confrontation can only further divide the Black community into supporters and ardent opponents of violence. Ironically, the rapid incorporation of Blacks in Pretoria's armed forces will also further this divisive process.[18]

In spite of these obvious historical differences, parallels between Afrikaner ethnic mobilization and Black nationalism in South Africa abound. Buthelezi's Zulu cultural and political movement, Inkatha, explicitly uses cultural revival of Zulu history as a means of political mobilization. Others place their hopes on the labor front. Once the emerging unions can use the growing Black purchasing clout effectively in consumer boycotts, an economic basis of Black power will have been laid similar to that Afrikanerdom achieved with *Volkskapitalisme* in the 1920s and 1930s. After the cultural and economic mobilization has succeeded, so its advocates expect, it can finally be extended to the political realm to reap the ultimate victory of state power, as the National Party did in 1948.

The obstacles in the path of the Afrikaner ethnic revolution were formidable, as are those in the path of Black nationalism today. The most obvious similarity is disunity. Bitter interethnic and regional antagonism between the wealthier and liberal Cape Afrikaners and the poorer Transvaalers has dominated

most of the last hundred years of Afrikaner history. Anglicization held real allure for the intellectual elite, both informally, as a means of career advancement, and, for a while,
formally, as official state policy. Feuds among the three Calvinist churches fragmented the *Volk*. The present dislocation of
large numbers of surplus Black laborers finds a precedent in
the internal stratification among Dutch Afrikaners between
the wealthy farmers and the *bywoners* driven from the land in
the wake of the development of commercial farming. Above
all, the state protection upon which the poor Whites have historically been dependent parallels the welfare measures any
South African government will inevitably have to adopt in order to create a semblance of stability. Just as the Afrikaner
nationalists had to wrest state power from their British adversaries through a long struggle and despite various setbacks, so
Black nationalists will gain their rightful share only by making
inroads into the White minority monopoly in a long effort for
liberation on various fronts.

One factor that militated against Afrikaner nationalism
should, in contrast, greatly aid Black cultural ethnicity: the
tradition of African communalism. While the burghers' geographic isolation, origins, and farming methods fostered extreme individualism, the close kinship ties in rural African
society tend to reinforce ethnic solidarity. Unlike the independent Boers, the African subsistence farmer was bound to his
chief for land allocation. Many mutual social obligations
within the clan established cohesive bonds, backed by a much
higher degree of state organization and group awareness
among the Blacks than among the Dutch Afrikaner farmers
in the late nineteenth century. There was nothing voluntary
about military service in the Zulu armies, nor did this military
service devolve largely upon the poorer people, as was the
case with the powerless *bywoners*, who were overrepresented
in the ranks of the Boer commandos. The Zulu equivalents of
field-cornets could not afford to show contempt for the re-
mote central authority, and in traditional African hierarchies
a disciplining conformity, very unlike the individualistic
equality traditional among the Boer settlers, was rigidly en-

forced. In short, Black society, particularly under the pressure of uniform racial stigmatization, may not have to work to ferment the cultural ethnicity that Afrikanerdom had to forge with great effort but may be able to build on a pervasive sense of objective, uniform oppression.

These obvious similarities between Afrikaner and Black nationalism may well be outweighed, however, by the structural and historical differences between the two situations. The decisive differences become clearer when one isolates the two principal means by which Afrikaner nationalism has been mobilized: language and religion. Using heritage-language as a means of cultural mobilization is feasible when 90 percent of the population is engaged in agriculture, as were Dutch Afrikaners in 1875; primary producers need little interaction with the society at large, except through bilingual brokers or merchants. However, African mobilization must use the language of the oppressor. The alternative—insisting on Zulu, Xhosa, or Sotho to communicate in an interdependent industrial setting—bars its adherents from jobs, education, and career opportunities that depend on a mastery of official languages. The indigenous language is used as the medium of resistance, a secret underground code during the struggle for equality, but it is not the language of material success. These oppositional modes of African expression are nevertheless not perceived as being in need of rescue from the danger of Anglicization, let alone absorption into Afrikanerdom. Ethnic entrepreneurs need not struggle to save Zulu or Xhosa from extinction in the way that Afrikaans-speakers had to fight against the inroads of English. Throughout South Africa and regardless of ideological outlook, Black students want to be educated in English, but without giving up their linguistic heritage. Indigenous languages, as in the rest of Africa, retain regional importance even though they dwindle to insignificance in the arena of national politics.

If indeed one African language, for example Zulu, were to emerge as the unifying symbol of liberation, it would not only alienate non–Zulu-speaking Africans but also isolate the two million so-called Coloreds and one million Indians, who have little historical relationship with African culture. The solidarity of "Black consciousness" that includes the three designated racial groups is based on the political factor of common discrimination, not on common cultural affinities. The weakness of the movement lies precisely in this abstract political bond, which is not backed by shared everyday experiences and perceptions. Conversely, the present government policy of co-optation to wean away sections of the two middle groups from Black solidarity builds on the cultural distinctiveness of Indians and Coloreds. The separate languages, religions, foods, customs, and socialization of the three Black groups are as hard to mold into a cohesive culture as is the proclaimed internationalism of the socialist class movement. Through differential privileges in education, politics, residential areas, and economic opportunities, Pretoria has cunningly reinforced this historical cultural hierarchy rather than letting common political grievances assert themselves. Just as the British empire-builders in the nineteenth century considered Afrikaners as "pre-fabricated collaborators," so does the present South African government now treat Coloreds and Indians, thereby strengthening its base.

Ethnic entrepreneurs used religion, in addition to language, as a crucial tool for mobilization.[19] Without the predicants of the Calvinist churches to give impetus to the ethnic movement, Afrikaner nationalism would be inconceivable. While neotraditionalist Afrikaners redefined the religious congregation into an ethnic community, this option is not open to Blacks, who embrace a multitude of religions. Not only are virtually all Christian denominations and sects represented among the subordinates, due to the indefatigable missionaries, but so are Islam, Hinduism, and a variety of powerful indigenous offspring of Christian and native fundamentalism (Zionism).

Black theology, with its concern with material and political in addition to spiritual suffering, has been suggested as a unifying religious bond. But Black theology is largely confined to its intellectual advocates. Whereas in Latin America liberation theology is embedded in a centralized Catholicism, South Africa has no unified, pervasive church.

Moreover, even Black theology binds its adherents to the world of their adversaries. It encourages, not a separate religious ethnicity as in Lebanon, Northern Ireland, Sri Lanka, or Sudan, but a perception of common fate with White Christians. The Black theological stance toward South Africa is to lament the behavior of fellow Christians who are failing in their duties as brothers and sisters. Salvation is to come from moral persuasion and protest. Black theology does not uphold a separate identity and initiatives fundamentally at odds with the world-view of the adversary, as a self-confident Afrikaner Calvinism was with Anglican, Jewish, and Catholic faiths.

In the absence of an unconstrained political leadership, it remains for Black clergy to articulate Black grievances authentically. But this "clerictocracy" becomes divisive as soon as these leaders focus on their religion. The worldwide Islamic revival, and some Hindu factions, for example, fragment the Indian community, which had been much more united in a secularized political front. Divided religious, even more than linguistic, ethnicity ultimately serves to fracture rather than bond.

While the ideological confusion characteristic of early Afrikanerdom and contemporary Black politics alike could perhaps be successfully molded into a linguistic and religious ethnicity by Afrikaner cultural entrepreneurs, the greatest potential for Black unity does not come from a common culture or even racial classification, but from a common economic deprivation. Middle-class Afrikaner ideologues were able to channel the economic frustrations of poor Whites into a cultural movement. Does this option give hope for success to their Black counterparts now?

For most South African Blacks today, cultural heritage is gradually being replaced by what has been referred to as economic ethnicity. The massive dislocation and economic insecurity of both township dwellers and the rural population have increasingly made traditional customs obsolete. The general exploitation of African workers at the bottom of the pay scale and labor hierarchy promises to become the grievance that bridges Black cultural heterogeneity. In this sense, economic ethnicity is identical to class grievances. Because of the vast numbers of Black workers and the economic squeeze in advanced capitalism, any plan for material co-optation of the Black working class faces much greater obstacles now than was the case with poor Whites previously, for there are few cultural foils to camouflage continuous relative deprivation.

Contemporary political practice increasingly emphasizes this economic solidarity. The emerging Black union movement insists on independent workers' organizations. They see this as a necessary guarantee against being hijacked and used to further the goals of political middle-class nationalism. Indeed, just as the Afrikaner-educated petty bourgeoisie exploited their uneducated brothers for a "common" cause, so Black politicians are likely to use workers for their own ends. The intense debate over union strategies, particularly over how deeply unions should become involved in manifestly political issues at this stage, reflects the fear of falling into the trap of false ethnicity. Unlike the early Afrikaner unions, the contemporary Black unions are relatively immune to the exhortations of outside professionals but, rather, rely on shop-floor democracy to determine policy. This real organization from below also makes it likely that the common grass-roots sentiments and everyday experiences of union members will in the long run prevail over the tactical quarrels of the union leadership which dominate at present. An economic ethnicity consisting of a shared identity as Black workers could perhaps affect the balance of power, in spite of continuing ideological splits and leadership rivalries.

Such a belief casts doubt on some assumptions of the cultural pluralist school, particularly the tendency to reify ethnic groups and treat them as monolithic "givens." As Paul Brass has pointed out, pluralists ignore crucial intra-group conflicts such as union competition for members and vested interests of rival leaderships in the same ethnic or class group.[20] Occupational stratification and diverse political outlooks within each ethnic group often fracture the cultural bond.

A leading proponent of cultural pluralism, M. G. Smith, assumed a "cultural incompatibility" among the various sectors.[21] He concluded, therefore, that only the domination of one part or the alien rule of the colonial power could guarantee a stable coexistence for the culturally heterogeneous parts in a single state. Apartheid ideology postulates a similar cultural incompatibility in the name of racial self-determination. However, what incompatibility in religious practice or ethnic customs there may be can easily be confined to the private realm. What matter are collective and individual life chances, determined in the public arena by access to political and economic power. Except among the ruling minority, there is widespread consensus that the Western democracies with common citizenship rights and at least nominal equality of opportunities should provide the model for a nonracial South African state. There is nothing incompatible in the cultures of the sectors that would prevent such an arrangement; it is thwarted only by the privilege maintenance of the dominant section. Even more than the economic ethnicity of relative deprivation, political ethnicity—a shared determination to overthrow White rule—can be used to unite the culturally heterogeneous groups in South Africa.

The assumption of cultural antagonism made by the cultural pluralists is derived from the study of isolated cultural institutions and relatively self-sustained ethnic economies in preindustrial societies. These allegedly insurmountable barriers disappear in the light of the common, albeit differential, involvement of industrial citizens in an interdependent postindustrial economy. Cultural preferences, differences in norms and values, are completely overshadowed by the common interest of all subordinate members in divided societies (such as South Africa) in equal wages and opportunities, reasonably priced consumer products, Western standards of housing and education, optimal health care and recreational facilities, individual security, and public recognition of merit rather than skin color. Intergroup conflict occurs over differential allocation of these resources and not because of cultural differences. The latter merely serve as a smokescreen to justify and obscure the unequal distribution of life chances in the name of cultural pluralism. It is a sign of the progressive state of contemporary African nationalism that it has given priority to political economic frustrations rather than cultural substitutes. Despite the South African all-pervasive racial ordering and ethnic manipulation, the contextual nature of ethnicity is apparent even here. The changing political nature of ethnicity stands revealed most clearly in the defiance of the state's efforts to manufacture Black cultural nationalism through Bantu education and state-sponsored cultural revivalism.

The greatest obstacle to ethnic and racial mobilization among Black South Africans remains, ironically, the state's policy of racial categorization. As has been elaborated elsewhere, South Africa is the only multiethnic society in which ethnicity is imposed by the government. Everyone is forced by law to belong to one of four official racial groups, regardless of individual perceptions or preferences. This imposed group membership has resulted in ethnic categories, but not in ethnic communities. Objective compartmentalization has undercut subjective identity as members of the official categories. Leaders who want to tap the cultural symbols of the racial group for political identity formation will find themselves essentially pursuing government policy. The threat of this stigma hampers use of the symbolic resources of the underprivileged, which ordinarily could be a powerful tool in the hands of ethnic elites. Issues of boundary maintenance, which preoccupy ethnic mobilizers elsewhere, are drowned in a groundswell of sentiment for a common, nonracial South Africanism. Official racial policies under the guise of cultural self-determination have evoked mass preferences for, not multiracialism, not even solely a liberal nonracialism, but a decided anti-racialism. In this way the policy of imposed ethnicity has discredited any ethnic or racial backlash by the disadvantaged. The potential counter-racism of the oppressed so far scrupulously avoids falling into the ideological trap of the oppressor.

Even at its height in the late 1970s, the Black Consciousness movement of the educated middle class was not anti-White per se, but rejected the paternalistic tutelage of White liberals who had dominated the apartheid opposition for so long. Black Consciousness aimed at psychological liberation from internalized colonial attitudes but hardly tried to build a Black counterculture that would have been incompatible with the dominant norms.[22] The older and increasingly legitimate resistance movement in the form of the Congress organization has always pursued an explicitly nonracial policy, despite various attempts to reverse a sometimes controversial stance.[23]

In short, Afrikaner mobilizers used grievances about culture suppression for political ends. Black nationalism has, instead, economic and political complaints. Black cultural revivalism is, on the contrary, part of the state's separate-development policy, an obvious attempt to fragment Black unity and impede Black competition through traditionally oriented Bantu education. Thus any flirtation with a divisive past is thoroughly discredited by modern African nationalists. The official policy of separate development, so to speak, has to a large extent preempted racist Black cultural revivalism.

White liberalism also contributed to the relative lack of racial polarization in what is often portrayed as an escalating race war. White responses to Black frustrations were at all stages sufficiently varied to prevent a Black generalization of all Whites as evil. White stereotyping of Blacks always exceeded Black stereotyping of Whites.[24] The handful of Whites who, in the course of "the struggle," suffered lifelong imprisonment (Bram Fisher), died under police interrogation (Neil Aggett), were banned for decades (Helen Joseph, Rowley Arenstein, Beyers Naudé), or became public symbols for Black civil rights (Helen Suzman) turned Black judgments from grounds of race to that of morality. Together with an array of charitable organizations, from the Black Sash to churches, anti-government English newspapers, universities, and liberal parties, the Black elite could always find powerless White allies. The ethnic concentration of political control in the hands of Afrikaners partially concealed the silent collusion of the conservative English beneficiaries of apartheid with racial domination. English business, posing as a victim of petty bureaucratic ideological obsessions that hampered the free market, added its share to the ideological confusion about the identity of the enemy. All these factors have so far impeded a clear racial mobilization against a racially exclusive ruling group.

In 1872, when the Cape Colony was granted "responsible government," the hitherto manipulated rural poor not only gained access to the political arena but also acquired a motivation for engaging in politics. Gradual Afrikaner political mobilization became imperative for simple economic survival. If farmers wanted just taxation and their share of credit, labor supply, and state expenditures, they had to ensure that their concerns were represented in parliament against entrenched imperialist interests.

Now, a hundred years later, although Blacks have many of these same economic interests, they no longer depend to the same extent on the political arena. Not only have the powers of parliament been preempted by a vast state bureaucracy and other agencies such as private monopolies, but the economic success of the individual Black businessman is contingent on his apolitical stance. It is going along with the status quo, not ethnic resistance, that guarantees Blacks jobs in the civil service and private sectors. To be sure, collectively Blacks would benefit from a reversal of political power. But only a minority in any ethnic community will be prepared to act to achieve long-term collective goals at the expense of personal advancement. In short, the dependency of Blacks on an industrial economy controlled by Whites forces most subordinates into one or another form of collaboration, whether they like and admit it or not. This limits the appeal of both linguistic and religious ethnicity as means of unified political mobilization.

It forces the excluded to aim straight for political power by whatever means the fragmented factions deem feasible. Black politics will most likely run the gamut from more violence to increased collaboration. Rather than an increasingly unified movement to conquer political power, internecine strife is likely to shape and weaken Black challenges in the absence of ethnic cohesion apart from the invidious racial mark. Even this common bond is being eroded by increasingly sophisticated strategies of co-optation of a Black professional bourgeoisie into a nonracial system of consumer capitalism.

Class and race still overlap in South Africa almost completely and thereby provide the ideal condition for an ethnic ideology which does not even have to camouflage internal stratification. However, the educated professional leaders of the Black masses, more than Anglicized Afrikaners in the cities ever were, are constantly lured by the material spoils of political acquiescence in an advanced capitalist society. Their career chances may be blocked in the civil service of the central government, but some of their expectations are, to a certain extent, fulfilled in the vast bureaucracies of Bantustans and, increasingly, in the administration of "own affairs."

If the Black elite is to profess solidarity with their fellow Blacks, it will be in reaction to their continued political exclusion from real power. It is the insult, the blow to their self-esteem, and no longer mainly material deprivation, that makes many materially better-off subordinates ally themselves with their worse-off fellow group members. Under the conditions of entrenched racialism, the elite needs at least a rhetoric of solidarity for self-legitimation of its privileged status. But in a very real sense it is only with the aid of large numbers of mobilized workers that the political entrepreneurs can hope to gain the central kingdom, or at least a greater share of the pie. The lack of much common ground except skin color severely impedes this attempt. On the other hand, the intransigence of the dominant group in failing formally to remove race from the criteria of social stratification helps to surmount the obstacle of cultural heterogeneity. Even substantial reform from above can no longer assuage the demand for a new order. Apartheid is viewed as irreformable. Only when Africans are recognized as playing an equal role, not as objects of administration but as administrators in their own right, will the post-apartheid state have arrived.

3

Conflicts
in White Politics

WHILE MUCH OF THE LITERATURE distinguishes
between pragmatic (*verligte*) and reactionary (*verkrampte*) outlooks, important developments are obscured by this simplifi-
cation. At present four competing definitions of Afrikaner
policy vie for hegemony among the divided *volk*. They may be
labeled those of the labor racists, the orthodox ideologues, the
ruling technocrats, and the critical moralists. Each ideological
outlook and policy prescription derive from a distinct constituency within the Afrikaner ranks. From a common rhetoric
quite different priorities emerge.

This analysis assesses the strategies propagated by the four
groups in order to cope with their different perceptions of
crisis, their potential or actual political clout, and their suscep-
tibility to outside influence.

The Labor Racists

The labor racists of the Herstigte Nasionale Party (HNP),
which had split from the Nationalist Party under B. J. Vorster
in 1969, were, politically, left out in the cold when in the late
1970s the government favored business interests over conflicting White-union demands for job reservation and differential
labor conditions. To be sure, in the Afrikaner state the worker
section has at no time been the dominant voice. But with the
working-class Whites historically constituting up to one-third
of the Afrikaner voters, organized Afrikaner labor exercised

virtual veto power on crucial issues of Black employment. The ethnic mobilizers of the Broederbond—their "good financial standing" being a criterion of admittance—nevertheless integrated the poorer "brothers," both ideologically and politically. With the increasing stratification of Afrikanerdom and the declining percentage of White manual workers generally in the 1960s and 1970s, together with the imperatives of new labor policies on the mines, the White workers were dropped from state protection.

Why did this Afrikaner class coalition fall apart, despite its strong ideological coherence? Why did so strong an ethnic bond as that belonging to a powerful nationalist movement in the end prove so weak that its alleged invincible unity disintegrated precisely when the challenge to Afrikaner rule deepened? Among the many, necessarily simplified, answers one stands out.

During the boom of the 1960s and early 1970s two shifts in traditional labor practice became imperative: first, the increased capital-intensive production demanded a stable, urban, semi-skilled (Black) work force, in addition to the traditional policy of relying on rotating, cheap, migrant labor; and, second, skilled (White) workers, protected by the color bar, were mostly upgraded into the technical/supervisory positions of mechanized production. They were not, however, able to fill the increasing demand for skilled technical manpower. By insisting on the color bar and blocking African advances, White workers created a major impediment to economic growth. This obstacle could not be removed by the employers alone without the collaboration of the state. The defeat of the Mine Workers Union in their last strike, together with the decline of the South African Confederation of Labour and its associated unions, signaled the demise of the traditional protective labor policies.

So desperate is the Mine Workers Union for members now that it has begun to recruit among White workers in the parastatal companies who feel threatened by Africanization as well as potential privatization. Interestingly, the declining White unions are adopting the general workers' principle just when the Black and nonracial unions are moving toward industrial organization.

On the political front, the Afrikaner establishment succeeded in purging the followers of Albert Hertzog from its crucial political institutions, particularly the Broederbond in the early 1970s. Many of those later to be supporters of the Conservative Party, who at that time held prominent positions in the Nationalist establishment, played an active part in the bitter in-fighting. In the 1972 purge of HNP sympathizers from the Broederbond, each member had to sign an oath that he "was not associated with the HNP either through membership or cooperation, and if [he] was associated, [he would] undertake to end this association immediately." The leaders of the HNP have still not forgiven A. P. Treurnicht, then chairman of the Broederbond, and his supporter Vorster for HNP's expulsion from Afrikanerdom's most influential organization. This history accounts for a variety of contemporary personal incompatibilities, in addition to the difference in class base of the two groupings on the political right of the Nationalist Party. Despite the obvious advantages of avoiding a split vote now, this hampered a merger and initially even an electoral pact against the Nationalists.

Until 1986 the HNP had succeeded in only one by-election (Sasolburg), although the recession and free-enterprise policies combined with cuts of traditional subsidies, as well as substantial sales-tax increases, fueled the resentment of marginalized White labor and farmers as never before. The electoral power of the combined right-wing vote would also be curtailed by the proposed redrawing of constituency lines which, ironically, would eliminate that gerrymandering of rural voters from which the Nationalist Party had benefited in the past. In the unlikely event of a serious right-wing threat to the ruling technocrats, the Progressive Federal Party could well hold the balance of power, provided White democracy still exists. Its abolition in South Africa is not as simple as the example of authoritarian-corporate regimes in Latin America seems to suggest.[1] No minority government in South Africa can ignore the issue of legitimacy among Whites. If the executive state became a technocratic military dictatorship, it would still have to accommodate both substantial sections of the White right-wing and liberal factions. Any further absorption of political power by the present government would be fiercely resisted by the conservatives, whose collaboration in the civil service and the army would prove essential.

In the meantime, Jaap Marais, the leader of the HNP, who is an outstanding orator, can accrue credit for having castigated the dictatorial tendencies of and betrayal by the Nationalist Party long ago, while his competitors remained opportunistic accomplices to the crime of destroying Afrikanerdom.

Semi-militarized fringe groups such as the Afrikaner-Weerstandbeweging (AWB) operate in the shadow of the HNP. They imitate uniformed Nazis to defend "the honor" of the Afrikaner people, mainly against prominent defectors from the ranks. These pathological fundamentalists are responsible for some physical attacks upon Afrikaner intellectuals and English liberals, very much in the style of vigilante groups in the American South during the civil rights struggle. These groups, often in collusion with local police, form the potential reservoir of "death squads" in the Latin American tradition, although the South African government has occasionally clamped down on these fringe activities.

The discourse among Afrikaner nationalists is best summarized in party posters at the October 1985 by-elections. The National Party (NP) poster said, "Don't shoot. Think"; the HNP reversed it to proclaim, "Shoot. Don't think." The CP leader Treurnicht suggested that the security forces should be "unleashed." He portrayed half-hearted repression as the cause of continued unrest. Another poster with a young blond girl admonished: "Don't repeat Rhodesia for her sake," equating majority rule with child molesting. The influx of Rhodesian Whites into South Africa after Zimbabwe's independence has also added to the appeal of the right wing. The open expression of conservatism and racism by some English South Africans has been welcomed by the Conservative Party, although it dilutes its Afrikaner exclusivity.

The Orthodox Ideologues

In contrast to the racist rhetoric of Marais, the orthodox ideologues in the Conservative Party avoid openly reinforcing
grass-roots racist sentiments. Andries Treurnicht and his
aides cultivate respectability. Their main constituency lies in
the lower echelons of the vast civil service, which comprises 40
percent of all economically active Afrikaners, and what is
called the petty bourgeoisie, the lower middle classes. Conscious of their newly acquired white-collar status, they wish to
keep aloof from *lumpen* ethnics. Their vague party program
mixes pre-Verwoerdian ideology with calls for a Colored and
Indian homeland in order to ensure White self-determination
and avoid power-sharing. Thus the Conservative Party distinguishes itself by completely ignoring the reality of an interdependent economy, let alone the political wishes of the subordinate population. Contrasting "sharing of power" with an
advocated "division of power" remains meaningless in the absence of any workable plans to achieve these goals.

It is ironic that the catchword of *power-sharing* precipitated
the split since, as was admitted, this was never intended to
mean loss of Afrikaner control. Colored and Indian "leaders"
enjoy the style but not the substance of office. Complex constitutional arrangements ensure that Afrikaner nationalists
still dominate the system completely. Not even the hypothetical possibility of a temporary loss of power exists, since alliances between Coloreds and Indians and the White opposition
are ruled out. In fact, the proposals substantially strengthen
the ruling group's hold on political power, by legally supplant-
ing traditional democratic procedures with administrative
fiats.

One reason for the latent appeal of conservative ideology
undoubtedly lies in the occupational position of many of its
adherents. Most civil servants are sheltered from the harsher
economic realities by job security and state protection. They
are perturbed by the prospect of competing with members of
former outgroups. Moreover, the labor control board officials,
the Afrikaner policemen or teachers of "Christian-National"

education, who are themselves only subalterns receiving their orders from above, were previously rewarded, in part, by their conviction that they were serving a good cause. With the old apartheid certainty in disarray and the meaning of their work in question, they cling to a glorified past order with great zeal, regardless of the consequences.

The intense ideological mobilization through Christian-National indoctrination in separate schools for Afrikaans-speaking White children now backfires on the technocratic Nationalists. Teachers—who are comparatively poorly paid, and 70 percent of whom are women—constitute a latent support-group for the orthodox ideologues, particularly in the Transvaal. In an ironic reversal of an earlier cherished practice, the Minister in charge, Gerrit Viljoen, felt obliged to caution teachers against bringing party politics into education, since this "could cause alienation between parent and child."[2] The sectarian nature of White education is best reflected in the existence of two teachers' organizations in the same province, the Transvalse Onderwysersvereeniging and the (English) Transvaal Teachers' Organization, who complain principally of the nepotism and indoctrination of the Afrikaner-dominated educational bureaucracy.

Another group still powerful in molding sectarian attitudes is the Afrikaans clergy, although they are by no means as ideologically homogeneous as the church front would like to suggest. Treurnicht, himself a former cleric, devoted much time to the house meetings of dominees, while Chris Heunis, a government minister, railed against "theological racism which will destroy this country."[3] When two Afrikaner churches, the leading Nederduitse Gereformeerde Kerk and the smaller Hervormde Kerk, were finally expelled from the World Alliance of Reformed Churches at its Ottawa meeting in 1982, the expected soul-searching in South Africa was awaited in vain. The action was simply rationalized as another part of the international "total onslaught" against the country. Pleas by more enlightened ministers for a unified and desegregated church were rejected as "untimely" by the majority and by the conservative church hierarchy.

The Kerk, like other ethnic organizations, is constantly criticized for failing in its moral and spiritual leadership by adopting a noncommittal, self-righteous stance on politically divisive issues. However, with a divided membership and with the
conservative flock in a clear majority, vested organizational
interests in preserving unity win, not unpredictably, over
moral duties. The increased factional politicization of the constituency after the split of the Nationalist Party has resulted,
paradoxically, in an apparent depoliticization of the official
stance of its auxiliary institutions. Even an overtly political organization such as the Broederbond is now politically so par-
alyzed that it denies any internal differences. The choice such
organizations face is either to split or to confine themselves to
noncontroversial cultural issues. For the time being, at least,
the crucial support institutions of Afrikaner nationalism are
opting for formal unity and factional in-fighting over institutional influence rather than for pursuit of the party example.
This leaves to the political arena less opposition than ever to
its control over the fate of the *volk*.

What makes people accept one or another explanation of
reality remains one of the most vexing questions in the social
sciences. The Marxist answer, "class interests," is shown to be
inadequate when people in the same class adopt conflicting
ideologies. Whatever makes equally wealthy farmers in the
Transvaal, or teachers in the Free State who have identical
material interests, nevertheless define their political stances so
differently escapes economic reductionism.

The former politicization of the Afrikaner civil service with
wide discretionary power, based on the underlying consensus
of the incumbents, also seems to backfire now. No longer do
all officials automatically implement all orders from above;
rather, they interpret them according to their own views. The
admission by Ministers that their staffs are undermining official policy is not merely a rationalization for inertia. Intra-
departmental conflicts increasingly create problems for administrative efficiency and state coherence. Various incidents
indicate that officials are increasingly coming to act without
orders from above. The continuing pattern of deaths of de-

CONFLICTS IN WHITE POLITICS 65

tainees in police custody, for example, despite the worldwide outcry after the assassination of Steve Biko, first president of the South African Students' Organization (SASO) seems to suggest that the technocratic upper echelons are too weak, if not unwilling, to put their house in order. The reluctance to persecute the perpetrators may well also be due to the fear of appearing "soft" on security, thereby providing the right wing with another cause. In short, deracialization means detribalization of the South African civil service, to be replaced with a bureaucratic professionalism of adherence to rules rather than exercise of discretion.

South Africa has so far only experienced the beginnings of the kinds of death squads Latin American regimes often employ. Unrestrained killing of suspected dissidents remains a distinct possibility if the legitimacy of authority is eroded and if the combatants perceive mediators as the main stumbling block to a polarized commitment. At that stage, the ground may well be prepared for a dictatorship taking over with widespread popular approval, based on the sentiment that Marx once ascribed to pre-Napoleonic France: "Better an end with terror than terror without end." At present the ruling establishment perceives itself as accountable at least to its domestic constituency and world audience. Compared with the potential for repression in modern, scientific barbarism, the bungling, paternalistic autocracy of Afrikaner nationalism could come to seem authoritarian dilettantism. Particularly when a civil war legitimizes extraordinary measures, there are few moral precepts that effectively bar large-scale atrocities or even genocide, although there are clear limitations to this in South Africa. For example, an academic supporter of Treurnicht, Hercules Booysen, warned: "This country can be put on fire, not only by Blacks, but by Whites too. Apartheid has, to a certain extent, given Whites a false sense of security. But take away the system and see what will happen then."[4]

Traditional democratic theory insists on a depoliticized military combined with civilian authority's clear control over strategic issues. How fully the barracks are under the command of an elected government and parliament is considered to determine the division between democratic and military rule. In White South Africa, as in Israel, this distinction does not apply. Increasingly, the entire society is becoming militarized. In these states the boundaries between politicians and the military are fluid: personnel are interchangeable, and the two spheres merge. In Latin America the armed forces are usually politicized; in the beleaguered ethnic state, however, the polity becomes militarized. The political power of the State Security Council, in which military influence is strong, epitomizes this trend.

A suspension of White democracy and the establishment of a reformist military dictatorship are often mentioned as an alternative to Black and White extremism. However, great obstacles bar fulfillment of this technocratic vision. First, unlike the military in Latin America, the South African military does not constitute a separate caste; 90 percent are conscripts. These draftees reflect the divisions in White society. Their morale, already questioned by the army's use in the civil unrest, would be further undermined if they were called upon to serve a military dictatorship. The fewer than 10,000 professional soldiers could not run an advanced industrial society against widespread resistance. Second, the South African military is still, at least in theory, steeped in the British tradition of loyally serving the civilian government in power.[5] That does not preclude that senior officers be politicized and take an active part in intergovernmental rivalries. It is well known that high-ranking members of the South African Defence Force (SADF) frequently counteracted the Department of Foreign Affairs' policy of peaceful neocolonial relationships with neighboring states by actively working to destabilize "Marxist" governments. South Africa's political isolation has above all cut off its military personnel from foreign training and posting opportunities. That, in turn, has led to a parochial and regional outlook at the expense of realistic, global assessments by many senior personnel. Third, the close working relationship between the military and the ruling National Party that consolidated with the ascendancy of former Defence Minister P. W. Botha has made the military an integral part of government decision-making, so that there is no need to take it over formally. Unlike the situation in several states that have experienced military takeovers, in South Africa the army leadership is on the same ideological wavelength as the government. Support for either the HNP/CP or the official opposition, the Progressive Federal Party (PFP), is negligible among South African colonels, according to all available information. However, among the police, and especially the Security Police, right-wing sentiments are known to be widespread. The technocratically minded police leadership faces frequent difficulties in enforcing the chain of authority on relatively autonomous area commanders. It is in this arena of undereducated, low-status-conscious, and overworked guardians of the state that right-wing sentiment finds sympathy, though not necessarily formal recruits.

The Ruling Technocrats

While the conservatives attempt to make the fiction of partition convincing, the ruling technocrats articulate the pretense of power-sharing. On 2 November 1983, White voters in South Africa decided by a two-thirds majority in a nationwide referendum to approve a new South African constitution. The new political dispensation still excludes the 73 percent of the population that is African from participation in central political decision-making, but includes, symbolically, the 10 percent so-called Coloreds and 3 percent Indians in separate parliaments. The Coloreds and Indians now play the minor role of educating Whites in nonracialism.

The majority of White South Africans pride themselves on having voted for progressive constitutional change. They perceive themselves as having agreed, for the first time in history, to share power with people of color. The modest beginning is said to lead inevitably to more change later. A "step in the right direction" is said to be better than the status quo that would have prevailed had the die-hard racists won.

Much of the support for the flawed constitution came, somewhat hesitantly, from traditional critics of apartheid policies, particularly in the English business sector and parts of the English press. The influential Johannesburg *Sunday Times* and *Financial Mail*, for example, backed a yes vote while the Durban *Sunday Tribune* and the *Cape Times*, owned by the same group, advocated a rejection of the proposals. The Afrikaans press, as well as the government-controlled radio and television were of course unequivocal in their stance; this, despite the large ultra-right opposition in Afrikaner ranks, which makes up to 40 percent of the total Afrikaner vote, particularly in the most populous Transvaal. Their reasoning presents an interesting case of self-delusion.

While hardly anyone praised the constitution as a recipe for future stability, it was supported as an apparent improvement on the status quo. Had the government been compelled to reconsider the issues by a loss of the referendum, it would have had to compromise to the right and not to the left. Very likely a successor to discredited reformer P. W. Botha would have attempted to reunite Afrikanerdom. Foreign investors would have viewed a no vote in the referendum, for whatever reason, as a refusal by White South Africa to change: after all, the cautious move toward a more representative government represented progress, surely to be followed by later political inclusion of the Black majority.

These assumptions are clearly fallacious. Could the Pretoria regime renege on its steps toward modernizing racial domination? Could it afford to go back into the laager in the 1980s? In the light of the origin of this constitutional change—the need to accommodate new social forces—it becomes clear that a return to an old order is not on the cards. Nobody can say that the traditional apartheid order fit the requirements of a deracializing capitalism in an interdependent, advanced economy. The problems of stretched manpower needs and the legitimation crisis of Pretoria are not to be solved by perpetuating the status quo.

The strength of the ultra-right in South Africa notwithstanding, a return to the status quo and simultaneous economic stability would simply be impossible. To be sure, the

Conservative Party still speaks for a substantial section of the White population. However, this represents a declining constituency and ideology in terms of social forces relevant in the future. Regardless of the outcome of the referendum, South Africa would sooner or later have had to come to grips with its economic advancement and political lag, even under an ultra-conservative regime.

The option of stalling reform, therefore, no longer exists. If it were tried, it would highlight the inherent contradictions of the South African political order to such an extent that no sane government could keep itself in power and hope to remain part of an international economy. Real isolation, not just rhetorical condemnation as at present, would be the consequence. The price of stalled reform would be a declining domestic economy with much more serious instability. With hopes for reform dashed, there would be an internal and external loss of confidence of such depth that the various latent cleavages would break open uncontrollably. Belief in an evolutionary progressive political development, however slow, forms an essential part of the psychological glue that holds this deeply divided society together. If the illusion of genuine reform provides the necessary climate for business as usual, it must be reinforced by more legitimate political arrangements. "Power-sharing" and "more representative government" trigger such approval.

The new politics, however, are still being devised by non-African group representatives, albeit no longer by Whites only. To have Coloreds and Indians determining the political role of the majority population in cahoots with the ruling section can only aggravate intergroup tensions, particularly between the majority and the newly co-opted middle groups.

It is true, though, that the reform process, once started, may develop its own dynamic. Botha has reiterated that there is no hidden agenda, but he could hardly say otherwise in the face of right-wing accusations of betrayal. In any case, unintended consequences always arise. The pressure for inclusion of Black Africans built up sooner than the regime realized in

1983. With a caucus less ideologically oriented than they had expected, the more pragmatic policymakers were eventually forced to recognize reality, particularly when interacting with a wider circle of interest groups and ideological outlooks under the new dispensation. Technocrats are not incapable of learning lessons about the rising costs of maintaining privilege. However, intentions or the goodwill of constitution-makers are not at issue. The tragedy lies in the fact that the new rules invite conflict rather than minimize it. They waste precious time in letting excluded forces build up outside the political system instead of anticipating the pressure before the dam breaks—with dire consequences for all.

The referendum debate showed the official opposition, the Progressive Federal Party, under its leader F. Van Zyl Slabbert, to be more principled than its critics will admit. The party, often denounced as the political arm of English business, did not waver, despite assumed majority support among its supporters for the new deals and most leading English businessmen deserting their political home. On this issue, the PFP leadership stood for the long-term interests of White security against the short-term views of their traditional supporters. These were blinded by their newly found access to the corridors of political power.

Afrikanerdom has split most traumatically over the new constitution, despite Nationalist control being firmly consolidated. The so-called power-sharing was interpreted by the far right as compromising Afrikaner sovereignty, the thin edge of the wedge by which big business would sneak in color-blind profit interests rather than guarantee traditional White protection.

Ironically, this accusation contains some truth. The irony lies in the severe constraints Afrikaner political culture imposes on any serious technocratic attempt at conflict management. The present regime fears the far right as a much more immediate threat to its power base than the left. Given its ethnically bound constituency, it cannot open itself sufficiently to the tainted liberal spectrum without disintegrating as an Afrikaner party, cannot embrace genuine reforms without jeopardizing its basic Nationalist support structures. Considering the cold war that the limited reforms caused in all Afrikaner institutions, Botha indeed probably "went as far as he could." Many English-speakers, themselves as conservative and as solid beneficiaries of apartheid as the ruling section, wanted to give the government credit for its "courage" and not lose such a valuable ally. Herein lies the main explanation for the 66 percent yes vote in the referendum. However, accepting the ethnic limits of reform politics, the regime cannot go as far as is necessary to prevent future conflict. A new constitution that is imposed by one section rather than being freely negotiated by representatives of all major interest groups forces the excluded group to seek redress by other means. In the meantime, compromise and moderation become discredited as "leading nowhere."

How far many White South Africans still are from understanding basic premises of conflict management is shown in the reasons many "progressive" academics advanced for their support of the new dispensation. They made the point that an all-inclusive democratic system "will only be achieved if the actual beginnings of mixed government show responsible leadership, an overriding willingness to cooperate and a deeply felt dedication to eradicate prejudice and fear."[6] These condescending preconditions imply that the newly included have to prove their worthiness before they can expect further concessions. This insistence on proper behavior views political conflicts, which a constitution is supposed to regulate, in terms of paternalistic rewards contingent on the learning experiences of the rulers. Powerful as the White rulers may be, real power-sharing will not arrive in South Africa as a result of the excluded demonstrating non-threatening conduct. On the contrary, only real threats and pressures force enlightened rulers to compromise. The South African conflict does not concern the eradication of prejudice and fear; this will always exist among mobilized competitors. How the conflicting claims and perceptions can be channeled into mutually acceptable compromises remains the fundamental issue of successful constitution-making.

At present there are constraints on and limits to the abandonment of legitimacy claims. South Africa cannot afford to abolish all safeguards of Western legalism in favor of Latin American or Archipelago-style repression. The South African state perceives the need to bring itself more closely in line with its Western allies as well as to keep from becoming totally unacceptable to all Blacks. Above all, the predominant sentiment among the White section requires that its rule must be perceived as just and humane by the Whites themselves. Here the still strong relics of the liberal and Calvinist traditions merge. They demand, in addition to technocratic efficiency, legitimation and accountability for the powerholders. Too crude and ruthless a police action shocks even dulled Christian sensibilities. More Bikos, Aggetts, and deaths in police custody confirm the propaganda of the enemy. They reduce South Africa to the level of Third World dictatorships—but South Africa prides itself on upholding the rule of law while others have sunk into nepotistic despotism.

If White rule were to degenerate into an unlegitimated police state, ideological cleavages would open within the White camp that would weaken its fragile racial cohesion. White morale would be further undermined and the crucial self-perception of fighting for a just cause would be lost. The uncritical loyalty demanded from all South African patriots against "the total onslaught" would be exposed as a mere clinging to undeserved spoils. Few would want to risk their lives without a glorifying ideology; survival of privilege alone is not a tenable cause. Mere survival ideology represents the lowest common denominator of a divided ruling class in crisis. Economic growth also offers little reason for self-sacrifice. The garish obscenity of Sun Cities surrounded by starving peoples testifies to the moral decay of its defenders; this becomes much more visible when the other side primarily asserts a humiliated dignity and aims to rectify so gaudy an injustice as racial debasement and birthrights denied. This, then, stands at the core of the South African legitimation crisis for the Whites.

The Critical Moralists

The outcome of the ideological debate about the nature and future of Afrikanerdom depends also on the *critical moralists* (a term coined by Johan Degenaar, a political philosopher at Stellenbosch). They have a dormant, unorganized constituency. With the politicization of the Afrikaner cultural institutions through the split in the Nationalist Party, the dissenting theologians, non-nationalist students, and intellectuals do play an important role in redefining Afrikanerdom. Only a stereotypic view of Afrikanerdom can conclude that "Afrikaners do not produce critical self-analyses."[7] The writers, academics, and even journalists in the media that question the government have set in motion a process that continually challenges the legitimacy claims of the powers that be. Unlike English liberals, whose emphasis on universal values led them to denigrate Afrikaner ethnicity, critical moralists speak from the inside, as Afrikaners. Most will not join or even vote for the Progressive Federal Party. In the general election of 1981, only 5 percent of Afrikaners—compared to 25 percent of those with university education—voted for the PFP. Their political ideals are nevertheless close to those expressed in the PFP program and strategy. The critical moralists are concerned to separate Afrikaner cultural achievement from its oppressive political implementation. This demystification of Afrikaner history constitutes an important step toward a reconciliation between African and Afrikaner nationalism. The critical moralists are supplying new perspectives in a time when "Afrikanerdom's ideology is what each day's problems demand."[8]

The PFP faces a constant dilemma: should it adhere to non-racial principles, or should it engage in the politics of power? A decision to aim to capture a larger share of the White vote would require diluting its principles. Such pragmatic compromise would still fail to capture political power and would in addition lose the moral appeal that has made the party attractive to both a liberal White and a Black minority. With a constituency whose support for party politics is "soft," i.e., motivated less by firm ideological convictions than by dislike of the nationalist alternative, the PFP has to walk a tightrope between moral purity and reasonable voter representation. Given the essential conservatism of middle- and upper-class PFP supporters, there are clear limits to pursuit of a principled anti-racist policy. Perhaps more than half of the traditional PFP voters defected from the party line by voting yes in the constitutional referendum in November 1983.

The PFP does not constitute a party on the "left," as Nationalist Afrikaners commonly believe. Much like the British Liberal Party or the German Free Democratic Party (FDP), it represents the more enlightened and secularized sections of an urban, mostly professional stratum who equate traditional conservatism with outdated bigotry. In South Africa, moreover, the party is still strongly identified with the English section of the population, although it has been headed by an Afrikaner since 1979. The strength of the leadership, particularly that of F. Van Zyl Slabbert and Helen Suzman, the two principal public figures of the party,[9] lies in their cool dissection of the South African polity as well as in their impeccable record of civil rights defense. As a consequence, the PFP policy is seen as idealistic rather than aiming at practical goals; while many White voters may secretly admire the convictions of the PFP, they do not wholly trust it to guarantee White interests. In a crisis, White South Africa, including the majority of English voters, will put its faith in the National Party, with its proven record of racial priorities.

The PFP, then, is in practice confined to political education rather than functioning as a potential alternative government. As long as the extreme right wing is no threat, there is little chance, let alone likelihood, that a technocratic National Party will need PFP support for a coalition government. The liberal apartheid opposition fills a useful role in breaking political taboos about the likely future South Africa, thereby ideologically paving the road the government will inevitably have to trudge some day. A clear example of such taboo-breaking is PFP advocacy of federalism, which has not yet been formally

The Politicization of Innocence

This is the first time I have ever written to a newspaper. I am 19 and I was so shocked and repulsed by what I saw today that I felt it necessary to let you know how I feel about what is going on in Hout Bay.

My father has a youth Bible class at our house every Sunday and every Sunday they go up to the squatters on the mountain to bring them soup, bread, clothes they have collected, plastic for their houses and blankets.

The squatters are genuine, loving, normal people just like you or me. They, too, have feelings, emotions and feel pain and anguish. Yet today some people came from the Divisional Council and smashed up all their homes without any notice or warning.

Most of the men were at work and the women and children watched helplessly. I just don't know how these people from the council could have gone home at night with no conscience or guilt after smashing down 45 homes of men, women and children.

I went up this evening to bring these squatters soup and bread, more plastic and clothes. I want to know why, if they had to do it, they did it today when they knew it was going to rain, rather than the last few days when it was so warm?

I sat with some of the children this evening and at first I felt sympathy and sorrow, but it fast turned to anger. If I felt like that, can you imagine how they must have felt?

Please, it would mean so much to me and other teenagers (and grownups) who are friendly with these people if you could possibly publish who the people responsible for this destruction are. All we know is that they were from the Divisional Council.

People like this think they are doing so much good for the Government and the country, but they are doing more harm than good. They are causing hate and pain where it is not called for.

(The Argus, *24 August 1984*)

embraced by the ruling party because of the opposition's historical monopoly of the concept.

It remains to be seen how the drive to recruit Blacks into the PFP after the repeal of the Political Interference Act in 1985 will affect the party. An experience that the disbanded Liberal Party had twenty years earlier may perhaps be repeated. As Peter Brown remembers it, "The party started life with a basically laissez-faire economic program tempered by welfare statism. Its membership was predominantly White. It ended life in the throes of a hectic debate on a new, essentially social-democratic policy and considering changing its name to the Social Democratic Party of South Africa. Most of its membership was Black."[10] Now, though, twenty years later, Black politicization has developed beyond reformist multiracialism.

If the official liberal opposition can nudge the government into more widely acceptable interim solutions and real negotiation politics, it will have succeeded, given its structural constraints, as it will have served the cause of civil rights by holding the regime accountable for its violations. By constantly challenging the self-legitimations of rulers, by contrasting reality with false promises and potentials, the liberals may indeed uphold the long-term interests of capital against short-term calculations, as critics have charged, and may strengthen the South African system by wrapping the harsh edges of economic exploitation and political oppression in the bandages of false charity and illusionary goodwill. But only a dogmatist can reject immediate reforms in favor of a distant utopia. The claim that heightening present misery provides a shortcut to revolution is not only empirically false but also morally despicable when made by those who will not themselves be the victims. The derision with which many left-wing academics greet liberal attempts at realistic mediation and reformist improvements only demonstrates their own political paralysis.

4
Conflicts
in Black Politics

Political Alliances

THE CONSTITUTIONAL REFORMS have not only divided the three Black racial groups among themselves but have repoliticized a stale debate about strategies. Just as the Afrikaner right wing found it impossible to create a depoliticized stability, so Blacks are embroiled in ideological and strategic conflicts. The emergence of the National Forum in June 1983 and of the United Democratic Front a few months later revived the debates between Congress-oriented Charterists and Black Consciousness adherents. Even Chief Kaiser Mantanzima, surprisingly, declared that he would strive to reintegrate the Transkei into a reformed Republic of South Africa (RSA) and made overtures to Buthelezi in response to the constitutional anti-Black alliance. The Nationalist Party split in 1982 provided the legitimacy for the Colored Labor Party to join the government camp. It proved the "sincerity" of the reform. Had the same proposals been made by Vorster as prime minister, they would have encountered far stronger suspicion, even outright rejection, with the conservative ideologues being perceived as holding veto power.

The effects of state manipulation of its Black opposition can best be gauged by looking at the strategies of four principal Black tendencies. Despite repeated calls for unity of the oppressed, all four are locked into a bitter struggle for support among the vast majority of non-participants. By allowing the Black opposition more terrain on which to function rhetorically but denying them an institutionalized role in central political decision-making, the state has both weakened and strengthened its opponents.

The disarray in Black politics is widely misinterpreted as a conflict between radicals and moderates, collaborators and boycotters, liberals and communists, Black racists and nonracists, or, worse, Zulus and Xhosas. All Black politicians express abhorrence of apartheid and a desire for unity. Why, then, the intra-Black cleavages?

The most sensible analysis distinguishes four different groupings with distinct strategies and ideologies. On a broad right-left spectrum they can be labeled: patronage-client alliances (independent homelands, urban community councillors, Labour Party, National Freedom Party); pragmatic institutional opposition (Inkatha/"unity unions"/Solidarity Party); extra-institutional protest (UDF/ANC/"community unions"); anti-capitalist forums (National Forum/Cape Action League [CAL]/Azanian People's Organization [AZAPO]).

Patronage-Client Alliances

Certain groups collaborate with the government-devised machinery in order to reap benefits for their narrow constituency. In "independent" homelands (Transkei, Ciskei, Bophuthatswana, Venda) an administrative bourgeoisie is financed mainly by revenue transfers and displays the symbols of independence. The degree of internal legitimacy varies. The situation in Bophuthatswana, with some mineral resources, a bill of rights, and a relatively professional administration, contrasts slightly with the general underdevelopment, graft, feuding, and autocratic behavior in the other homelands.

The official rationale for taking "independence" was given in all cases as increasing the chance of self-determination by shedding the burden of direct Pretoria rule. In Chief Lucas Mangope's words, Bophutatswana opted for "independence" as "the only way to obtain for our people freedom from the constraints of a system imposed by a government they did not elect."[1] In some cases, such as that of Ciskei, "independence" was negotiated after expert commissions advised against it and reported that 90 percent of Xhosa speakers in their surveys favored a unitary political system.[2] A subsequent referendum nevertheless produced a majority of registered voters in favor of independence, as a result of the boycott of the referendum by opponents and of intimidation of voters.

Urban community councils are even more discredited. Many are known for achieving personal enrichment through the dispensation of lucrative licenses, and for general ineffectiveness. Rent and transport fare increases initiated by the unrepresentative councils are therefore opposed by many township residents.

The Colored and Indian majority parties that administer "own affairs" (welfare, education, health services) justify their participation in the tricameral parliament as contributing at least to small-scale improvements, compared with extra-parliamentary boycotts, which they see as impotent. In their view, they engage in power politics as opposed to mere protest politics, although they are basically clients and rely on concessions. David Curry, then the National Chairman of the Labor Party, defended his party's stance by designating boycotting a tactic, not a principle: "It is within the system that we must take the initiative because our people are not strong enough to change the system alone from outside"; he refuses "to become prisoner of our situation."[3] Similar justifications were advanced by the Indian parties; "Solidarity" party leader J. N. Reddy stressed their "critical participation" in order "to create a political power base."

Stripped of the rhetoric, the participation of respected leaders such as Curry and Reddy reflected the fact that the government had raised the status and actual power of racial self-government sufficiently to entice active politicians to risk the hostility of the boycott faction. Only political participation could promise short-term supply of such immediate community needs as improved housing and welfare provisions. Participation was, then, presented as a valid way for "collaborators" to extract new benefits for their constituency as well as for themselves personally. The popular image of the collaborators, nevertheless, is that of stooges, naively deferent and easily conned into a false harmony by their shrewd masters. In the words of Fatima Meer: "Men elected carefully for their back-slapping conviviality and their ability to get on with each other, will get on with each other and slip into easy consensus."[4] The actual relationship of collaborators and masters is far more complex. There are rules of reciprocity. The collaborators, although without power of their own and with little legitimacy, nevertheless practice what may be called the politics of embarrassment.

The strategy of embarrassment rests on two grounds: the public image of the ruling group, and its self-image as a builder of successful, benevolent domination. This must be demonstrated by the voluntary participation of subordinates in the rituals of the regime. The ceremonies for the opening of parliament, for example, provide conspicuous platforms for image-making. The new legitimation of multiracialism is destroyed if Coloreds or Indians boycott the public processions. Nationalist technocrats feel rejected and their policy failure is laid bare without the now fashionable multiracial visibility. The more exotic the new faces, the better the show.

A former South African Indian Council (SAIC) chairman reported that he was frequently requested to fly to Pretoria or Cape Town for a short meeting with "the Minister," who wanted to be seen "consulting with the Indians." Often the common three-minute appearance before the television cameras was the sole purpose of such a trip. This informant finally refused point-blank to meet unless meaningful discussions were guaranteed, by setting up an agenda beforehand. Through these contacts the intermediaries of subordinates can gain some concessions.

When a tight network of control discriminates at every level of daily life, the victims need to seek remedies wherever they can find them. Here the collaborator offers himself to alleviate grievances on an individual basis. His real or putative influence with the dominators makes collaboration with the collaborator the only avenue for prompt redress. In his own perception the middleman becomes indispensable:

> Sir—when doctors are given eviction orders, they come to the South African Indian Council; when doctors have premises problems they use the SAIC; when doctors want a foreign Indian bride to be brought into the country they seek the assistance of the SAIC; when doctors have problems relating to their foreign (White) wives, they have confidence in the SAIC.
>
> I can confirm that at present the SAIC is handling about 80 such problems. They realise that their problems are safe in our hands.[5]

The collaborator construes the predicaments of his clients as identification with the institution.

In routine harassments by the White apartheid bureaucracy, the official subordinate representatives can intervene successfully. An example, cited by the same informant, was that of Indians applying for gun licenses. They had to be approved by the White officials in the former Department of Indian Affairs, and were usually turned down. The SAIC succeeded in altering the procedure so that applications went directly to the police and in consequence reached an approval rate of 80 percent. Passports, zoning changes, and numerous other small concessions resulted from the successful intervention of well-connected intermediaries.

As is well known, their formal legitimacy rests on a mandate from an average 20 percent of the eligible (as opposed to registered) voters, that, however, varied from 5 percent in urban constituencies, to 50 percent in some rural constituencies of the Labor Party. Their future legitimacy will largely depend on how much they can deliver. In the meantime they exercise power over many realms of everyday life; even their boycotting opponents have to deal with them in order to carry on ordinary activities.

Pragmatic Institutional Opposition

In contrast to the direct clients of the government, pragmatic institutional opposition is not directly involved in the decision-making process, but adopts a more ideological stance against the apartheid order than the collaborators can afford. Nominally they operate within the rules, which they try to use to maximum advantage in the absence of feasible alternatives. Above all, Inkatha and the registered unions (to be discussed below) distinguish themselves by political clout that rests on a growing *organized mass constituency*. The threat of use of such a mobilized base in consumer boycotts and industrial action is far from idle and cannot easily be countered by the government. Such an independent power base frees these groups from the role of client and bestows bargaining power on them. In particular, the unions are not direct beneficiaries of the state, but simply recipients of legal rights and protection through registration, in return for performing certain stated duties.

However, while few challenge the right of Black unions to pursue an independent policy based on membership priorities, Inkatha is widely ostracized for undermining political unity and the common struggle by using apartheid-created institutions. The movement, with (by its own count) over one million members, is widely denounced as a tribal, populist, petty-bourgeois force with little standing in urban politics except among traditional Zulu migrants.[6] Members are said to be forced to join the movement to gain necessary material benefits, with little knowledge of, let alone commitment to, its policy. In confrontations, one informant charged, Inkatha's impis (traditionally armed warriors) "act like stormtroopers." Authoritarian regimentation is said to prevail, as evinced in the assaults on dissidents. Buthelezi is accused of acting as auxiliary to the police by ensuring that the Durban townships do not join the countrywide boycott and protest movement.

In denial of the accusation of being essentially a tribal movement, Inkatha can point to a small number of non-Zulu members.[7] Inkatha's stance on ethnicity, moreover, is unequivocal. Its general secretary, Oscar Dhlomo, asserts: "We abhor ethnicity in so far as it is used to determine people's political rights."[8] However, for Buthelezi, a self-confident ethnic identity is an asset in political resistance: "My pride in being Zulu in no way detracts from my contribution to the struggle for liberation as a South African. In fact my contribution is enhanced by my awareness of being a Zulu."[9] This is not a naive apolitical retribalization. Neither a romanticized cultural revival nor a rootless denial of a historical identity is invoked. Against the latter in particular, Buthelezi asserts the equal value of the ethnic contribution to an overriding South African nationality: "No Zulu today talks about the re-establishment of a Zulu Kingdom. We are South Africans with a Zulu contribution to make. It is an historical absurdity to assert that only those who have shed their cultural identity can shape history in the right direction."[10] This is in keeping with progressive worldwide ethnic expressions of political claims. In South Africa, criticism of such an attitude stems from a fear that they are playing into the hands of the White adversary. Much of course depends on the kind of ethnic awareness. Black Consciousness, for example, a broader-based, more inclusive formation, greatly assisted the psychological liberation of the colonial mind. Whether an awareness of the Zulu tradition of political resistance and conquest can politicize its adherents without estranging them from fellow Blacks from other cultural traditions remains to be seen.

Buthelezi tends to refer to the late conquest as a warning to Pretoria as well as to the ANC. In a letter to Oliver Tambo he bluntly reminds him: "In this part of South Africa, we come from warrior stock and there is a resilient determination in KwaZulu and in Inkatha which even the full might of the State will never be able to flatten. Do your colleagues really think they can flatten us on the way to their envisaged victory?"[11] When Buthelezi allegedly made a similar reference to an Indian audience (strongly repudiated later), warning of the danger of a repetition of previous interethnic clashes, he tarnished his universalistic image considerably.

Unfortunately, little reliable research exists on more recent ethnic attitudes in Natal. In indirect questioning Hanf found a 60 percent majority of African respondents tolerant of or indifferent toward Indians.[12] Our own research indicates a much higher degree of latent antagonism toward and resentment of Indians among African high school students than rejection of Africans by their Indian counterparts. Brewer found among his Kwa Mashu sample an "absence of any ethnocentrism" that "made them unwilling to countenance a political solution where one ethnic group would dominate, even if it were their own."[13] In this respect, Inkatha's educational work and Buthelezi's stress on power-sharing may indeed have defused a situation of official differential privilege where the middle group is almost certain to be scapegoated in lieu of getting at the real source of frustration.

There seem to be two strands of imagery that prevail in Natal. Buthelezi is cast as anti-Indian by Indian sympathizers of the UDF, who intend to rally support. When Buthelezi reacts to these accusations by berating Fatima Meer or ANC spokesman Mac Maharaj,[14] he reinforces the anti-Indian image among outside observers unfamiliar with the political undercurrents of the strategic dispute.

The other strand operates at the popular level: Indians are better off than Africans and are seen as fraternizing with Whites under the tricameral constitution. Buthelezi, in unison with the UDF, had publicly warned Indians against the Whites. These calls were widely heeded, but the low 20 percent participation in the August 1984 election did little to save Indians from African rage. In the Vaal unrest a month later, several dozen Indian shops and homes in Evaton were indiscriminately looted and gutted. The fact that some Indians were perceived as having joined or having been permitted in the White ranks automatically made all Indian shopowners suspects and potential traitors. Above all, the poorer Blacks complain about price-gouging by the Indian merchants. Some pay protection money to local Black warlords, who are sometimes affiliated with political factions. If the protection money does not trickle down to underlings, they can spark a looting.

All these factors played a role in the more serious August 1985 rioting in Inanda near Durban in which the historic Gandhi settlement, popularly associated with UDF supporters, was wrecked. Looting African mobs faced Indian vigilantes, screaming, "kill the kaffirs." An estimated 70 people died both in intra-Black and interracial fighting. Whole areas were tem-

porarily evacuated by Indians. It was Inkatha that finally held
an interracial mass meeting and restored a semblance of order
in the sprawling squatter camp after the White authorities had
cunningly withdrawn. Novelist J. M. Coetzee has aptly commented: "Though the mob probably did not think of itself as
performing a symbolic act, we may read the sacking of the
Gandhi museum as its verdict on the relevance of nonviolence
to the South Africa of the 1980s."[15] It must be added that the
tragedy also signals an obvious educational failure of the anti-
apartheid forces, both UDF and Inkatha, to make much head-
way in nonracialism against the apartheid doctrine, for the
looting had clear racial overtones. Inanda is the only area in
South Africa where Africans and Indians live side by side,
albeit in different classes—though many Indians, too, dwell in
shacks. The riots confirmed the success of the state in alienating the divided segments from each other through separate
institutions and differential incorporation.

However, the Black-Indian antagonism remains a minor aspect of the more serious simmering intra-Black civil war. The
creeping revolution against apartheid has, above all, polarized
apartheid's victims. The more cautious leaders in all camps
must now attempt to restrain overzealous supporters after
having exhorted them to wake up. All committed factions increasingly use violence against each other. Against the UDF's
goal of making the townships ungovernable by attacking
counsellors who in Natal are sometimes Inkatha members,
Buthelezi pits a strong resolve: "We will clean out hornets'
nests and we will banish from our midst the agents of death
and destruction who want Black to kill Black."[16] On the other
hand, there are almost daily indications that the "armed propaganda" of Inkatha's rival has caught up with the mood of
the frustrated: "'We are going to do everything we need for
our liberation,' the speaker said. Anyone who doubted this
needed only to see 30,000 people rising to their feet, pretend-
ing to hold guns pointed at the ground, running on the spot
and chanting, 'soldier, soldier,' in unison. They needed to see
the crowd jumping to their feet and the chants 'Viva Tambo,'
'Viva ANC' and 'Viva Communist Party of SA.'"[17] This pic-

ture from the Eastern Cape, which could also fit the Transvaal, is blurred by the Inkatha strength in Natal.

The various strategies and attitudes prevailing in different parts of the country need explanation beyond the persons and organizations involved. Why is Natal different insofar as Inkatha's insistence on nonviolence and evolutionary change is concerned? First, the late subjugation of the better-organized Zulu nation at the turn of the century accounts for a greater traditionalism in self-consciousness and ethnic cohesion compared with the more atomized African population, conquered a hundred years earlier elsewhere. And second, in Natal the presence of a large Indian population in skilled and lower management positions blocked the advance of many Africans in the industrial economy and relegated the majority of Zulu workers to low-skilled positions. In the Eastern Cape and on the Rand, the demand for skilled Black labor—and with it better education, greater self-assertion, and inevitable politicization—was always higher than in Natal. Both the absence of a substantial middleman minority as well as the higher concentration of sophisticated manufacturing (e.g., the auto industry) in the other industrial centers assumed a much broader Black economic incorporation and wider permanent proletarianization than in Natal. Here oscillating migrant labor is still most common.

In any ensuing confrontation, Inkatha can still fall back on a vast traditional hinterland and mobilize support while the civic organizations in the Eastern Cape are hemmed in between White overlords on the one side and formally independent Bantustans on the other hand. On the Rand in particular, Black politics is an entirely urban affair, cut off from rural roots, while in Natal urban and rural subcultures interpenetrate in close spatial proximity. In this respect, Buthelezi can base his leadership claims on elected democratic legitimacy as well as hereditary right. The different political styles flowing from these expectations sometimes pose contradictions. For example, the adulation of Buthelezi by his followers does not differ much from the lavish praise of autocrats in most independent Black African states. An editorial of the official magazine for the KwaZulu government read: "Prince Dr. M. G. Buthelezi, the President of Inkatha, the moving and guiding spirit behind Inkatha and the political philosopher of our time and age, challenges all men of vision and goodwill of whatever race or color to abandon the policies of the past for faith, for hope and for trust in each other."[18] Such tones, often reinforced by an egocentric style of speech, are anathema to those politicized urbanites who view themselves as equal to any leadership aspirants. On the other hand, Buthelezi, with his shrewd analytical capacity, stands head and shoulders above all other homeland leaders, quite apart from his different policy. To lump him together with other "homeland puppets," as the ANC now does, is propaganda rather than reality.

In the 1960s the ANC itself had recognized the special value of the Zulu tradition by urging Buthelezi to work under the umbrella of the apartheid system. He can claim that, as an active ANC member, "I was doing what I was doing with them and for them."[19] The working relationship between ANC and Inkatha collapsed in 1979 when Buthelezi apparently was asked to recruit for the ANC and refused. Recruitment would not only have been illegal but would have made Inkatha a subsidiary of the ANC. Stress also developed after a cordial official London meeting between the two sides in 1979 which Buthelezi made public in order to dispel the aura of secrecy and conspiracy that the encounter had acquired in the watchful perception of the South African special branch. The ANC accused Buthelezi of betrayal of trust.

Inkatha perceives itself as "the modern expression of the aims and objectives so clearly stated by the ANC's founding fathers."[20] It rejects the notion that it is "a third force" and insists that it represents the continuity of Black opposition. However, unlike the ANC Mission in Exile, Inkatha proudly claims democratic accountability. Because the ANC Mission in Exile is prevented from "consulting with ordinary South Africans," Buthelezi argues, it is out of touch with grass-roots feelings and has no real right to speak on behalf of Black South Africa on such issues as disinvestment. While the ANC is upheld by the mystique bestowed by illegality and the UDF by extra-institutional protest, Inkatha tumbles into the fray of pragmatic politics.

In his competition with the purist image of the ANC, whose internal heritage he claims, Buthelezi, however, overreacts. For example, Buthelezi contends that "within South Africa, it [disinvestment] is championed solely by those who seek to establish a non-capitalist state through the use of violence."[21] In a speech to an American audience he portrayed himself as an apostle of free enterprise and charged: "The ANC's Mission in Exile aims to establish a revolutionary government presiding over a Marxist state."[22] As will be discussed below, this ascription of non-capitalism through violence to all UDF/ANC leaders or sympathizers is hardly accurate.

While Buthelezi admits that the threat of violence "plays a positive role in the process of bringing about change" and while he expresses understanding of the ANC's military strategy, his organization rejects violence more for pragmatic than for moral reasons. Violence or "the politics of anger" will be suicidal in the South African situation, exploited by "vultures of death" for ulterior motives. Anger is portrayed instead as "a national asset" that is not to be squandered but is to be given "constructive objectives." Like Bishop Tutu, Buthelezi deplores Black/Black violence as counterproductive "barbarism" that "feeds the racial prejudice which looks at us as no more than kaffirs."

Unlike Tutu, however, Inkatha asserts that the ANC Mission in Exile "was never given a mandate to declare the armed struggle."[23] It considers as "madness" the economic sabotage counseled. "Only a man who has abandoned all decency will destroy the factory where he works to earn the money to buy food and clothing."[24] According to Buthelezi, Blacks do not want to "starve for Oliver Tambo." They vote with their feet when they queue in front of factories for job vacancies. In the ANC's definition of decency, however, "we, for our part, would be less than human if we were to sit back and accept that we should continue to be oppressed and exploited."[25] Buthelezi retorts that he "will not be dictated to by South African exiles who sit drinking whiskey in safe places."[26]

This polarization in Black politics nevertheless reduces In- katha from the *national* movement it claims to be, to a regional group, although the Zulu ethnic group represents the numer- ically strongest segment. If the trend toward a Lebanization of South Africa continues, some Black leaders are in danger of becoming regional warlords at the expense of national in- tegration. Their strong ethnic base gives them veto power over any settlement that excludes them. The alternative can be seen in Zimbabwe, where the exclusion of an authentic na- tionalist segment in the form of Nkomo's Zimbabwe African Peoples Union (ZAPU) forces resulted in a simmering civil war. In this respect the dismissal of Buthelezi as another Mu- zorewa hardly accords with his Zulu power base, which is much stronger than even Nkomo's Ndebele constituency.

Making South Africa "ungovernable" in order to facilitate liberation risks having a post-apartheid society that also will be ungovernable, as a result of irreparable damage done to the country's economy. A responsible conservatism, according to Buthelezi, is becoming more popular the more frequently the township confrontations show the senselessness of de- struction. Here Buthelezi may overestimate the "very substan- tial spinoffs" Inkatha is said to receive. Buthelezi's nonviolence lacks the mystique of a Gandhi because he is not himself seen to have renounced privilege. While the Inkatha leadership has never been close to the Nationalists, and Buthelezi person- ally has had only a few frosty encounters with Botha, he is nevertheless perceived as being on their payroll. The govern- ment machinery in Ulundi displays virtually all the symbols of an independent state, from the black Mercedes cars of Minis- ters to the KwaZulu legislature's impressive building. Its "own sources of revenue" in its annual budget fell from 22 percent in fiscal year 1974/75 to 18 percent in 1981/82. The KwaZulu government can rightly argue that Pretoria owes its underde- veloped hinterland such subsidies, but its image of credible resistance suffers nonetheless.

Pretoria has made no attempt to accommodate and incor- porate this "loyal opposition." Dozens of antagonistic encoun- ters have taken place, from the outright rejection of the mod-

erate Buthelezi Commission Report in 1982, to the attempted
Ingvavuma land deal with Swaziland, to less publicized events.
So far KwaZulu and Inkatha are not treated as a unique op-
portunity for practiced multiracialism, but as just another
Bantustan that can eventually be brought in line.

Typical of this attitude is a personal interview with a senior
civil servant in August 1983 in Pretoria, worth reporting
verbatim.

> *Question:* What can Pretoria do to force Buthelezi into in-
> dependence?
> *Answer:* We have a number of options. (1) We can *eliminate*
> Buthelezi. However, this is not in line with the Afrikaner's char-
> acter and will never be pursued. (2) We can *starve* him. We can
> give more development aid to the other independent states and
> that will affect KwaZulu's overall economic position. (3) We can
> *bribe* Zulus. This would not work with Buthelezi himself but with
> some of his followers. We can use the king against him and par-
> ticularly after the death of his mother, who is ill, the Zulu dy-
> nasty becomes open to all kinds of influences. It is difficult as
> long as KwaZulu is a one-party state, and Buthelezi knows this
> by stressing Inkatha's unity. Finally, and that is the option I fa-
> vor, (4) we can *nibble away* at him like we did with the Ingvavuma
> issue.
> *Question:* But that backfired, the government lost, Buthelezi's
> standing increased, and Inkatha's membership doubled? Even
> Tutu joined in.
> *Answer:* Yes, the government lost temporarily and Buthelezi
> won. But the impact of what the government can do has not
> been lost. Nibbling away at Buthelezi's obstinacy in various ways
> remains the optimal long-term option.
> On the other hand, we also need Buthelezi. Areas under his
> control have generally been quiet. As long as he uses Inkatha in
> a responsible way, Buthelezi is no danger. My father would have
> said, why do you give the bloody Kaffir a platform at all? Why
> don't you lock them all up? But we can't do this anymore and
> overcrowd Robben Island with people who disagree with us.
> The government needs Black leaders to talk to and that is what
> we are trying to achieve.

Inkatha practices an appealing pragmatism in the face of
such hostile exclusion. It does, however, lack a program of
action and even expresses pride in that lack: "Inkatha has
never adopted a view about the nature of the South African
state in medium or in long term."[27] This absence of ideological

hopes beyond nonracial power-sharing serves, paradoxically, as a bond. In the absence of a clear program of action, the coalition of diverse elements that constitutes Inkatha holds together better without divisive theoretical debates. By focusing on immediate problems that rural and urban, young and old, educated and uneducated, moderates and radicals share, the coalition avoids internal policy rifts. No wonder, then, that "ending discrimination" was most important to over three-quarters of a sample of Inkatha respondents in Kwa Mashu, while only 8 percent stressed "one man, one vote."[28] The same survey showed that Southall's[29] account of a lack of urban support for Inkatha proved "entirely erroneous," at least as far as the Durban townships were concerned. Nevertheless, most African urban areas are clearly divided in their attitude toward "homeland" administration: any attempt to expand that jurisdiction would be militantly resented by large sections, as the example of Lamontville has shown. Can a new unity of the anti-apartheid forces be expected to emerge for a national convention?

The new constitution was vehemently opposed also by the Progressive Federal Party and Inkatha. The United Democratic Front did not invite the PFP and Inkatha to join them. While their inclusion in the "front" was advocated by some of its organizers, the final conclusion was that the heterogeneous constituency of the new movement would be unable to tolerate groups who work within the system. A broader and more effective alliance for a specific political end was sacrificed for the sake of closer ideological cohesion. The proclaimed ideological unity of all opponents of apartheid would have been cracked by widening its anti-apartheid base. Hence, the United Democratic Front, committed above all "to uniting all our people wherever they may be," has accused Buthelezi and his colleagues "of grinding the defenceless masses under the yoke of oppression" by voluntarily manning Bantustan institutions.[30] The UDF will not cooperate with these institutions even if they agree on the goal of fighting an exclusive constitution. Buthelezi, on the other hand, has argued that only his takeover of government-imposed structures prevented them from being used by the government for denationalization. He has referred to the UDF's rejection of his invitation to talk to the KwaZulu legislature as "no more than the spit of venom coming from the ANC's Mission in Exile."[31]

UDF opponents will not share a platform with Inkatha or let Buthelezi speak at a neutral meeting. It is precisely because Inkatha's demands for nonracial democracy are identical to those of the UDF but pursued through different means that Buthelezi is rejected as a more dangerous enemy than the Nationalists.

Extra-Institutional Alliances

According to Buthelezi, "For people who are bearing the yoke of oppression and who are forced to live on a day to day survival basis, the world becomes a very immediate place."[32] The material world is slightly less immediate for the more secure and better-off urban Blacks. This group, including professionals and a growing bourgeoisie in the Indian and Colored segment, forms the main constituency of the extra-institutional protest alliance. The constituency of the UDF is best described by the unwitting self-definition of "the people of South Africa" who intended to send a message to Nelson Mandela in a march to Polsmoor prison on 28 August 1985: "We, the people of South Africa, represented by the UDF, university students, school pupils, academics, teachers, lawyers, doctors, clerics and other concerned citizens."[33] This group includes many radical White students, as well as disenchanted liberals and moral socialists.

Although membership claims tend to be extravagant in South African opposition politics, the UDF can plausibly claim to be the umbrella body for several hundred organizations, albeit with some overlapping membership. Since the UDF is not a membership-based group but a front organization for independent constituent groups, persecution of the UDF leadership does not necessarily destroy the movement the way the "beheading" of similar opposition has in the past. Not being a political party with a disciplined membership, however, leaves the amorphous alliance open to frequent internal policy conflicts. In contrast to Inkatha, which an observer described as an army without generals (but with one supreme commander), the UDF has many generals but an undisciplined army. It serves more as an embodied sentiment than an effective tool for action. However, there can be no doubt about the depth of militancy and widespread legitimacy of the most popular anti-apartheid movement. The UDF inherited the revered ANC mantle, and several ANC veterans figure as its patrons. Indeed, it has been accused of being a Marxist-inspired organization in which anti-capitalist agents manipulate naive fellow travelers, idealistic students, and well-meaning churchmen. Ironically, the same group is suspected by the socialist, Black Consciousness Left of harboring petty-bourgeois tendencies.

The all-class appeal of the UDF rests on the degradation caused by past government policies. Out of a combination of ignorance and arrogance successive Nationalist administrations have engendered such deep antagonism and suspicion through rejection of the civil rights pleas of the reformist opposition that alternative forms of resistance became desirable. In this view, Nationalist Afrikanerdom has forfeited the right to rule over or even to participate in a post-apartheid government. Now the turn of the new forces has finally come. Pretoria has mismanaged the reform process by its exclusion of Blacks in the new constitution. This was the final proof of the failure of institutional politics. Time has run out for the National Party, despite its new rhetoric. For the UDF/ANC alliance the time for upping the stakes and seizing, not sharing, power has arrived.

While the ANC pursued a policy of isolating Pretoria internationally, the new internal movement simultaneously sharpened its anti-American stance in response to Washington's "constructive engagement" policy of friendly relations with South Africa. In the past, leading South African activists cherished easy access to American media and diplomatic representatives as much as the latter valued contact with the opposition parties in South Africa. But in August 1983 UDF spokespersons decided not to invite United States representatives to their first national congress in Cape Town. All other Western missions did receive official invitations. UDF executives were also expected to refuse all formal social contact with official United States representatives. When Senator Edward Kennedy visited South Africa at the personal invitation of Desmond Tutu and Allan Boesak in 1985, the invitation was vehemently criticized not only by Black Consciousness supporters but by the left within the heterogeneous UDF as well.

The broad UDF coalition is held together by "the politics of refusal." The United Democratic Front evolved as a strategy of boycott and non-collaboration with the new constitutional reform proposals. In line with Gandhi's nonviolence, the Defiance Campaign against pass laws in the 1950s, the bus and school boycotts, and workers' stay-aways in the 1960s and 1970s, the strategy aims at political mobilization as well as paralysis of the enemy. Protest politics in its most dramatic form exposes the illegitimacy of unjust domination. At the core of the strategy lies the belief that obstructionism will eventually succeed. People cannot be ruled forever without participation in their own oppression. The coalition will not be party to any state initiatives. Although this absolutist stance on a tactical issue has engendered lively criticism within the Front, those advocating more pragmatic flexibility have usually subjected themselves to "organizational discipline."

Both the left and the right of the Black political spectrum have criticized the high price of the boycott strategy. It represents one-sided moral politics, without necessarily offsetting the suffering with an equal price paid by the opponent. The stay-aways are not trials of strength with recalcitrant employers, but mere warnings of dissatisfaction. The state and employers can dismiss the gestures in a callous assessment of the balance of power. For this reason many Black unions show reluctance to join strike calls from outside their ranks. They eschew the politics of theater in favor of building strength on the shop floor for the real tests. This view questions the primacy of the political that the UDF strategy implies. Equally controversial is the charge that the UDF/ANC is essentially using defenseless children as cannon fodder. The strategy to create liberated no-go areas in the townships, controlled by "people's committees on every block" and patrolled by small mobile units of "fighting youth," may harness the frustrations for ANC goals but exposes the activists to the full might of the better-equipped state.

For the first time in Black politics, in 1983 physical violence between the committed factions became a regular occurrence. In early 1983 rival student groups battled at the Natal University Medical School. In the School in Durban—one of the rare places Africans and Indians have close social contacts, a few hundred students studying and living together—a fistfight broke out between Black Consciousness and Congress supporters. Several students needed hospital treatment afterward. Significantly, the division occurred on ideological, not ethnic, grounds. Similarly, the clashes between Inkatha supporters and UDF students at the University of Zululand, culminating in five deaths on 30 October 1983, two days before the White constitutional referendum, was only the most widely reported incident of a series of hostilities. Antagonisms between supporters and opponents of constitutional participation among the Colored and Indian population have flared. Verbal attacks have accelerated. Confrontations between AZAPO and UDF adherents continued until in 1985 Bishop Tutu arranged for a temporary halt to open hostilities.

The heterogeneous UDF coalition is often said to lack ideological coherence. On the economic future of post-apartheid society the UDF and ANC spokesmen speak as ambiguously as Inkatha. They combine demands for the nationalization of key industries in the Freedom Charter with vague notions of a mixed economy in which, the leftist critics fear, White capitalists would merely be supplemented by Black capitalists. Indeed, in Mandela's social democratic vision, smashing monopolies will "open up fresh fields for the development of a prosperous Non-European bourgeois class. For the first time in the history of this country the Non-European bourgeoisie will have the opportunity to own in their own name and right mills and factories, and trade and private enterprise will boom and flourish as never before."[34] Such aspirations have been criticized from the left as proof of petty-bourgeois tendencies. The Charter's notion of several "oppressed nations" is said to overlook the increasing internal stratification among Africans, Coloreds, and Indians that has emerged since its inception. The privileged strata of these seemingly homogeneous aggregates "are pulled in the direction of the ruling classes in the South African state."[35] How a working-class leadership can be consistent with the antagonistic class character within and between "nations" remains unexplained. But for the two-stage theory of liberation espoused by the ANC, the construction of socialism amounts to a slow process that "is not consummated but begun by a successful revolutionary seizure of power," during which "a vital role, under restrictive controls, may still be required of a private . . . and exploitative sector."[36]

In its organizational self-understanding "the ANC is not a socialist party."[37] It can achieve the mobilization of a Black proletariat, the peasantry, and the middle classes in a democratic all-class common front. Thabo Mbeki, the official ANC publicity spokesman, ridicules what he calls the pathological fear of the petty bourgeoisie. In light of the White monopoly bourgeoisie, the enemy is not "the barber at the Soweto street corner." Because Africans, Indians, and Coloreds "are denied the right to self-determination regardless of class," national oppression and not class forms the essence of apartheid.

The controversy has led to the expulsion from the ANC of a group of Marxist Whites (Legassick, Hemson, Ensor, Petersen) in the late 1970s for consistently attacking the socialist credentials of the ANC, South African Council of Trade Unions (SACTU), and Communist Party (CPSA) alliance. Earlier, eight "Africanists" were expelled for taking the very different position of "chauvinistic ghetto nationalism" that criticized the multiracial character of the organization. The 1985 ANC decision to elect non-Africans to the ANC executive (in addition to the previous membership allowance), together with the growth of socialist ideologies among the former Black Consciousness movement, ensures that the national question, the two-stage theory, and the populist character of the extra-institutional UDF/ANC alliance remain on the ideo-logical agenda of Black politics.

The intellectual elite in South Africa who subscribe to the "politics of abstention" run the risk of preening themselves on their moral purity at the expense of effective intervention. They may lament the evil but still shy away from attempting feasible improvements, waiting instead for a utopian libera-tion. These appealing dreams of paradise color even more deeply the strategies of a socialist alliance that propounds a "workerist position." It is this purist academic elite, the former Black Consciousness adherents and vocal rivals of the UDF/ANC coalition, that forms the fourth tendency in Black politics.

Anti-Capitalist Forums

The importance of the Black Consciousness Movement of the late sixties and seventies lies in its initial emphasis on psycho-logical liberation. By stressing the need for Blacks to rid them-selves of self-racism, of an internalized slave mentality, the movement laid the basis for a self-confident, assertive young leadership. At the same time these new spokespersons severed the historical ties of traditional liberation groups with White liberalism, under whose condescending tutelage so much of the classical protest had occurred. It also transcended the im-plicit racism of the earlier Pan African Congress (PAC) posi-tion by including other discriminated groups (Coloreds and Indians) in its orbit, unlike PAC, which insists on an exclusive African (as opposed to a Black) leadership role. However, the Black Consciousness Movement neglected economic issues, save for the propagation of Black communalism.

Under the influence of Sath Cooper's prison studies and the work of theorists such as Neville Alexander, the 1983 Ham-manskraal Manifesto shifted the theoretical focus to the issue of "racial capitalism." Now the Black working class is seen as the savior. Above all, this position is distinguished from that of the Congress alliance by its deep suspicion of the national Black bourgeoisie, notwithstanding that most of the constituency of the National Forum belongs to this class. Its anti-capitalist rhetoric is much more orthodox than that of the traditional Congress supporters. Neville Alexander states: "In South Africa, as in any other modern capitalist country, the *ruling class* consists of the owners of capital, which is invested in mines, factories, land, wholesaling and distribution networks and banks."[38] His UDF critics charge that such a view not only overlooks all the refinements of class analysis in the last decades but also fails to take into account the autonomous role of the state. Politicians and bureaucrats, both White and Black, are now as much part of "the South African ruling class" as are managers (as distinct from owners of capital).

Against the Freedom Charter's frequent references to "the people of South Africa," Black Consciousness (BC) has redefined the "Black and White together as equals, countrymen, and brothers" and has narrowed the definition of true Black patriotism. There is much concern among BC adherents that the Charter embodies essentially liberal principles that are cooptable by a capitalist nonracialism. AZAPO-BC philosophy aims at going beyond a mixed economy in which state-controlled production would coexist with private enterprise. For BC advocates, social democracy is not the goal, but treason.

These definitions inspire an almost paranoic obsession with potential sell-outs. Speeches are heavily laced with references to counter-revolutionaries blunting the militancy of the workers. Far more than the White racist, the enemy within the ranks is the one who needs to be watched for and "flushed out." "It is a proven fact that it is the less obvious of the enemies of the revolution who compromise and destroy the revolution. They are more dangerous than the secret police."[39]

Unlike ANC/UDF, who, according to ANC president Oliver Tambo, do not exclude a dialogue with Pretoria on "how to extend democracy," AZAPO is deeply suspicious of a National Convention strategy. Negotiations between petty-bourgeois politicans are considered the ultimate sell-out to preserve capitalism, a conspiracy to cheat the masses out of socialism: "The Botha-Malan junta has a master-plan to ensure the survival of White supremacy in our beloved Azania. This master-plan has been hatched in conference halls in Washington, D.C., London, Paris and Bonn."[40] While this statement correctly identifies a common ideological affinity between Black non-socialist nationalists and Western capitalists, it overlooks the fact that such a pact could only occur at the price of Black political and economic incorporation.

If this vigilance interferes with the pursuit of unity, unity is abandoned. "Unbridled and unprincipled alliances are not synonymous with unity."[41] BC reserves the right to scrutinize the conditions under which unity is achieved. Although it recognizes unity as a prerequisite of a successful struggle, it is less interested in the outcome than in the purity of the process.

One of the more remarkable points of "The Azanian People's Manifesto" demands the "development of one national progressive culture in the process of struggle." This demand contradicts the Freedom Charter's explicit recognition of different "national groups." It goes against the Charter's acceptance of people's right to use their own language and to "develop their own folk culture and customs." While the Charter seeks "equal status" for ethnic groups in the courts, schools, and other institutions of the state, BC rejects the very concept of ethnicity as divisive. In particular, the separate organizational mobilization, for tactical reasons, of anti-apartheid forces in the Congress movement is considered to reinforce enemy divisions. The National Forum rails against the revival of the Transvaal and Natal Indian Congress.

Whether disparaging self-chosen cultural diversity as a worthy goal or recognizing it as a historical reality in South Africa, BC strives for cultural uniformity. "One national, progressive culture" seems to imply state-enforced linguistic and educational indoctrination. A similar problem seems to exist with regard to religious diversity. Most apartheid opponents adhere to some form of either Christianity, Islam, Hinduism, or Judaism. The degree of secularism is remarkably low in South Africa. For the first time, however, there is evidence of cautious rejection of religious consciousness. While Black (Christian) theology inspired much of earlier BC ideology, speeches now warn "against following religious ideologies which have no material base in our own existential situation."[42]

Socialist BC adherents' self-chosen isolation from the mainstream sentiment of their constituency is most clearly demonstrated in the new emphasis on the Black working class as the sole leader of the struggle. Since BC adopted a socialist stance in 1983, many of their speeches have contended that the working class alone can end the system because they alone have nothing to lose. They thereby relegate three other groups to the role of mere entities for mobilization. These are the urban and rural poor, together with the radical sections of the middle classes.[43] This distinction between the poor and the working class is never explained, nor is why they should be susceptible to mobilization by another group. The differential legal rights and statuses of squatters, migrants, and workers with permanent urban residence rights are ignored in the exhortations for unity. This unity supposedly lies in their shared racial/capitalist oppression. But this objective situation may be experienced quite differently by different groups. To desperate rural work-seekers, those with jobs in the cities represent a privileged class. Many townshipdwellers see the migrants as cheaper competitors or as an underclass.

The obstacles to "the solidarity of the working class" are heightened in South Africa by the objective differential oppression which makes the lot of the urban group more tolerable than that of the excluded rural sections. To expect unity in such a situation demands sainthood of ordinary people. As the history of unionism has shown in more favorable circumstances, unions frequently settle for benefits for their members rather than solidarity with more disadvantaged groups. If the issue, for example, is shared employment, unions frequently choose fewer men and women at work as long as those on the job receive higher wages and easier conditions; if the issue is squeezing out advantages for a small group by inflicting hardship on the general public, the selfishness of the organized recognizes few bounds. Why should

South African Blacks be expected to behave more altruistically than the rest of humanity?

Another contradiction in BC's insistence on the unity of all anti-apartheid forces simultaneously with the exclusion of all other persons with similar goals concerns the role of "progressive Whites." Against the charge that AZAPO's Black exclusivity is itself racist, its adherents point to their own powerlessness, claiming that the power to oppress is an essential ingredient of racism. While the White liberal was branded as the arch-enemy when SASO started the movement in 1968, the example of Neil Aggett, who died in detention, and of other committed White activists has made untenable the earlier position of resentment of all sympathetic Whites. Some spokespersons would now allow Whites to play a part in the struggle as long as the leadership remained firmly in the hands of the Black working class. This second-class role should ensure that the Black cause is not hijacked by opportunistic Whites. Others define Blackness no longer in terms of skin color but as a state of mind, a consciousness that is accessible to sympathetic Whites and unobtainable by Black collaborators. In line with its class approach, the Cape Action League, for example, would reject Black middle-class organizations as affiliates but would accept individual Whites. White groups such as NUSAS and Black Sash are kept at a distance because of their privileged class base. The BC aversion to White democrats has obstructed work with the unions, whose cause they champion. The role "vanguard consciousness" ascribes to sympathetic allies exerts less appeal for disenchanted apartheid opponents, for whom liberal criticism is insufficient, than does the nonracial alliance of the UDF charterists.

Yet some African nationalists continue to feel suspicion toward members from other racial groups in the liberation effort. The prominence of non-Africans in BC has led to veiled accusations of manipulation by neonationalist opponents of its philosophy. They cast the Indians and Coloreds in the same role as White liberals or communists in earlier phases of Black protest. Thus the editor of the official magazine for the Kwa-Zulu government asserts: "Now instead of Whites in NUSAS, it is the Indians and Coloreds who dominate BC." He accuses the organization of "preferring to have an African figurehead" and adds with a nationalistic "clarion call" that "Blacks in South Africa will not be liberated by Russia or Asians, but they will liberate themselves."[44]

At the same time, growing rejection of racial compartmentalization has led to criticism of White liberal intellectuals for insufficient participation in the Black cause. Herbert and Absolom Vilakazi have castigated the "shameful, condescending distance English-speaking universities keep between themselves and the existing Black universities." Low-status "bush colleges" are abandoned to Afrikaner academics who teach natives in the higher interests of Afrikaner nationalism. The Vilakazis conclude: "Supporting the African cause also means that White (liberal) intellectuals should as much as possible participate in the sharpening, clarification and debate of the major issues of the African cause . . . for the cause is theirs, too."[45]

AZAPO presents itself as explicitly anti-imperialist, anti-racist (not just nonracist), anti-sexist, and anti-capitalist. In addition, it raises "the land question." Against the Charter, which stipulates that the land belongs to all who live on it, AZAPO emphasizes initial conquest. Restitution, expropriation, and land reform presumably are necessary items on the post-apartheid agenda. The alien-settler position of Whites is contrasted with the inherited rights of indigenous peoples. This insistence on original landownership may win far stronger support from Blacks than the coalition's insistence on "proletarian hegemony" ever could.

In summary, four trends in Black politics can be delineated (necessarily somewhat simplistically). First, the increasing Black politicization cannot be stopped by the state. The state can attempt to suppress or manipulate its articulation, but the need for a better-educated, skilled work force will inevitably continue to increase the number of politically informed workers, regardless of agitation and repression. This strategically placed work force will have the clout to win satisfactory political incorporation.

CONFLICTS IN BLACK POLITICS

Second, better occupational positions bring status and material benefits which its owners are reluctant to risk. Unlike landless peasants, rootless unemployed, or students, urban adult Blacks have much to lose in an escalating confrontation, quite apart from religious and ideological prohibitions against engaging in outright warfare. The demonstrations are carried out by the youth, while the employed parents suffer mainly from status grievances as a result of the racial order.

These tendencies result in the paradox of increased material incorporation with simultaneous political and emotional alienation from the existing order. The individual can resolve this dilemma in one way—by increased rhetorical militancy, our third trend. This will make for much more intense debate on the ideological terrain on which the polity is contested but does not necessarily spill over into revolutionary praxis on the part of the organized and employed work force. Radical symbolic resistance, rather than real struggles for state power, can be expected. As far as the other segments are concerned, the South African industrial complex is both too flexible and too strong to be overthrown by guerrilla action, let alone by traditional protest politics.

In these intense ideological debates the state has all the advantages of manipulative interference based on consumerism and the control of the major socialization agencies. The media and the educational institutions have been dominated by establishment perspectives, denying politicized minorities the organizational resources to build themselves into a cohesive opposition. However, a fourth trend is for the opposition forces to carve out niches of dissent within the major institutions, particularly the schools, the media, and the bureaucracy. Institutional guerrilla warfare in addition to extra-institutional resistance is likely to characterize the scene, as long as technocratic liberation fails to fulfill its promises.

Explaining Political Violence

Probably government will send strong instructions to its bureaucracies to suspend the more heavy-handed practices of the past. But the

police, the administration boards, the security police and even the
military are not docile house-dogs to be called so easily to heel after
their long years of near-autonomy. Any of them is perfectly capable
of perpetrating an inconvenient atrocity at the worst time.

(Work in Progress 35 [1985])

When Justice Donald Kannemeyer, appointed to investigate
the shooting of twenty unarmed marchers to a funeral at
Langa township on 21 March 1985, finally submitted his report, the findings merely confirmed widespread suspicion.
The police had willfully discarded conventional riot-control
weapons in favor of lethal guns; they had made inciting re-
marks that may have triggered the violence; they had fabri-
cated and exaggerated evidence after the shooting; and, finally, they had lied to their own Minister about the events. Too
narrow a focus on the responsibility of the police for the political violence, however, can lead us to overlook the wider system of which the "security forces" are merely a part. The incidents at Sharpeville and Langa, and other shootings of
unarmed demonstrators, are not a form of brutality peculiar
to South Africa. Colonial history provides many examples of
worse massacres.[46] However, the unrestrained use of deadly
force against collective protest characterizes an early phase of
coercion, still practiced in "backward" states out of the lime-
light of world attention. Police forces in more developed societies now tolerate nonviolent protest in order to benefit from
the manipulation of dissent.

Police forces everywhere tend to act independently. Strong
control is needed to keep them from taking the law into their
own hands. A continuously reinforced professional code of
conduct is essential to restrain overzealous police officers. In
volatile racial confrontations in particular, professional skill
can soothe embittered feelings just as prejudiced and weak
leadership can heighten antagonisms. Establishing genuine
communication between the two sides usually achieves the
former goal, while a traditional assertion of dominance leads
to increased mutual hostility.

South Africa provides a daily model for unprofessional police conduct. Despite the sophisticated rhetoric of accommo-

> ### The Making of Revolutionaries
>
> *He was placed in a room with about 20 other boys between the ages of nine and sixteen. Policemen took their names. One of several policemen then allegedly said "give them gas" and produced a can which he shook and sprayed into the faces of three boys. They fell to the floor screaming. He said the gas was in a long slim canister with a red knob and "burnt" the eyes and throat. One of the policemen then allegedly told the boys to run outside. As they ran down a corridor, policemen stood on both sides and sjambocked (whipped) them as they passed. They ran into a yard "where police vehicles were parked" where they were told to wash their faces. A police officer then said they had been warned. If they were picked up again they "would sit" for three years.*
>
> Cape Times *(4 September 1985)*

dation at the political level, law enforcement generally operates in a direct, brutal, and traditional master-servant relationship. Here apartheid reveals its raw nerve.

Once the authorities receive the slightest provocation, they tend to go well beyond restoring order. Unrest allows the individual policeman to act out his deep-seated racism. The occasion is used for crude pedagogy. In the context of the Crossroads upheavals (see below, p. 109), for example, Francis Wilson quotes a Cabinet Minister as talking of destroying Crossroads in order to "squash that spirit of defiance, that unhealthy community spirit."[47] Authoritarians are not willing to accept limits on control of outgroups, let alone tolerate successful resistance to imposed designs: law and order must be enforced at any price.

Where police forces around the world use sophisticated riot equipment to control stone-throwing crowds, the South African police use guns. Birdshot is frequently fired to maim. By appearing without protective uniforms, the police provoke stone-throwing, which gives them an excuse "to shoot in self-defense." Normal riot gear or staying within their vehicles is perceived by police as demonstrating weakness. The camou-

flage uniforms generally worn signal that a war is on and resisters must not expect mercy. The Afrikaner rugby mentality
is carried over to the township streets. Not for South Africa is
the universal principle of restraint in using force against civilians. The toll of dead and injured in regular confrontations
testifies to an official callousness in containing South African
conflicts.

The technocratic leadership has not yet dared to curb individual sadism. Plans for an interracial training program that
would professionalize, educate, and sensitize the poorly paid
force from the lower echelons of Afrikanerdom have not been
successfully implemented. While responsible politicians express pro forma concern or even condolences, every policeman knows where politicians' real sympathies lie. Supervisors
exert little pressure to curb an inflammatory situation. To be
sure, the Minister of Police can no longer afford to repeat
sentiments like Jimmy Kruger's on the police killing of Steve
Biko: "It leaves me cold." Although dozens of commissions of
inquiry have been set up, not one culprit has yet been con-
victed. The declaration of a state of emergency in 1985, by
itself not necessary to contain protest, mainly served to indem-
nify the police and place them above the law. When opposition
members bring up affidavits of police brutality in parliament,
fellow parliamentarians treat them as a joke: "They sat there
laughing and joking as if there was nothing wrong," said John
Malcomess when he presented eyewitness accounts of the
Langa shootings.[48] The dominant reaction to the Kannemeyer report was not guilt or shame, but self-congratulation
that such independent inquiry is possible in an authoritarian
state, coupled with glee that the judge had refuted opposition
allegations of a higher death toll.

For the victims, on the other hand, riots provide an opportunity to assert identity. They are not primarily interested in
victory. Denied their dignity everywhere, they defy the de-
grading routine for a few moments of heroism, an affirmation
of their humanness. Particularly for adolescents, participation
in demonstrating crowds gives meaning to a meaningless existence. They can bask in the illusion that their spirit can over-

come superior force. For a fleeting moment, the clenched fists and unequal weapons have assured recognition and equality—regardless of costs.

The mass celebration of anger at political funerals, contrary to the appearance, really reflects the absence of community. Apartheid lowered people to the deepest degradation of the human condition. The possibility of gaining identity does not exist. Above all, apartheid has liquidated a spirit of belonging for Blacks. The popular soccer games, like the funerals or Zionist church field services, serve as one of the few sorts of occasions when the powerless can momentarily borrow power from the crowd. For a short time they leave their anonymity and gain the larger identity of the occasion.

When defiance of the police provides a welcome opportunity to demonstrate heroism, the very presence of the authorities becomes a provocation. Many accounts have pointed to the incitement of unrest rather than its suppression by the police: "Wherever they [the police] appeared with their vehicles people began to gather and riots followed. If the police had not made continual appearances in the townships and if they had stopped patrolling with their helicopters, there would have been no such warm riots as the Vaal area experienced."[49] The frustrated policemen are as keen "to teach a lesson" as the children are to prove their worth. The mutual brutalization then encounters few limits. With a low degree of professionalism, both White and Black policemen are ready to run amok.

Increasing numbers of reports of unofficial "hit lists" and unresolved killings of activists hint at a slow drift into a situation of death squads and reprisals. The June 1985 state incursion against exiles in Botswana, *The Economist* commented, "puts South Africa in the same camp as Libya and Iran."[50] Nevertheless, South Africa's Whites supported the alleged retaliation after two grenade attacks on Colored parliamentarians. The mass-circulation *Sunday Times* in the language of fascism praised the "deadly competence" and lauded the counterproductive assault: "The terrorist needs to be brutally reminded of the credibility of South Africa's deterrent."[51]

The Death of a Policeman

Constable Farmer, a coloured, was killed in Browning Avenue at about 1:40pm when an emotionally charged but peaceful funeral procession of about 5000 people moved through Salt River for the burial of Mr. Ebrahim Carelse, shot by police a week earlier.

This is one man's story of the crucial 15 minutes in Browning Avenue which left one man dead and another badly wounded:

There was a police car, with a white and a coloured policeman sitting in it, parked across Browning Avenue in the direction of De Waal Drive.

I saw a group of people approach these two men and tell them their presence was very provocative because they were white.

The policemen said they had a right to be there.

The small group of people gathered around the car told them to move because their presence would cause trouble.

I think I knew that there was going to be trouble at the time, so I moved in that direction.

The white policeman got out and ran away. This is significant because no one gave chase after him or tried to stop him.

It was just a case of a scared white man running away.

The second policeman got out, pointed his gun and shot.

In fairness to him, he was in a most precarious situation. I saw him rising up, shooting and saw a man jerk backwards into the crowd.

The policeman, whom I now know as Farmer, began running down towards Main Road. He ran right into the crowd which had come to see what had happened.

The crowd moved in on him.

I shouted over the megaphone to him to keep on going towards the cemetery, in an attempt to stop what was happening. But by this time the crowd was more interested in getting hold of him.

Timmy MacKay, the man Farmer shot, was shouting hysterically—I think not in provocation but because he was shocked and upset.

I heard someone say that Moulana was on top of him. I fought my way through but the policeman was already like pulp. I helped Moulana to cover him, then Moulana passed out.

The policeman was clutching on to Moulana—he knew he was his only saviour. He was very confused and bloody and still shouted "I am the law." It was the only attempt he had left to try and save himself—by proclaiming his authority.

The Star, *IE (16 September 1985)*

Such tones bode ill for compromise between the government and its opponents. The more each side defines the other as evil and engages in what Allan Boesak has called "holy rage," the less politics works. According to surveys, police and army behavior is approved by 74 percent of Whites, who view the army forays and township battles on their evening television news very much as Americans watched their soldiers in action in Vietnam. The difference lies in the low number of White casualties so far and the fact that South Africans are watching a civil war literally only a few miles away. So oblivious is White South Africa to the "outbreak of social rage" that a leading journal can seriously declare the unrest as being without cause: "As far as can be judged the Grahamstown and Port Elizabeth incidents were largely motiveless—unless they are regarded as the sudden release of frustration."[52]

While the unrest is generally confined to specific grievances of the permanent urban population, migrants in single-men hostels or even illegal squatters on occasion offer physical resistance when they consider their lives threatened. In the Crossroads case, reporters on the scene observed: "By midmorning, streets surrounding Crossroads had been cut off with massive trees and concrete blocks. Burning vehicles and tyres signalled the start of the confrontation. For the first time in the Cape, police found they would have to deal with organized street-fighters. First, running about at random, were a few demonstrators willing to take the risk of a buckshot wound as they distracted the marksmen. Behind them, marching with corrugated iron sheets as shields, came others chanting war-cries. They sheltered those carrying stones and petrol bombs."[53] Soon after these events the government canceled plans for forced removal of the Crossroad squatters, against protests by the Afrikaner right wing.

The savagery on the victims' side, the dancing around charred bodies of suspected collaborators, equally denies any notion of racial solidarity. Black traders, Black shopkeepers, and anyone considered to be benefiting from the system became prime targets. These groups in the townships were largely identical. The Black traders rarely identified with any political movement. They usually refused to support community projects or individual calls for educational support. This self-isolation reinforced the perception that they took money freely but never gave back. Their relatively large houses in the midst of matchboxes seemed amply to demonstrate their opportunistic greed. In the end, any house with more than two bedrooms was liable to be attacked.

The police were traditionally uninterested in intra-Black violence and were in any case unable to quell it. Township dwellers had to protect themselves against criminal gangs on Friday evenings, petty thieves on overcrowded trains and buses, and the assaults and rapes common on weekends. The flourishing Black taxi business owes its success largely to these conditions of lawlessness. The atmosphere of general anomie, with the lure of plunder joined with political legitimation to attack the property of "sell-outs," proved irresistible to the masses of unemployed and drop-outs. The fire-bombings and lootings in some cases did not even stop with goods. One eyewitness reports: "Some people even cut pieces of meat from a living cow which escaped. It ran about without some parts."[54]

Terror became confused with liberation. The UDF/ANC call to make South Africa "ungovernable" lent respectability to the horror that soon would not distinguish between friend and foe. Let loose without a disciplining organization guiding the action, with the authority of most teachers discredited and with parents absent, the fury of excited youngsters recognized no bounds. Themba Molefe has pointed out that family life in the townships has lost its meaning because many fathers, due to unemployment, have lost control of their children, "who only consider where to get the next cent."[55]

Initially their main targets were the community councillors and policemen employed by the system, regardless of their individual record. Even popular and competent councillors were forced to resign. The Black administrators of the impoverished dormitories of White affluence were held responsible for the infuriating rent hikes that sparked unrest in the midst of widespread layoffs. Elected by a turnout of less than 10 percent, the councils lacked legitimacy. The system irreparably collapsed when it faced its first test. It had no taxation authority to supply it with funds, no moral authority to command compliance, not even the physical force (apart from vigilante groups) to protect itself. Even more than by the direct attacks on corrupt councillors, the system of indirect rule was affected by a form of passive resistance—refusing to pay for inferior services. The *Financial Mail* reported: "Either out of conviction or out of fear of paying tribute to a hated system, tens of thousands of households are withholding payment of rent and services levies."[56] Many could not in any case afford to pay. However, rent increases only triggered expression of deeper resentment. Where rents did not go up and are generally low, as in the KwaZulu–administered Durban townships, similar protest, albeit expressed differently, nevertheless took place.

After the 1976 unrest at the latest, grievance procedures should have been established that would give warning before situations became inflammatory. What has been achieved in the industrial relations system could surely have been instituted at the community level. Instead, Pretoria relied on discredited urban councillors to mediate rent increases and transport charges. Predictably, these frequently corrupt opportunists became the immediate target of outrage, in the absence of opportunity to target the real causes of the misery.

Black administrators of the flashpoints of anger are hardly responsible for the grievances. As mere dormitories of White wealth, the townships could not become financially self-sufficient even if they were granted taxation authority. The low rentals that are all the poor can afford merely perpetuate the cycle of meager services and inadequate housing. Only if the wealthy, White parts of the cities were obliged to pay for their servants' quarters could an improvement be envisaged. Above all, business could assume responsibility for the housing of employees; the firms are after all the main beneficiaries of having the Black proletariat at their doorsteps. Whether the proposed levies on the White sector will achieve real improvement in Black townships remains to be seen.

In addition to their unrepresentativeness, the political stu-

pidity and personal calibre of some of the community councillors made them a liability to their patrons. Thus Soweto's
ousted "mayor" Ephraim Tshabalala publicly stated that
apartheid was created by God, that victims of unrest should
not be allowed burial in local cemeteries, and that government
should ban commemorations of the 16 June 1976 Soweto
uprising.

Beyond these causes, how can one explain the astonishing
initial lack of attacks against Whites and the concentration on
the auxiliaries of apartheid? In the tradition of reference
group theory, analysts have distinguished three relationships:
(1) "A comparative reference group is the group whose situation or attributes a person contrasts with his own." A comparative reference group can be either positive or negative, de-
pending on whether a person wants to share the situation of
another group or whether he wants to dissociate himself from
this group. (2) "A normative reference group is the group
from which a person takes his standards." The individual
would like to share the values and lifestyle of this group but
does not compare himself with it. Finally, (3) membership reference groups involve the particular subjective roles of individuals. Feelings of relative deprivation arise only when a person shares some common quality with the reference group
and therefore compares himself with it.[57]

It can be hypothesized that Whites constitute a normative
reference group for many Blacks in South Africa but do not
yet figure subconsciously as a realistic comparison group. The
apartheid divide and differential racial life-chances have penetrated ordinary perceptions to such an extent that the "we
would like to live like them" demand has not yet become a real
aspiration. At the same time, the White life-style has become
the standard from which successful Blacks derive their norms
in a Western consumer culture. This explains youngsters'
hatred of successful Blacks and the relative paucity of attacks
on White businesses. The Black traders, shopkeepers, and
professionals constitute the obvious comparative reference
group, which does not deserve its higher status as long as the
rest suffer. They are accused of having sold out and become

the scapegoat traitors, while the Whites are seen as behaving as expected. The concentration of militant unrest in the Eastern Cape region, compared with the initial uneasy calm in Natal, has highlighted other specific causes of grievance. The South African recession affected the motor industry particularly severely, and 60 percent of industrial output in the region emanates from this sector. Car sales dropped from 32,000 in June 1984 to 17,000 a year later, after tax changes. As a result, the three motor assemblers in the area, General Motors, Ford, and Volkswagen, employed only 11,334 people in March 1985, from 17,048 in December 1984. To the thousands laid off or permanently jobless must be added the masses of disaffected youth. Many schools had been closed for months because of unresolved educational grievances and the firing or relocation of popular teachers. More than half of the Black township population is under the age of 18. Even if their parents had managed to put their children through school, the sacrifice promised to be of little value, given the educational inequities and lack of job prospects.

Above all, the Eastern Cape has the longest tradition of resistance and political activism in South Africa. After the Xhosas were finally subdued in a series of frontier wars during the first half of the nineteenth century, a strong missionary presence secured a relatively high level of education. Lovedale High School and Fort Hare University became symbols, far beyond the South African border, of an African intelligentsia. It was there that the South African Native National Congress originated in 1912, and there that Biko lived. Already in 1886 Blacks constituted 47 percent of the electorate in the five Eastern Cape constituencies. When subsequent administrations attempted to reverse or repress this political tradition, the political alienation found expression in labor militancy and community activities. In Natal Buthelezi's Inkatha directs and disciplines political activism, but in the Eastern Cape frustrations exploded in angry resentment. The absence of credible Black leadership had backfired on the originators of the frustration, who thought they had restored calm through repression.

However, beyond the wide range of specific causes for continuous militancy, a new qualitative factor transcends particular grievances. The "nascent rise in revolutionary consciousness" points to a total rejection of the social system even if it addressed specific complaints.[58] This new militancy can no longer be appeased or intimidated; it is ready to die for a cause. The hysteria that sweeps the school and townships resembles the Children's Crusades of medieval Europe. Immune to the strategic reasoning of parents, teachers, or even Bishop Tutu, it cuts its deadly path outside conventional politics and traditional ideologies. Political socialization now starts with tear-gas fumes. Ten-year-old boys address one another as "comrade." Liberation lyrics, township columnist Maud Motanyane observed, have become part of the children's nursery rhymes. Most popular are militant political songs such as "Siyaya e Pretoria" (We Are Marching to Pretoria). Real fighting with the police has replaced games of cops-and-robbers. Since the language of adult public speeches has shifted to the vernacular, the children can follow them. This new political atmosphere cannot be dismissed simply as the inconsequential excitement of youngsters. It was the COSAS students who initiated the most successful two-day stay-away in the Transvaal on 5–6 November 1985 and who built street barricades to enforce it.

The universal generation gap acquired a new political significance in the African townships, because parents and teachers are generally considered to have accommodated themselves to the apartheid order. Most teachers lost the respect of their students through a combination of professional incompetence and political docility. As rightless objects of a feared bureaucracy, the teachers themselves became conditioned to blindly following the orders listed in circulars or issued by authoritarian inspectors. Some school principals resorted to calling in the police upon the slightest provocation. In the absence of progressive leadership from intimidated teachers, a permanent out-of-class student population became the most significant political force. The idea of "liberation before education" captured the imagination of youngsters who experienced their brand of inferior racial education as "poison." To politicized pupils, a curriculum geared to normal functioning in an abnormal environment betrays the morality of learning. Despite a substantial expansion of Black education in terms of enrollment, teachers, schools, and capital expenditure, the system failed to elicit the perception of legitimacy from its beneficiaries.

The rejection of depoliticized formal education led to remarkable efforts at political self-education. Unlike the Chinese cultural revolution, in which Mao used organized youngsters to terrorize his bourgeois opponents, the rule of the "comrades" is largely self-inspired and self-directed. "They" rule by example, rumor, and excess. Entire townships have participated in consumer boycotts. However, the calls to refrain from shopping in certain stores primarily succeeded not because Black consumers had suddenly been immunized against the lures of capitalist commodities, but because the students demonstrated their ability to enforce collective action. In this reversal of roles from traditionally deferential children to commanding political activists lies the far-reaching impact of the social revolution in the townships. House-to-house instruction draws the passive majority into "the struggle" to the extent that they are compelled to change their lifestyle. During "Black Christmas" 1985, for instance, rumors circulated that youth waited at bus and taxi stops and asked to smell workers' breath for any trace of alcohol and punished women with permed hair. Shebeens (illegal home pubs) closed, and dances and concerts were cancelled. Overnight, demoralized townships became moralized.

Barrington Moore has identified three psychological preconditions for rebellion. These human qualities are, first, "moral courage, in the sense of a capacity to resist powerful and frightening pressures to obey oppressive or destructive rules or commands. The second quality is the intellectual ability to recognize that the pressures and rules are in fact oppressive. This recognition can take the form of moral awakening in terms of existing but largely suppressed standards of behavior. The third capacity, moral inventiveness . . . , is the

capacity to fashion from existing cultural traditions historically new standards of condemnation for what exists."[59] On all
three counts the open repoliticization of the Black spectrum
in the 1980s has made considerable progress.

Can the beleaguered regime increase its repression? Will
South Africa follow the path of the Nazis in the thirties, with
worse to come as the pressure increases? An American observer has commented: "If the government is willing to fire
automatic weapons into crowds of Black mourners, knowing
that those whose good will they covet are watching, what
would they stop at if their very survival were at stake? Is it
really credible that the most sophisticated military on the continent would balk at carpet-bombing the Black townships if it
came to that?"[60] While the regime undoubtedly has the capacity to annihilate large parts of its subject population, it cannot
afford to do so. Unlike the Nazis, Pretoria cannot risk collective punishment of Black townships. It can set up gulags for
its unemployed "trouble-makers"; it can restrict access to cities; but it cannot create arbitrary and indiscriminate terror
without alienating the larger part of its productive force.
Whites are dependent on their antagonists. They have to seek
a minimal legitimacy if they want to be able to rely on a majority of as yet uncommitted workers. When the army conducted
house-to-house searches in Sebokeng, it proclaimed in leaflets
that the soldiers were coming as friends to protect the people
from themselves.

It seems that the anomie in many townships has now
reached such a point that in the long run only two measures
can guarantee a return to stability. First, the general terror
reflects not, as the government asserts, political organization,
but a lack of it. Sooner or later, then, the government will have
to allow legitimate, representative political organizations, because they alone can end the political alienation and confine
followers to rule-bound activities. Ironically, it may turn out
to be the great historical mission of the ANC to contain the
anomie rather than instigate revolutionary destruction. Only
widely acclaimed legitimacy of an authentic resistance movement can redirect frustrations into responsible channels. Sec-

ond, even with freedom of political activity, the bottled-up intra-Black class conflict in the restricted areas of townships makes further strife likely. The solution to this is to allow anyone who can afford it to settle in any other municipal area. This necessitates the repeal of the Group Areas Act in order to allow market forces to play themselves out. Only this residential integration along class lines can allow the emergence of a Black middle class that does not have to live in fear of being instantly expropriated by the masses of the less fortunate.

The economic and demographic situation now calls for more than concessions. The limits of repression are evinced in rising costs both at home and abroad. The government, let alone the Whites as a ruling segment, is not a monolithic entity; it also has to accommodate its own dissenting forces. Thus the rising costs result in continuous splits and compromises with Black demands. The unintended effect of these appeasements and attempts at containment is, frequently, to strengthen the opposition. The best example is the growing clout of unions, which had to be allowed to secure labor peace. Can mutual pressures result in diminishing the dichotomy between Black and White rule to a point of minor relevance? In such a largely deracialized arrangement of genuine power-sharing, the issue would no longer be race but class, not ethnicity but ideology: how will the conservative forces respond to the claims of socialist-oriented redistribution through the state; how can nominal equality of opportunities be translated into equality of results?

Prospects for Negotiations: The ANC and Pretoria

On 13 September 1985, four leading South African businessmen—the chairman of the giant Anglo-American Corporation and three South African editors—met the leadership of the exiled African National Congress in Luangwa National Park at the lodge of Zambian President Kenneth Kaunda, who presided over the unprecedented six-hour session. South Africa's president had warned the industrialists publicly that they would legitimate "terrorists," but in the end the government took no action against the contact, which some believed Pretoria had even welcomed informally. However, two leading Afrikaner industrialists, Anton Rupert and Fred du Plessis, withdrew from the delegation after Botha's reference to "disloyalty."

The historic episode highlights the new fluidity of business-government relations as well as the status of the outlawed Congress movement. Since having been expelled from Mozambique a year earlier, the ANC could rightly claim credit for three major achievements: it had undermined White solidarity; it had reached a high level of mass mobilization; and it had won unprecedented international legitimacy.

The accord signed by South Africa and Mozambique at Nkomati had destroyed hopes of external liberation and forced South African Blacks to focus more realistically on internal means for political reform. The ANC is undoubtedly justified in feeling betrayed by front-line states. Not only was the ANC not consulted before the principles of the Nkomati treaty were agreed upon, but the conditions of the ANC's future operation in (and expulsion from) Mozambique proved rather "uncomradely," as one observer described it. The promised "moral, political and diplomatic support" of the ANC by Mozambique was restricted to a ten-member diplomatic office for which the organization had to submit names for approval. Of the suggested ten persons, six were rejected. Only four ANC members have been granted visa privileges to visit Mozambique at any time. It is clear that Frelimo wants to rid itself of the vestiges of an embarrassing ally sooner rather than later. In Zimbabwe, Robert Mugabe refuses training facilities, not only out of fear of reprisals but because the Moscow-linked ANC supported his rival Nkomo before Zimbabwean independence. The temporary Angola–South Africa military cooperation boded ill for the ANC training camps in Angola. With its Ho Chi Minh trails cut and its personnel officially expelled from Swaziland and Lesotho, the ANC faced difficulty in sustaining the level of sabotage. But the setback did not erase the ANC from the South African map. On the contrary, it was wishful thinking on the part of the SABC to state: "The ANC now is probably a spent force in South African politics."[61]

The new situation did not force the ANC to abandon its preference for military confrontations. The ANC's controversial strategy was to attack where its opponent was strongest and the ANC weakest. A more politically oriented opposition, using unions and other legitimate organizations, could concentrate on areas where the apartheid defenses are weakest and the opponents strongest. The journalistic focus on security considerations notwithstanding, so far Pretoria has shown only moderate concern about the occasional ANC incursions from abroad, though South African propaganda has exaggerated the ANC threat and the Cuban presence in Angola in order to mobilize White support at home. The South African army bombings of ANC shelters in Maputo, Botswana, and Lesotho were aimed more at placating domestic right-wing opinion. "Going soft" on the enemy would have undermined P. W. Botha's constituency, for 80 percent of the White voters approved of an aggressive policy of retaliation. When government leaders now plead for consensus, inveigh against confrontation, and warn of the costs of revolutionary turmoil, they repeat the grounds on which the liberal opposition has based its condemnations of apartheid for decades. But by co-opting this reasoning of doom, the government implies that it has sufficient foresight to avert disaster. It suggests that it can avoid the impending catastrophe if a racist constituency gives it unquestioning support for racial reforms.

The Nkomati peace pact, on the other hand, undermined one of the ostensible reasons for the reluctant reforms—the threat from an all-pervasive outside enemy. It rendered incredible the myths of the "total onslaught" and "the border," manufactured for domestic militarization. The menace of communism, still being proclaimed in an attempt to forge internal unity, seems increasingly less threatening in the light of the record. In contrast to Angola, Mozambique, the Soviet Union's ally in Southern Africa, is not even considered a genuine Marxist state by Moscow, but merely "socialist-oriented."

The Soviet Union remains the major arms supplier for the ANC and the South-West African People's Organization (SWAPO), but has no naval bases in the region, despite treaties of friendship and cooperation with Angola and Mozambique. Indeed, it is much more prudent for Moscow to let South Africa fester as the obvious racial sore of capitalism than to seek to escalate the risk of confrontation with the West in this distant arena. With relatively small expenditures for military hardware and diplomatic assistance, the Soviet Union reaps huge ideological benefits in public opinion from the Western ties with a colonial racist regime. For all these reasons, South Africa ranks low among Moscow's global priorities.[62] The Kremlin would be an unlikely source for active disturbance of the apartheid order. Indeed, even a government as concerned about Soviet expansionism as the Reagan administration nevertheless does not share the common South African perception of the Soviet Union as lying in wait to grab the subcontinent's treasures: "Southern Africa is, practically speaking, well outside the Soviet Union's zone of primary interest, indeed of its secondary interests. We believe that Moscow is aware of this fact and, in reality, spends little time thinking about the area," according to Frank Wisner, U.S. Deputy Assistant Secretary for African Affairs.[63]

Sanctions against South Africa are only rhetorically endorsed by front-line states, most of which are secretly participating in ending the economic isolation of the apartheid state. This forces the international anti-apartheid movement to plan new strategies. The likely outcome in the long run is a split between those committed to military confrontation and those willing to participate in internal reform. What shape such a division will take and who will align themselves on each side depend on what channels of legitimate political participation are open to radical apartheid opponents.

The present tricameral system constitutes a dead end for the vital African political incorporation. No internal, legalized ANC could participate in the system without committing political suicide. Even if Mandela were freed, and the government welcomed back exiles committed to peace and began to consult with the ANC/UDF about a new deal, any negotiations would require scrapping the whole constitution. Despite speeches emphasizing the need for an internal peace accord, the government has put forward no concrete proposals about how to accommodate Black demands for direct and meaningful participation in central political decision-making. In the absence of free political activity, activists are forced to work clandestinely in legal bodies and to politicize unions, church groups, and students. These activists no longer operate as a specific historical resistance movement and are no longer bound by the organizational discipline of a political movement. Such fragmentation may be celebrated as a victory by the powerholders, but it can backfire. It takes only a few alienated individuals to wreak havoc in an industrial society—as terrorism by fringe groups in the capitals of the world proves almost daily. Lucky the authority that can legitimately bind such individuals into cohesive organizations and institutions in which radical commitment finds peaceful expression.

Excepting the occasional car bombings in South African cities, the ANC leadership, including the Communist Party element, has so far successfully resisted pressure to resort to all-out terrorist activities such as killing White civilians. Despite the inclusion of Black and White bureaucrats in the approved target range at the 1985 consultative conference, bombs in supermarkets and deliberate attacks on civilians are still ruled out. The widening of the gap between external militants and internal militants who are no longer under the control of a tight authoritarian organization may well turn out to be a Pyrrhic victory. The strategic planners in the State Security Council may yet regret having achieved the fragmentation of a movement of great symbolic value for the mass of victims. They may yet long for the days when they could pinpoint a politically predictable and reliable opponent for negotiations instead of having to deal with unmanageable anarchists.

Such difficulties do not arise in negotiations between states. To conclude an external accord between two hostile but sovereign states is easier than to achieve the same results between diverse domestic parties. The question for South Africa remains: how can the situation of peaceful coexistence being worked out among the states of the region be extended to South Africa's more fundamental internal conflicts? A cohesive movement that could legitimately bargain for the oppressed may indeed be in the interests of those who most fear for their security. Alternatively, and most likely to develop, a Black pluralism of opposition groups with different ideologies and interests could strengthen the chances for a democratic system.

Pretoria and the ANC both now for the first time have good reasons to begin a dialogue, though the two sides may enter this *indaba* for quite different reasons and with different agendas. Lasting stability now depends more than ever on negotiations between Afrikaner nationalists and what are constantly referred to as "the authentic leaders of the Black masses." Of the many Black leaders with a following, the outlawed ANC, with its hidden constituency in the UDF, ranks top, although by no means alone, among politicized urban Blacks. With a remarkable insensitivity to the rejection of collaborating Blacks by the politicized group the approved leaders are supposed to control, the government officially insists on their leadership role while publicly ignoring the real representatives. This distance, however, only enhances the credibility of the rejected. Any Black leader who collaborates with the government almost certainly loses his following. Even if the exiled ANC president were to fly to Pretoria tomorrow, he would immediately be suspected of selling out a more militant internal leadership. Hence, both sides have a vital interest in keeping contacts secret, though for different reasons—Black activists cannot afford to be compromised, while Pretoria takes propagandistic risks in being cast as weak by negotiating with an official enemy. What, then, are the prospects for talks more productive than the informal individual contacts and proxy dialogues now taking place?

Pretoria's external aggressive destabilization and general militarization of the country have encouraged those who advocate traditional means of coercion. However, many are coming to realize that the township unrest may be contained militarily but can only be solved politically. Business leaders such as Tony Bloom have urged the government to realize the "historical inevitability" of talks with the ANC. Under the impact of successful strike action, in December 1984 organized business for the first time spoke out forcefully against the traditional repression of union leadership, on whom it increasingly depends for industrial peace. Although after a meeting with the Minister, the Afrikaner business sector retracted this position, the influence of business on government is likely to increase in the severe recession. With a worsening economic crisis, costly ideological projects will become the obvious target for savings. It is not true, as Basil Davidson asserts, "that nothing has been officially proposed, or even discussed, that could in any way improve the social and political situation of the Africans."[64] On the contrary, from a cabinet secretariat to the Urban Foundation of big business and the Human Science Research Council of academia, dozens of eager attempts are being made to find "solutions to intergroup relations." They mostly take a "management approach" that implies continued White control, albeit with sufficient modifications to appease, contain, manipulate, and co-opt Black militants. A minority seek an open-ended dialogue, and a still smaller group advocates serious negotiations about formulas of power-sharing that would be mutually determined, rather than imposed by one group upon the others.

Nevertheless, since 1980 when Ton Vosloo, editor of *Beeld*, became the first prominent nationalist to suggest that the government would eventually have to negotiate with the ANC, this proposition has gained wide currency among technocratic powerholders. It is speculated, for example, that the buying of *City Press* by Vosloo's Nasionale Pers group was intended to provide the Nationalist Party with a credible outlet in the Black newspaper market through which such a dialogue could be carried out and influenced. The sides have each stated their formal bargaining position: Botha wants the ANC to renounce violence; the ANC wants Botha to abandon apartheid. Within the wide meaning of these terms there may well be significant areas of common interest and potential compromise: federalism, economic regional development, decentralization of power to nonracially selected local authorities, and new citizenship regulations in an undivided South Africa with universal franchise. The crucial test will be to what extent Pretoria is prepared to abandon the imposed racial ordering of South African society in favor of voluntary group associations.

The flurry of statements regarding Pretoria-ANC negotiations are part of a West-supported campaign to parallel the Mozambican reorientation by drawing the ANC into the Western orbit. Success in this effort would signal a far greater danger for Pretoria's hard-liners than having the ANC safely labeled *communist*. Nonetheless, it would obviously suit South Africa if the ANC were to suspend its military activity as part of a formal summit agreement. While the summit is a distant possibility, a truce is not. The government has no intention of offering the ANC a share in political decision-making. By showing willingness to talk, Pretoria hopes to exploit differences within the ANC and eventually to split the organization into so-called radical communists and compromising nationalists. Pretoria's goal remains to crush the opposition rather than incorporate them as a partner in power.

The ANC, meanwhile, is under pressure, by more than the futility of military action in South Africa, to reassess its armed struggle in favor of political dialogue. A repetition of the Zimbabwean example of liberation is nourished more as an inspiring vision in the industrialized South than as a realistic option. ANC president Oliver Tambo's proclamation, "We are not bothered by the strength of South Africa. We don't think they are strong at home. We will prove that on the ground," may be bravado or propaganda, or Tambo may indeed believe this to be the case.[65] Whatever the case, such a misperception of the opponent's strength on the part of committed activists is likely to lead to losses that a realistic assessment of power differentials could avoid. Failure to deliver the promised liberation depoliticizes. Unfulfilled expectations turn into cynicism, just as the prospect of obtainable alternatives can politicize.

Samora Machel of Mozambique and Kenneth Kaunda of

Zambia in particular now are subtly pressuring the organization to fall in line with their own designs. In the past such
front-line persuasion often determined specific stances of liberation movements, even if the guests perceived their interests
differently from their hosts. The greater distance between
some front-line states and the ANC, together with the attempt
to shift more responsibility for the ANC to an inefficient Organization of African Unity (OAU), however, will lead to a
decline of front-line influence on the ANC. For example, the
ANC leadership in Lusaka prefers to have contacts directly
with Afrikaner nationalists rather than conducting them
through the good offices of its host, as was the case with the
first official SWAPO-Pretoria encounter.

Trained cadres in the field reportedly occasionally operate
outside approved guidelines. Students fresh from South Africa joining the battle for training often are more militant than
those who have undergone lengthy periods of preparation
abroad. Internally, the organization is latently divided between those who favor an escalation of military action against
"soft" targets, regardless of the casualties involved, and those
who merely want to use an occasional bomb as a reminder to
Pretoria to start negotiating. This split does not necessarily
coincide with the often-noted division between alleged militant Marxist and moderate nationalists. Those with allegiance
to the Communist Party tend to have a greater concern for
organizational public relations and the international ramifi-
cations of a "terrorist image" than those with a less clearly
articulated ideological commitment. Last but not least, relics
of the Christian tradition of nonviolence and Gandhian paci-
fism still linger in those of the ANC leadership who were once
deeply involved in the passive resistance campaign. While the
Communist Party ideologues start with a long timetable for
the structural transformation of the adversary, most of the
leadership is concerned about premature action. Now that vital connections to the operational zone have been cut by the
Nkomati accord, the guerrillas operating inside South Africa
are more difficult to control and to discipline. The External
Mission has already had to apologize publicly for embarrass-

ing mistakes by its militant cadres. Added to the problem of public image is concern about the very real possibility of more brutal repression if the amount of sabotage increases.

An exiled movement that is politically active worldwide in addition to giving military training abroad to an estimated 6,000 guerrillas cannot escape problems of internal discipline. Thus a report on the decisions of the second consultative conference in Kabwe (Zambia) in June 1985 recorded: "ANC 'draft-dodgers' will not be allowed to opt for Moscow as an alternative to the more austere Angolan camps, where the ANC leadership has been increasingly concerned with a breakdown of discipline. A rebellion there was ruthlessly put down last year. Among ANC exiles who have become accustomed to the comforts of Western life-in-exile, mention of Angola is comparable to the connotations Siberia has for the Soviets."[66] The conference also felt the need to adopt a strict military code of conduct for all ANC members, laying down rules governing relationships with persons of the opposite sex, drinking habits, and the company kept by ANC members abroad.

Above all, the exiled ANC leadership faces growing competition from a new generation of internal militants. Out of the country for twenty years, the veterans of the struggle are pressed to make a choice as to how long waiting for liberation should last. The ANC has to assert its symbolic role as the oldest resistance group, since the union movement refuses to subject itself to the organizational discipline of populist political leadership. Most of the union officials now have a vested interest in their own workers' organization as against a party political organization. Breyten Breytenbach, after eight years in South African jails as the result of an ill-conceived recruitment trip, has speculated that "the ANC External Mission, in the grip of the dogmatists, will be stronger than the ANC inside the country, and probably they will shut them out in any ensuing power struggle."[67] It is much more likely that the opposite will happen: internal activists are more steeped in the realities of the struggle and therefore will eventually wield more influence.

In all likelihood the revered Umkonto activists captured in Rivonia, who have now been in South African jails for twenty-five years, are the last Black leaders with a wide enough legitimacy to negotiate with Pretoria without being compromised. But in 1985, only 6 percent of the White electorate supported the unconditional release of Nelson Mandela.[68] For Mandela, Walter Sisulu, and Govan Mbeki, on the other hand, to maintain purity is the only way to maintain dignity after heroically sacrificing their lives for a cause. So far, Pretoria has undertaken nothing to recognize publicly the principled justness of their opponent's cause; few face-saving proposals have been made to allow negotiations to begin. But the longer the wait the greater the likelihood that the restrained militancy of the ANC will be overwhelmed by the unrestrained rage in the townships. A new generation of ANC leaders then will have to follow rather than lead.

For all these reasons, the external ANC leadership, too, cannot reject the idea of serious negotiations. Pretoria would thus grant recognition of the ANC's legitimate role, and the exiled faction would gain a platform from which to assert its hegemony over internal competitors, particularly Inkatha and independent unions. However, it is difficult to envisage what role the ANC (banned as a political organization in South Africa since 1960) could play as an *identifiable* organization if it is demilitarized, as South Africa demands as a precondition for talks.

A national convention—even if perceived as an ongoing process rather than a one-time summit meeting—must deal with the existence of substantial opposition groups that do not subscribe to ANC or UDF strategies. Buthelezi's Inkatha movement stands out as a force that could sway the balance in any concerted action. A future majority government under ANC control could hardly expect to create stability without also recognizing the strength of Inkatha. Despite the failed 1979 talks in London between Inkatha and the ANC, and the subsequent mutual hostility, there is less antagonism toward Buthelezi among some ANC officeholders abroad than among UDF activists in the Transvaal. Unlike the UDF leaders who rejected an alliance with Inkatha in the constitutional struggle, most exiles are prepared to accept Buthelezi (but not the Mantanzimas and Sebes) at the conference table. In their view, Buthelezi is too shrewd a tactician not to side with the emerging new power group. Buthelezi, on the other hand, much more realistic in his evaluation of adversaries and appropriate tactics, will not succumb to pragmatic manipulation. In the unlikely event of an ANC faction succeeding in pressing the United Nations to declare their organization the sole representative of the disfranchised South African people, the rupture with competing anti-apartheid groups would become permanent. A permanent rupture would be equally certain following the assassination of Buthelezi, which he claims has been ordered by the ANC. But if the broad spectrum of internal opposition can reassert itself in a united democratic Congress movement, the present ANC itself could change. Breytenbach does not see "any chance of the ANC transforming itself into a free democratic organization," for it is "the victims of its friends, its history and the conditions imposed on it by the struggle for freedom in an arena controlled by a cruel and criminally irresponsible adversary."[69] But there is no sociological law that says that authoritarian characteristics and moral conduct must be adopted by its opponents. If organized resistance in South Africa can institutionalize authentic grass-roots influence similar to the functioning of most unions at present, rather than being manipulated from above by all kinds of external interests, then not only a free and democratic movement but also a much more powerful opponent to apartheid will have emerged. Tough negotiations will require coming to grips with realistic alternatives instead of indulging in self-deceptive dreams.

5

Compliance
without Consent

Legitimacy, Hegemony, and Ideology in the Ethnic State

SOUTH AFRICA PRACTICES THE TEXTBOOK CASE of legal violations of legitimacy by denying the majority population equal political rights. With an ethnic minority in power and the majority disfranchised, illegitimacy becomes the norm. This means that a legitimation crisis is being institutionalized. This permanent emergency may actually constitute an asset for the minority as long as it does not seriously threaten security. Crisis keeps the constituency mobilized and provides a reason for assuming wide discretionary power in maintaining law and order.[1] If the "total onslaught" were not real in some aspects, it would have had to be invented in South Africa.

However, in order to solicit compliance and ensure ingroup cohesion, the ethnic state must exercise power legally. Arbitrary terror would increase the costs of coercion and motivate more resistance. *Legality* thus becomes a substitute for *legitimacy*. The separation of legality from legitimacy makes it possible to rule illegitimately with the aid of the law. Divorced from substantive ideals with universal content, normative regularity becomes a reified faith in procedures, so that in the end legitimacy interests can succeed only by illegal means.

This "subversive" implication of the legitimation crisis is clearly recognized by the more sophisticated social engineers of the dominant group as well as by those who do not confuse the moral with the legal. In this situation, violations of the legal order become legitimate. Legitimate breaches of legality are now widely accepted and counseled as indicators of a mature, alert citizenry. In South Africa civil disobedience is forced upon those who not only deny the basic political legitimacy of the lawmaking process but are themselves placed outside the civil order as noncitizens by the very system they are expected to perceive as legitimate. Can a dominant ideology obfuscate or reconcile this dilemma?

In most critical analyses of the role of ideology it is assumed that an officially propagated value system (ideology) is primarily directed at its victims. The beneficiaries of a dominant ideology explain their role by false claims which they want the dominated to believe, because this facilitates domination. This view implies that the ruling group knows and agrees upon its real interests; it has only to manipulate its opponents in order to achieve its goals. The manipulators are presumably not misled by their own propaganda. However, an effective ideology, it can be argued, must address both antagonists. Both subordinate and superordinate groups must find their lives made intelligible in a dominant ideology. In short, the ruling group too must feel morally comfortable with its ideology. A dominant ideology must, therefore, not only rationalize its exploitative features but also encompass its opposite.[2]

Colonial administrative ideology never treated its objects as mere labor units. The "civilizing mission" struck a chord in its carriers rather than its victims. It always shifted ambiguously between moral rationalizations and control functions. Domination that, for example, can honestly claim material progress for all its people, however differentially, is comforting to its adherents. It entitles its administrators to respect. In short, the perfect ideology interprets the experiences of both classes, allowing both ruler and ruled to embrace it, though for different reasons. When ethnic policy and ideology lack this common denominator of a widely acceptable principle—as in the case of racism and sectarianism—the system's moral legitimacy is particularly vulnerable.

State officials, of course, do not invent an ideology. Instead, they utilize prevailing values and myths and devise some order to them as brokers between competing priorities. What emerges as an ideological package of constantly reiterated themes must not be overrated in its coherence and rational planning to achieve its goals. It affects various audiences differently, and various aspects are emphasized according to the exigencies of the day. Questions of content and effect of state ideologies are subject to empirical investigation and cannot be answered by conceptual closure of a general theory of ideology.

A state of affairs must be distinguished in which a ruling group no longer indoctrinates its members as well as opponents with an elaborate defense of its behavior. This is partly due to the decline of a religious belief-system during periods of secularization, but is above all due to its having secured power.[3] It may indeed be argued that in South Africa White rule is no longer efficiently legitimized with an ideology of Afrikaner identity or racist doctrines, but now with bureaucratic notions of law and order, as in most other Western societies. This technological rationality in its extreme form needs simply to expose people to an overwhelming reality in which, apparently, no alternatives are possible or desirable, in order to achieve the necessary acquiescence and collaboration. This state of affairs is qualitatively different from conflict perceived and argued in terms of good and evil, particularly as far as the possibilities of change are concerned.

In a perceptive comparison between the conflict in South Africa and in Northern Ireland, Hamish Dickie-Clark has argued an essential difference between religiously perceived rivalry and racially defined competition: in the former, beliefs are "mutually exclusive" and held by "rival groups as absolute truths beyond all compromise."[4] Especially when these absolutist claims intend to dominate the secular public realm—by imposing sectarian legislation on such matters as education, marriage, abortion, public symbols, and other sacred rituals— the scene is set for intractable and long-lasting strife.

However, "keeping one's own identity," the phrase South African Whites use to justify their separatist policies, does not seem to have the nonbargaining quality of a religious conflict.

Though often argued in intractable terms and with the appearance of a firmly held belief-system, "maintaining identity" is, above all, the mask for monopolizing material privileges, power, and status. Assuming the hypothetical case that after a reversal of power the alleged obsession with racial purity suddenly became associated with powerlessness and loss of superiority, the slogan of "White identity" would have little appeal—as many examples of decolonization have shown. In other words, it is not racism as such, but what it stands for and protects that is at issue.

Apartheid must be seen as a tactical device, invented as a response to pressure, almost a last resort of token decolonization, reluctantly implemented whenever necessary and feasible. Grand apartheid lacks a motivating belief system, a utopia to strive for, a future to dream about. At the most it can present as its final outcome such a utopia as one of harmonious, peaceful relations between independent nations within a Commonwealth of Southern Africa. But even many apartheid apologists hardly believe in it themselves and merely sell it as the only solution available.

This raises the question as to how deeply held the racist notions in contemporary South Africa really are. Can they be shaken by a rational argument that points to an undesired outcome? Could reality break through enough that an entrenched racial domination would become negotiable? Important questions are: (1) to what extent is this conceivable? (2) what level of dysfunctionalism, conflict, and pressure must have been reached for this to happen? and (3) how many members of a racist oligarchy may be expected, how soon, rationally to exchange an accustomed privileged life for an uncertain option? These questions demand speculation about the degree of commitment to the stated claims, and perhaps a differentiation between core beliefs and peripheral outlooks, where changes are more readily conceivable.

Unfortunately, much of the social science literature on ideology, particularly from political scientists, fails to analyze the degree of conviction in professed claims. Instead, a rhetorical reality is frequently taken at face value and an elaborate ideology is discerned when the claimants do not really identify with it themselves or merely use claims to manipulate an opponent. A genuine commitment to and basic belief in a given rationale seem to be preconditions for calling it an ideology in the sense defined above. Propaganda and other cynical devices do not constitute an ideology. Nor does mere compliance under pressure of group sanctions. It lacks the legitimacy of a motivating ideology. While in the attitudes and behavior of individuals all these elements, including self-critical doubts, are usually present to various degrees in an inseparable mixture, the task of the political sociologist should be to discern the dominant collective outlook, to weigh the scanty evidence for past and future trends as reflected and crystallized in the policy decisions of the power elite or majority opinion.

There are few contemporary cases for a comparative analysis, though the Israeli example is often cited as a fitting analogy by radical Third World spokesmen as well as conservative Western observers. The experienced diplomat George F. Kennan, in discussing the "very real problem" of maintaining "historical and cultural identity," has noted: "It is an identity in which, as in the case of the Israeli, national components are mixed, for better or worse, with religious ones; and the Afrikaners are no more inclined to jeopardize it, by placing themselves entirely in the power of a surrounding foreign majority, than are their Middle Eastern counterparts."[5] Kennan overlooks the fact that South African Whites are already largely in the hands of their adversaries economically though not (yet) politically. In South Africa the challengers are not a "foreign majority" but a domestic native labor force on which the entire system is dependent and for whose regimentation it was largely created. The hollow religious overtones of the Afrikaners' "civilizing mission" as a "chosen people" ought not to be confused with the zeal of Jewish exclusiveness in a "promised land" in which their very presence is challenged. The legitimacy of the "White tribe" in Africa, on the other hand, is widely accepted among its antagonists. As the Lusaka Manifesto of 1969 has already pointed out, it is, at least in theory, only the racial monopoly of political power, not the White identity or right to share South Africa, that constitutes the contentious issue. If the understandable White fear of an equally understandable African reversal of domination could be somehow assuaged by cast-iron guarantees for minority rights in a united South Africa, new prospects for a negotiated coexistence might emerge.

Compliance through Coercion

What needs explanation above all else in South Africa is not repression but the relatively smooth achievement of compliance through coercion. How could an authoritarian regime with little domestic legitimacy continue, until the mid 1980s, to detain annually for political or security offenses fewer than a thousand persons out of a population of twenty-eight million? Why did South Africa ban only eleven persons in 1984–85, when in comparable military technocracies from Turkey to the Philippines, from Korea to Chile, from Cuba to the Soviet Union, tens of thousands of political dissenters are persecuted?[6] The question is even more puzzling in light of the legally entrenched racial order that grew up along with an advanced industrial economy.

Despite the 1985 state of emergency and civil war in the townships, the historical overall picture is one of compliance with unjust laws, obedience to a customary hierarchy, and acquiescence with, though not consent to, grossly unequal life chances. Only rarely do the many commentators note this strange paradox. "The startling fact about South Africa," editorialized the liberal *Washington Post* at the height of the 1984 Vaal disturbances, "is not that an occasional riot or police action brings White repression and Black unrest into the news but that there is, relatively speaking, so little evident protest." The writer provides two facile answers: "The immense blanket-like White police apparatus, Soviet in quality, makes protest prohibitively costly for most of the people most of the time. Moreover, among the politically powerless Black majority there is a wealth of patience and stoicism that is awesome, verging on the incomprehensible, especially in light of the massive provocation and offense to which Blacks are routinely subject."[7]

In the literature on apartheid this issue of compliance is obscured by the dominant focus on resistance. In the liberal and Marxist traditions alike political protest is celebrated; the further exiled writers live from "the struggle," the more dissent is glorified. Conservatives, on the other hand, easily construe pragmatic acquiescence as consent. Their assumption of the South African state's legitimacy reveals an approach just as biased as that which underlies the romanticized emphasis on repression and courageous resistance.

All modern societies are held together by a variety of integrating mechanisms. Especially in divided societies like South Africa, four overlapping forms through which dominant groups achieve compliance may be distinguished: coercion, dependency, co-optation, and legitimacy.

Coercion, or the threat of sanctions, is of course the most obvious form of political control. Batteries of draconian laws and a multitude of state agencies concerned with security are used to imprison, torture, restrict, or intimidate dissidents. The state reacts to resistance from below as well as tolerates degrees of politicization that in turn spur state repression. Periods of tightened coercion alternate with times of liberalization. The controversial constitutional reforms of 1983–84 made it opportune for Pretoria to allow a national Black protest movement to reemerge. The United Democratic Front demonstrated to the right wing that the National Party had not betrayed its origin. An open Black protest movement also legitimized the reform debate until the politicization in its wake reached a critical threshold. Virtually on the eve of the Colored and Indian elections, a great part of the UDF leadership was detained and the emerging legitimacy of the elections was destroyed. Since the protest movement constituted no threat to the more sophisticated electoral co-optation attempt, the government action could only be explained as irrational. It set the stage for a further politicization on the issue of schools and that of rent and transport fee hikes. The subsequent township unrest culminated in strikes and official emergencies. When the army was called in to back up an exhausted police force in systematic and indiscriminate township searches, traditional coercion reached a new height. The number of political detainees (as calculated by the Detainees' Parents Support Committee) swelled from 264 in 1982, to 453 in 1983, to about a thousand in 1984, and to several thousand in 1985, not counting the hundreds of people killed in escalating political violence since.

Still, there are constraints on the use of coercion by even the most ruthless government. The escalating violence revealed the need for the state to develop cheaper and more efficient ways to secure compliance. Coercion erodes a much sought-after international legitimacy, increases resistance among its victims (e.g., leading them to join the underground), and is inherently unstable and costly. While all governments always fall back on coercion in a crisis, the recurrence of crisis in White rule forces Pretoria to shift its enforcement of compliance away from coercion. This necessity for new forms of political policing is clearly realized by the more sophisticated of the government supporters. For example, parts of the Afrikaans press, now acting as sympathetic critics rather than being shackled to absolute party loyalty, frequently advise less heavy-handed coercion: "We hope that a new era of greater wisdom and a more sensitive approach has dawned, not only in the case of Dr. Naudé but also in similar cases; also that it, together with the freeing of various detainees, is part of a more subtle strategy on affairs concerning people's freedoms."[8] Other voices praised the government for not acting against the South African Council of Churches although the Eloff Commission had set the stage for repressive measures. In school disturbances the authorities initially adopted a non-confrontationist stance. In industrial disputes police were being used less frequently and the state was in the process of withdrawing from the market by increasingly privatizing system maintenance. When even the Reagan administration hints that some detainees should be freed as proof that "constructive engagement" works, Pretoria is under great pressure to tread more softly.

The replacement of old-style coercion by a more subtle strategy reflects the professionalization of control as the authorities become aware of the costs, in resources and legitimacy, of excessive suppression. It reflects, not less concern with security, but a more effective use of the tools of the trade, which decreases the casualties of political policing while increasing the results.

The revival of coercion always remains a last resort. The laws still on the books serve as a reminder of this option. They will not, therefore, be abolished, as liberals advocate. As long as individual cases function as a general deterrent, the state does not need to raise the level of coercion. For example, the tortures and suicides in prison are regularly publicized, deleterious though they may be for external legitimacy of the regime. Breyten Breytenbach, whose exposure of prison brutality was nevertheless allowed to be published in South Africa, has explained the contradiction: "Not only are these acts not disavowed in practise—the 'antiterrorist strategists' *want* their opponents to know that, when captured, they will be brutalized. The clearly signalled intention is itself part of the strategy. They believe that it is a simple matter of 'them or us,' and, cynically, that the ends justify the means. They also believe that foreign rulers and investors, despite hypocritical sounds of disapproval of necessity made from time to time, do in reality understand their politics."[9] Such intimidation, however, precludes genuine legitimacy.

Austin Turk has identified four worldwide trends in political policing, applicable to South Africa: increased field control; selective targeting; subcontracting; and internationalization of security.[10] *Field control* comprises the manipulation of resources and opportunities according to seemingly neutral or reasonable technocratic criteria. For example, making admittance to urban areas dependent on adequate available housing for the rural work-seekers achieves influx control more smoothly than pass laws. By turning the tap of subsidized housing, the authorities can regulate the flow of migrants much more elegantly than through street raids. Another powerful tool for steering political behavior is the

Traffic Incidents

Small incidents can turn into major rows when expectations are always geared to the larger problems of a racial polity. The Sunday Times *(24 August 1984) reports:*

An argument over a traffic ticket turned into a pitched battle involving traffic officers, members of the SAP and even the army.

It started when a driver was ticketed in Pretoria's Vermeulen Street yesterday. But the driver was having none of it and told the cop so in as many heated words. Their argument began attracting a crowd. A second officer appeared. Within minutes more than 100 people had gathered on the scene.

Then all hell broke loose. Patrol cars screamed in and cops on motorcycles fought their way through one-way traffic to get to the scene. The flashing lights and wailing sirens drew even bigger crowds.

By this time traffic in four-lane Vermeulen Street was backed up for several blocks. Police officers ordered people to move on. There was a roar and several punch-ups developed.

Soldiers then emerged from the New Liberty Life building, in which the Defence Force has offices, carrying submachine guns and rifles. But soon police had the situation under control. Later the police said a Black man was detained on a charge of assault.

simple channeling of development funds according to political preferences. Such political bias is denied by the Southern African Development Bank, but in this view, a homeland that refuses independence could find itself starved of aid and loans, which instead go to the "sovereign" states.

Selective targeting reflects the increased sophistication of authorities in dealing with their opponents. More thorough monitoring through computerized intelligence records and electronic surveillance paradoxically results in a more sparing use of terror. Instead of random persecution of potential resisters based on general suspicions, modern control specialists learn to distinguish real from imagined enemies. Streamlined bureaucratic procedures ensure more efficient action on better information.

Much is made of the ingenuity of new forms of resistance, but the forces of coercion show an equal degree of innovation in their brutality. The increased recruitment of Black police, including Black women, in the 1980s strengthened the law-and-order camp considerably (but the direct attacks on police-men in township unrests in the 1980s may well reduce Blacks' willingness to join the force). In short, the learning process of a romanticized resistance is not confined to the state's oppo-nents. The crisis managers, too, feed on the periodic crises.

Subcontracting or, better, the *privatization* of policing tasks in South Africa has taken various forms. In particular, private security agencies have experienced phenomenal growth and have been described as a recession-proof demand for security in the midst of economic insecurity. Whether the private po-licemen guard shopping centers, banks, or strategic installa-tions, they save the state valuable resources. The auxiliary role of private security services is gratefully acknowledged by the police who push for their legal upgrading: "Security compa-nies are a boon to the police. Their intimate knowledge of the layout of the buildings they serve, for instance, is essential at the time of a bomb threat. How would policemen entering a strange building know which parcel or briefcase should or should not be there. These security men need to be given status in terms of knowledge, training and expertise. The po-lice force is keen on legislation to upgrade the security estab-lishment. The formulation of this legislation has greatly in-volved the University of South Africa."[11]

The privatization of policing is now considered the most effective means of enforcing the restrictions of the Group Area Act. Against the steady trickle of Colored and Indian tenants into high-rise areas such as Hillbrow in central Johan-nesburg, it has been proposed that the property owner should carry the legal responsibility of ensuring that no accommoda-tion is let or sold to the wrong race group.

Increasingly, private business is drawn into law enforce-ment. When in March 1984 a new tax structure was intro-duced to equalize Black taxation principles with the existing White terms, the government, much to the chagrin of man-agement, left it to the employers to explain the higher taxes to their Black work force. It was only due to the fact that the majority of Blacks paid slightly lower taxes under the new unitary system that dissatisfaction with taxation without representation was not expressed in as militant a way as when the pension rules had been changed without Black consultation three years earlier.

In the 1984 township unrest, many residents refused to pay rent. Some unpopular councils then wanted to use employers as unofficial rent collectors. A proclamation ordering employers to deduct rental arrears from workers' wages was occasionally heeded despite employers' misgivings about becoming involved in contentious township politics.

The idea of privatizing municipal services in the townships is now discussed as a means "to defuse the political time-bomb."[12] The Western free-market system of privatizing large areas of public service, including police and prison facilities, could not, however, easily work in the South African climate of politicized resentment. Here a strong state is needed to back up private contractual arrangements at all junctures.

After defining the "homeland" citizens as aliens, the state switched enforcement of influx control to the Department of Internal Affairs, which controls immigration. The government cannot succeed in this task without private assistance. A new "Aliens and Immigration Law Amendments Act," a business weekly laments, "can be used to force employers, under draconian penalties, to become influx-control informers; and it also imposes drastic penalties on those who employ or house illegal aliens."[13] A proposed Orderly Movement and Settlement of Black Persons Bill increases maximum fines for pass law violations from R 500 to R 5,000 for a first offense. In the wake of the Riekert Commission recommendations, enforcement of the pass laws was taken off the street into factories, with the onus put on employers to keep "illegal" workers out. Indeed, the number of pass-law persecutions dropped dramatically, from 694,000 in 1968 to 172,000 in 1981. The simultaneous tightening of influx control measures led to fewer indiscriminate arrests but an increase of arrests in selected target groups such as female work-seekers in the Western

Cape. Above all, the state is in the process of withdrawing from labor disputes; the authorities would like these to be settled by regulated bargaining between representative unions and employers rather than through regular police involvement in spontaneous strikes and lockouts.

A major subcontracting of ordinary policing tasks is entailed in the homelands policy. With the sovereign Bantustans responsible for law enforcement in their area, Pretoria has turned over a cumbersome burden to frequently more ruthless junior clients. As has often been pointed out, the central authority thereby escapes the blame and can point to the subjects' own style of misconduct. However, making corrupt rulers administer their own people's poverty can backfire. The bizarre feuds, graft, and repression coupled with the total lack of legitimacy of the Ciskei rulers, for example, make their regime itself a security risk, counteracting the intended sophisticated methods of social control by inspiring greater resistance.

Finally, the *internationalization* of political policing is widely practiced in the industrial world. Satellites monitor intercontinental communication and computers scan international phone calls and Telex messages. South Africa, no doubt, is part of this network of control. With the signing of the nonaggression treatise in Southern Africa this control network is formally being extended, by the very authorities that had allowed some free niches, to include the unpoliced hinterland. Swaziland's collaboration with Pretoria illustrates this development.

Today, only in Third World countries that are unable to modernize their political policing can an overthrow of a government by internal rebellion be envisaged. Where an industrialized state can rely on modern technology and the loyalty of its security forces, its illegitimacy alone does not ensure its transformation. The degree of illegitimacy only affects the costs and the means of securing the state.

In South Africa, the coherence and effectiveness of political policing are guaranteed by the privilege of race, the very principle that causes the illegitimacy of the state. Despite the splits over strategies of privilege maintenance in the Afrikaner camp, all factions agree on the need to retain iron-clad control. With this commitment and the advantage of state control to ensure compliance, so far South Africa has virtually discarded the traditional assumption that a modern government needs to solicit moral legitimacy among the subordinates. Despite the high—but still tolerable—costs of illegitimacy, moral legitimacy matters mainly for the cohesion and motivation of the rulers. Only if the dominant group suffers from the illegitimacy of its racial domination will a consequential legitimation crisis arise. Herein lies the simultaneous vulnerability and strength of the present South African system.

Dependency and Co-Optation

With the ideological right wing limited in its influence on day-to-day decisions and a technocratic administration in power, the South African state now relies above all on *dependency* to make the mass of the population toe the line. Dependency comprises what Marx somewhere called the "dull compulsion of circumstances." To earn a living, to make ends meet, to avoid risks, to survive in a hostile environment absorb so much energy and impose such stringent rules of conduct that alternatives are hard to contemplate. The routine of the daily drudgery guarantees compliance almost by itself, independent of supportive ideologies.

Abercrombie and his associates have turned this simple fact into a well-reasoned refutation of the Marxist "dominant ideology thesis."[14] In a similar vein Barrington Moore long ago stressed the power of habit in the acceptance of injustice: "It seems more realistic to assume that large masses of people, and especially peasants, simply accept the social system under which they live without concern about any balance of benefits and pains, certainly without the least thought of whether a better one might be possible, unless and until something happens to threaten and destroy their daily routine. Hence it is quite possible for them to accept a society of whose working they are no more than victims."[15]

In South Africa, even radical disruptions of daily routine are frequently accepted because of this dependency. The potential for resistance to the continual uprooting of rural people, for example, was thwarted by a system of sophisticated relocations of necessities. Subtle pressure rather than crude force was being used in relocating long-established communities from so-called "black spots." Instead of moving in with a large police force, trucks, and bulldozers, and attracting worldwide publicity, the government moved essential services in order to force the people to follow. Schools and clinics were closed and the people referred to the new locations. As an incentive, better facilities were frequently provided there. In some cases pension payments were stopped in the old locality and those essential means of survival had to be collected in the designated new area.

Against such tactics popular resistance proves weak as long as the resisters are dependent on such state-supported services. Most theories about peasant uprisings have been derived from the workings of autonomous peasant communities of previous times. Where this relative self-sufficiency no longer exists, the state authorities have such a vast leverage over their dependent population that they can enforce virtually any orders as long as they do it in a sufficiently "rational" and underhanded manner.

Unlike traditional societies, an increasingly greater proportion of the proletarianized peasantry in South Africa is not only dependent on wage labor but is directly employed by the state. While much attention has been focused on the 35 percent of all employed Whites who work directly for the state, the implications for the civil servants from subordinate groups have hardly been considered. The respective figures for the other groups for 1983 are: Colored people, 25.5 percent; Indians, 16.5 percent; Africans, 19.4 percent. The more than a fifth of the employed subject population who are directly dependent on the state for their livelihood, let alone for individual advancement and promotion, are in practice removed from active resistance. Moreover, the Black state employees are inclined to identify with their work in order to give meaning to an often meaningless occupation. It is only a myth that the average Black policeman, railway worker, or letter-carrier could function as a saboteur with a deep-seated grudge who turns against the hand that feeds him whenever an opportunity arises. On the contrary, very much like the exploited domestic servants, the Black civil servants are on the whole loyal to their employer, not only because of the security that overt loyalty promises but also because of the status that a steady job and the authority of officialdom bestow. The harassment of Black state employees by the revolutionary forces may in fact drive the threatened dependents closer to their masters than to their opponents. After all, they have more to fear after a Black takeover.

The strongest manipulative weapon for ruling elites is a policy that employs *co-optation* and concomitant fragmentation. Throughout history, dominant groups have accepted selected outsiders. This aids in perpetuation of their rule by increasing their number while simultaneously weakening adversaries by skimming off the best talents. Oligarchies collapsed when elite boundaries became frozen and social mobility became barred by rigid membership definitions (such as race or ancestry).

In addition to encouraging educational and class stratification among Blacks, government policy places great emphasis on the urban/rural division. As has often been pointed out, influx control and pass laws, together with differential legal work and residence rights, favor the permanent urban dweller at the expense of the increasingly impoverished rural population. This fragmentation has superseded the old policy of highlighting ethnic divisions among the African population.

With parts of the Colored and Indian working class won over by the spoils of co-optation, the political fragmentation of a seemingly homogeneously discriminated-against population has in fact increased. The most far-reaching effect of the new constitution has been the deepening of political cleavages in the Indian and Colored segments. The intra-group divisions introduced by the co-optation policy have destroyed lifelong friendships, eroded social customs, and atomized formerly cohesive networks, particularly in the Indian group. At the same time, intergroup suspicion has been heightened by the co-optation policy, despite its large-scale rejection in the Indian and Colored polls.

A collective fate does not, then, necessarily unite. Discrimination is experienced in different ways. When certain sections enjoy privileges, they are set apart from the rest. The often-cited solidarity of the oppressed remains an ideal, not a reality. The unifying "anger which transcends all political differences between Black leaders and Black organization"[16] exists more in the perception of liberal outsiders.

The sexual division of labor also serves to fragment the Black work force. In South Africa, unorganized and low-paid Black women, already the most overburdened sector in an enduring chauvinistic tradition, are now also used to undercut higher-paid male labor. For this reason, in some sectors the Black unions can ill afford to continue organizational drives that ignore female workers.

Co-optation and fragmentation are not employed only when actual or potential resistance is most threatening to authorities, as sociologists usually conclude.[17] Coloreds and Indians posed no threat to the South African state, which could have ruled these groups more efficiently and with less expense in other ways than by granting them their own parliaments and a cumbersome bureaucracy of "own affairs." Nor was a costly conscription of the limited supply of White manpower the main reason for the co-optation policy. It stems, paradoxically, from the self-defined ideological crisis in Nationalist Party doctrine. The Colored and Indian token political inclusion as "groups without a homeland" made the grand-apartheid philosophy more consistent. Above all, it blurred the label *racist* even though it entrenched racial categorizations by constitutionalizing racial segmentation. The illusory racial power-sharing demonstrated to a prejudiced electorate that Afrikaner control is not jeopardized when non-White cabinet ministers have some jurisdiction. This proof of "successful deracialization" opened new possibilities for the political entrepreneurs to forge alliances with African adversaries by demonstrating the seeming irrelevance of color to friend and foe alike. In the rulers' self-perception they have finally shed their colonialism by relinquishing some administrative responsibility to subordinates, under the false label of power-sharing. P. W. Botha, in his opening address to the tricameral parliament on 25 January 1985, claimed that "a new era has dawned in which we have finally broken with the colonialist past."

In the literature, co-optation is usually portrayed as an issue of rewards. Whether a regime can afford inclusion and patronage of selected clients is considered crucial. However, the material incentives must not be overrated. Initially the symbolic rewards for collaboration may be sufficient. Being admitted to parliament, being recognized as equals, and being awarded formal citizenship can satisfy temporarily even if the spoils of the new status are not immediately forthcoming. In the long run, however, no symbolic rewards can compensate for continuing degradation and legal inequality. By jettisoning some of its racial symbolism for pragmatic control, the South African government bought itself time. It is now in the process of mustering resources (educational financing, township development, and career opportunities) as an incentive for conformity. Perhaps it is too early to tell whether the outlay is sufficient to make co-optation of selected groups succeed for the time being, but its chances of doing so should not be dismissed out of hand. Sam Nolutshungu asserts most eloquently the theses that (1) in a colonial relationship Blacks will never be successfully co-opted, and (2) that a racial state in any case is structurally incapable of deracialization.[18] Along the same lines, a growing orthodoxy views the attempts of an ethnic technocracy to reform from above as mere deception and manipulation. Neville Alexander states baldly: "A nonracial capitalism is impossible in South Africa."[19] The American sociologist Michael Buroway comes to a similar conclusion: "The survival of South African capitalism rests on the survival of South African racism."[20] "Apartheid capitalism," Robert

Davies and Dan O'Meara assert, "is fundamentally incapable of resolving the crisis without destroying itself."[21]

The false belief in the irreformability of the apartheid state does, however, have much to commend it insofar as the position of the Black bourgeoisie is concerned. What, realistically, are its opportunities even if central business districts are now opened? With whom are Black businessmen going to compete, and under whose terms, in an economy that is experiencing ever-expanding takeovers and monopolies?

The concentration of capital in the hands of a few restricts the Black businessman. New ventures on the part of already disadvantaged groups face both legal and factual impediments. How could Black entrepreneurs realistically expect to break into tightly regulated markets even if they had the means and freedom to do so? Black capitalists who try to capture the expanding Black consumer markets inevitably end up as junior partners and subsidiaries of established White interests. The often envisaged independent Black bourgeoisie standing as bulwark against militancy remains a pipe-dream as long as their entry to comparable wealth and power is in fact blocked and deracialized small-scale capitalism is still dominated by racial monopoly capitalism.

What options are open to such a frustrated Black bourgeoisie? If the history of Afrikaner mobilization against British imperial dominance serves as a guide, it will be African nationalism rather than interracial capitalism that proves attractive. A frustrated bourgeoisie wants to capture state power in order to alter the system that excludes it. Racial monopoly capitalism engenders "racist socialism." Marx envisaged for Europe a proletariat uprising; in South Africa it is not the proletariat that is in the forefront of militancy, but the frustrated bourgeoisie. Armed with the legitimacy of "free enterprise ideology," it can even use capitalist ideals of competition in the marketplace and traditional bourgeois political freedoms as its mobilizing weapons. So far, however, the militant speeches of authentic Black spokespersons mainly reflect the disappointment of exclusion from the spoils of capitalism rather than an uncompromising striving for an alternative state-run utopia. Behind the radical rhetoric, however, lies a violated dignity, an indignation over unearned denigration.

However, monopoly capitalism combined with the newly entrenched constitutional exclusion blocks all hope for Blacks ever to join the system in a legitimate way. Before the new constitution was passed, an evolutionary extension of political rights could be envisaged within the terms of White democracy. The racial ratios of representation under the present constitution do not allow African inclusion without loss of White control.[22] Now the 1983 system has to be broken down before any nonracial franchise can be expected. This built-in necessity for extra-constitutional confrontation further undermines the legitimacy of South African capitalist democracy.

The propagandistic notion of the irreformable apartheid state has also gained currency through the rejection of constitutional reforms that were implemented precisely to prove the new deal. Indeed, the low polls of 19.3 percent and 17.9 percent of eligible voters (as opposed to registered voters) in both the Colored and Indian groups in the August 1984 elections seem to confirm the failure of co-optation.

However, a closer analysis of the elections reveals a peculiar statistic: the participation rate was highest among the poor and least well-educated, and lowest among the middle-class sections in both groups. Among Coloreds, fewer than 10 percent of registered voters went to the polls in Cape Town, while some rural constituencies had a greater than 50 percent turnout. A less visible division prevailed among the 90 percent of urbanized Indians, with an overall participation of 18 percent.

Many factors that do not necessarily confirm the apparently overwhelming rejection of co-optation account for the figures. Above all, government itself undermined the controversial legitimacy of the election by two actions: (1) it did not hold a referendum in the two groups, contrary to the procedures among Whites and earlier promises and expectations; (2) the arrest of dozens of UDF leaders on unsubstantiated charges of intimidation on the eve of the election damaged the legitimacy of the contentious elections beyond repair. It forced many ambivalent bystanders into solidarity with the victims and directly contributed to the low percentage at the polls.[23]

The campaign over the constitutional reforms revealed support for and resistance to co-optation from unexpected quarters. Surprisingly, the policy of using government-created institutions most appeals to the lower-income and less-educated sections. For these groups, *economic* concerns rank first. In their view, employment opportunities, housing, educational and health facilities, and crime prevention can only be attained by cooperating with the ruling groups.

It is the urban-based, educated middle class, particularly teachers, lawyers, and other professionals, who most strongly object to collaboration. Theirs is primarily a *political* grievance and no longer an economic complaint. They object to the inherently unequal status of racial institutions per se. Now that teachers' and doctors' salaries have been equalized with the pay of Whites with the same qualifications, the status incongruity has become the point of offense. The cars these groups can afford and the houses they can purchase are no longer inferior to those of their White colleagues. However, they may not live in the central parts of the city, due to the Group Areas Act and their second-class citizenship. Collaboration is perceived above all as entrenching these invidious distinctions.[24]

This intra-group conflict, between professionals on the one side and political upstarts on the other, has been intensified by the overthrow of the traditional leadership hierarchy, particularly in the Indian community. Those with education and status (based on wealth and donations) were traditionally considered the representatives of the group. The bureaucratic bourgeoisie, however, is often recruited from among non-professionals. By handing over control of education and welfare to those "official" group representatives, the government made the professional elite dependent on the collaborating politicians. The officeholders, despised as they may be by the majority of the group, now nevertheless determine the chances of promotion of teachers and of licenses for businessmen.[25]

It is feared that the new patronage could even be dispensed according to sectional bias, although there has been no evidence of this as yet. In the past, the White overlords at least discriminated uniformly. The existence of the Black bureaucratic bourgeoisie opens the prospect of intra-group discrimination according to linguistic origin and politics. The policy of fragmenting the Black challenge and directing its anger inward against its own group members has thus again proven successful.

Paradoxically, the low poll has strengthened the position of collaborators within the new constitution. Because of the widespread rejection of its imposed constitution, the government finds itself under pressure to make the arrangement work through concessions. On the other hand, the bitterness of the constitutional debate and the firm rejection of collaborators by their urban constituency bind the clients to their sponsors, regardless of payoffs and lack of legitimacy. Not until the client's physical safety is in jeopardy and they cannot perform the assigned tasks of self-administration does the relationship crumble, as has occurred with many Black urban councils in the wake of the township unrest. Indeed, as David Welsh and other academics have pointed out, Black township councils will not receive popular backing as long as they are seen as a substitute for a political settlement at the national level. With threats to individual councillors, their families, and their properties, the government is unable to use local self-government as a means of stalling on power-sharing in central decision-making. The unrest indeed may have spelt the end of the experiment of using local councillors in similar ways, as Bantustan officials. The administration of townships and particularly rent collection, exacerbated by the lack of a meaningful tax base, proved impossible when the councillors, many of whom were corrupt, had to live and work among those on whose cooperation and goodwill they depend. This is not the case with homeland government officials, who not only command a source of revenue but enjoy, on the whole, much greater rapport with their constituency. Black urban administrations, however, will not become Bantustans even if their police force is doubled and their tax base strengthened by new levies upon the White sector. Such measures ease the problems of administration but do not create the identification and motivation so vital for productivity and smooth functioning of an industrial society.

However, of the three groups selected for preferential treatment—the African bureaucratic bourgeoisie in the homelands, the Colored and Indian junior partners in White control, and the permanent urban African working class with Section 10 rights—the last clearly will carry the most weight in any successful attempt to stabilize the system. If the permanent urban workers could develop an interest in keeping "Africa out of the cities," the government strategy could be quite successful. This group of urban insiders, Hermann Giliomee has pointed out, must be kept small enough not to constitute a threat but affluent enough to develop an interest in keeping out migrant outsiders who might undercut their wages if the co-optation strategy should work.

In a persuasive refutation of Nolutshungu, Wilmot James has argued that the small Black bourgeoisie does not wield sufficient clout in South Africa to be crucial to stabilization.[26] With their political and status grievances they are unlikely candidates for co-optation, as the continued militancy among university students and professional bodies confirms. In this respect the view of the colonized Black as non–co-optable may be correct. But the "government does not work with a middle class model of co-optation,"[27] which is indeed only one option among many. By aiming at the privileged urban insiders—the rapidly expanding numbers of skilled and semi-skilled blue- and white-collar workers—the co-optation policy may indeed succeed. For these workers the benefits of immediate material gains in wages and services may outweigh the losses inherent in status denigration by a racial state. If these benefits can be obtained by passivity many are tempted to remain silent.

This conclusion is supported by many surveys, above all Lawrence Schlemmer's thoroughly researched study on Black production workers' attitudes toward political options, capitalism, and investment in South Africa.[28] Compared with ear-

lier surveys, Schlemmer found heightened political consciousness, anger, and militant resentment of government policies.
Distrust of employers was widespread. Among the 551 workers interviewed, support for the ANC had grown. And yet
despite various strong indicators of grievances and militancy
the majority wanted to separate politics from their short-term
material interests. The use of unions for political ends was
supported only by a strong minority of 36 percent, even
among union members themselves. In answer to the question
"What can trade unions do for Black people?" only 3 percent
mentioned "work for political rights," while 54 percent referred to wages, dismissals, and other working conditions.
Seventy-five percent expressed agreement with foreign investment, because "it makes jobs for all people in South Africa." Schlemmer concludes "that they are no dull, apathetic
and crushed proletariat who must be saved from a morass of
false consciousness by liberated minds abroad." But he also
diagnoses a "split consciousness at the present time."[29] The
majority have not become ideologically estranged from the
capitalist system. They give priority to work opportunities.
However, a growing number, now almost one-third, do support protest strikes and the politicization of labor relations.

Since the Schlemmer survey, a marked change in the political climate has increased Black support for outside pressure
on the government. Bishop Tutu's 1984 Nobel Peace Prize,
with its subsequent publicity, has galvanized Black opinion.
When the media created an idol, it became a powerful influence in crystallizing vague attitudes. The rising unemployment, together with the army presence in the townships, reinforced the feeling that disinvestment could not worsen the
situation but could provide a last chance for change, short of
more violence. Hence, it is no surprise that later surveys, such
as the Markinor study for the London *Sunday Times*, found
that 75 percent of urban Blacks favor some form of disinvestment.[30]

Pretoria is perceived as being hurt by outside pressures, and
politicized Blacks increasingly approve of any damage to their
oppressor. Thus surveys conducted by institutions known to

be sympathetic to the ANC/UDF report that in their sample 36 percent believed the "armed struggle" was justified, while 28 percent condoned attacks on Blacks who work for the system. At the same time, 90 percent of respondents still favor genuine negotiations between government and "true leaders."[31]

Faced with this attitude of latent politicization, the wavering co-optation policy so far has shown few results. It would indeed be doomed to eventual failure even if it were to yield substantial rewards for the insiders, so long as racial stigmatization persists. The more people are freed from anxiety about immediate survival, the more they become concerned with aspects of esteem and politics. Privatization of public interests into a depoliticized consumerism—the Americanization of South Africa—can only succeed when status denigration is abolished through genuine deracialization.

Moreover, widening the gap between urban insiders and rural outsiders through successful co-optation would only increase the appeal of moving to the cities from the impoverished countryside. Influx would be even more difficult to control. An "orderly urbanization policy," as the new euphemism reads, means the abolition of influx control. The fate of urban and rural Africans can no longer be bureaucratically separated.

Moreover, the official emphasis on ethnicity contradicts the policy of fragmentation of Blacks into urban and rural segments. *Race* stresses the unity of urban and rural people. The co-optation policy of privileged urban dwellers at the expense of the rural underprivileged, in contrast, aims at a split along the lines of material benefits and rights. Only if the gains made by the urban dwellers outweigh the disadvantages of the common stigmatization can the co-optation policy succeed. All Black organizations, however, from the unions to the UDF/ANC and Inkatha, have memberships that include both migrants and urban dwellers and thereby counteract the attempt at cleavage.

In summary, the goal of co-optation cannot really be achieved without deracialization. Racial co-optation ignores

the need for esteem; the continuing stigmatization will undermine co-optation even if all races have equal access to material
rewards. The goal of "separate but equal" will remain an im-
possibility.

From a short-term political perspective, however, it must be
admitted that since the differential status and patronage to
some extent entice leaders and groups to work within state
institutions, the system has succeeded in isolating moderates
from so-called radicals. If the radical support proves stronger,
the stakes can be raised; indeed, without the presence of radical demands for boycotts, collaborators would have little
value to the state. It must, however, be remembered that acceptance of the rules of imposed institutions does not necessarily imply acceptance of their goals. Critical collaboration in
the absence of any realistic alternatives differs from opportunistic collaboration. The real test will come when more advocates of boycott decide to undermine and use the system from
within instead of denouncing it from outside.

Consumerism as a Substitute for Legitimacy

Compliance out of dependency or the expectation of reward
has to be distinguished from obedience out of a belief in the
value or *legitimacy* of an order. Acquiescence out of interest or
necessity can coexist with rejection of a political system as illegitimate. The four mechanisms, means, and motivations for
compliance can be summarized as follows:

Mechanism	Means	Motivation
Coercion	Law Enforcement	Fear
Dependency	Poverty/Inequality	Necessity
Co-optation	Patronage/Clientelism	Rewards
Legitimacy	Ideological Manipulation	Belief

Ignoring for the moment the complex relationship between
acquiescence and legitimacy, we can safely assume that the
South African state is not based on the consent of the majority
of the governed. Its legitimacy rests solely with the enfran-

chised White section of the population. From this perspective it makes sense to distinguish between the obvious importance of legitimating beliefs in the ruling section and the irrelevancy of the concept for the subordinates. Similarly, it is useful to differentiate between internal and external legitimacy. While the South African order has little internal legitimacy, it is evident that a valuable degree of external legitimacy is granted when even the Pope receives its Prime Minister.

In divided societies such as South Africa it is clearly the active partiality of the ethnic state that causes the majority to feel excluded from the polity. Unlike bourgeois democracies, in such states the polity and the economy are not separated; the state openly intervenes in the market on behalf of the dominant group. Legally economically unequal subjects operate within a political order whose symbols and raison d'être explicitly discriminate against them. If it is true that "a state's legitimacy depends heavily on the population's perception of the political system as reflecting its ethnic and cultural identity,"[32] then ethnic minority rule must be considered illegitimate. Not only is the majority population not normatively integrated into such a system, it is permanently excluded under conditions of institutionalized illegitimacy.

This situation poses fundamental ideological contradictions for a state that wants to reduce the inevitably high costs of coercion and co-optation. It has been contended in this analysis: (a) that South Africa has engaged in a process of political manipulation by shifting from a legitimating ideology of racial exclusiveness to the rhetoric of deracialized economic stability; (b) that, the official ideology notwithstanding, the control, security, and privileges of the ruling minority remain paramount; and (c) that state manipulation has had some success in addressing its ideological predicaments. How does a political system cope with such an ideological reorientation and yet stay within the confines of an ethnic state? How is compliance achieved through ideological manipulation?

If South African ideological control is compared with Orwell's model in *1984*, a crucial difference immediately becomes apparent. Far from regimenting the population into

ideological unity, South Africa aims at fragmenting nationalist sentiments by institutionalizing ethnicity. Instead of the
ideological conformity of fascist or Stalinist totalitarianism,
South Africa encourages depoliticized acquiescence. Heretical
thoughts ("thoughtcrimes") are tolerated as long as they fall
short of counter-mobilization. André du Toit has claimed that
"the extent of media manipulation and thought control is
probably much higher in White society and does not have any
impact on Black communities,"[33] but while the White constituency forms the sole source of legitimacy for the ethnic state
and, therefore, the principal target of media attention, Blacks
too are indeed being manipulated.

Some of this manipulation is traditional and primitive but
still effective, as when P. W. Botha spoke to one and a half
million enthusiastic followers of the Zionist Christian Church
on 7 April 1985 at Moria. In this address to the annual gathering of the largest church group in South Africa, Botha took
upon himself the role of a god-sanctioned ruler: "There is no
authority except from God. Rulers are not a terror to good
conduct, but to bad conduct. Do what is good, and you will
receive the approval of the ruler. He is God's servant for your
good." In his capacity as the earthly representative of the Almighty, he identified evil with ANC liberation, "the forces of
darkness." "We shall not tolerate people who come from far
away with evil minds to kill and injure innocent people." A
common Christianity was invoked as the basis of cooperation.
"There are countries where Christ is ignored. But we in South
Africa believe that we must first seek the presence of Christ
and many of our problems will vanish."[34]

However, Black identification with the apartheid system of
racial domination cannot be expected. In the absence of viable
Black political institutions, political conventionalism can identify only with discredited Bantustan traditionalism. A policy
of depoliticization seems the logical alternative when democratic participation is blocked and genuine political involvement inevitably leads to resentment and resistance.

Depoliticization, however, does not preclude dissent. Depoliticization only implies refraining from organized resis-

tance. The system can neither demand loyalty in the form of voluntary adherence to its premises—that is, engender legitimacy—nor insist on abstention from critique. Verbal condemnation by individuals, sometimes in very strong terms, is tolerated. Since the South African state has no sacred doctrine to guard, the yardstick for tolerance is the effectiveness of the critique. If the indignation is likely to lead to collective action, particularly outside approved institutions, it will most likely be quelled. But since most political dissent remains at the rhetorical level and lack of identification with the state is taken for granted, such dissent does not threaten ethnic privilege. On the contrary, rhetorical freedom helps to bolster Pretoria's democratic legitimacy both internationally and among its own White domestic constituency.

A state with no official ideology can tolerate the most exaggerated anger of its subjects, as is evinced in the popular "theater of the struggle." In Moscow an unofficial exhibition of modern art on the outskirts of town was bulldozed; the art of the South African victims, however, serves to keep them off the streets. Angry words as revenge for powerlessness can reinforce the powerholder. As an outlet for resentment the burning stage secures the daily drudgery. Few Blacks need to be "conscientized" by the depiction of brutal Boers when their daily reality surpasses the play. The radical playwright acts out the bitterness of revolutionary fervor where it does not harm the overseers of anger. A critic has aptly captured this defusing of tension through extremist rhetoric: "Is this really a danger to state security? No. The medium overrides the message. Maybe this is why we are allowed to watch the honkies being trampled on and the National Anthem being sodomized. We feel the clenched fists and the Azanian warcries, and we will say (with some relief): Well, this may not be a totally free society, but at least there is room for this expression. At least they can get away with this."[35] Insofar as a state tolerates its critical artists it incorporates and disarms them.

The contention that the White media have no impact on Black communities underestimates the powerful messages transmitted by radio, White and Black television and racial advertising. Market researchers found that 20 percent of Black households in the Rand area owned a color television. More than 30 percent of the rest intended to buy one as the highest priority among six appliances listed in the survey.[36] (Apart from purchasing power, the major obstacle to owning a television for many homes in the township market was the lack of electricity.) While not fully part of the consumer culture, urban Blacks are well on the way to becoming so. Other researchers determined that in 1984 687,000 Blacks tried losing weight (compared with 2.1 million Whites); 164,000 had taken out a life insurance policy during the twelve preceding months; 9.6 million adult Blacks owned a radio; and 1.9 million, a hi-fi set.[37]

At the core of the cultural diet on which Blacks are fed lies the message that happy Blacks are those who confine themselves to consumerism, who stay aloof from trouble-making politics, and who strive hard to live in harmony with their circumstances. The depoliticized image of material success aimed at Black purchasing power is, despite formidable obstacles, quite effectively paraded by the media. Educational and status achievements replace political involvement or ideological commitment.

For example, a Zulu-speaking Spiderman has made its appearance in comic books distributed by Metro Cash and Carry. The fact that the heroes uphold the moral values of the Western world is seen by their promoters as a bonus, as is the dubious contribution to Black literacy. "But can a Black child relate to these Whiter-than-White heroes? Oh, yes, says Raphael. Superman, Batman, and Spiderman have already been screened on TV2, and Bop-TV has bought the rights for further screening, proving that the characters are potentially as popular among Blacks as Whites."[38] Behind this Americanization of Black consciousness lies the commercial drive to bind the children early to brand loyalties to goods with which the comic-book characters are associated.

Western consumerism thus pollutes the attitudes of the excluded. The materially good life dangles in front of the poor as an ideal more tempting the less they can achieve it. Jim

Baley, former editor of *Drum Magazine*, concluded an overview of his long publishing experience: "My [Black] readers had always wanted to be as tedious, boring and tasteless as their White middle class counterparts, regrettable as it is to confess this."[39] This little-noticed value emulation distinguishes economically integrated South Africa from its segmentally isolated colonial counterparts. When people are treated as racial outcasts, deprived of individual status and collective dignity, ostentatious consumption may be the only avenue for assertion of individual worthiness.

In the colonial setting, insiders and outsiders lived separate lives in tightly insulated compartments. With the exception of a few top-level social contacts, colonizer and colonized stayed apart. Despite official segregation in South Africa, the common industrial economy changed this situation. The communications technology, in particular, intertwines insiders and outsiders through common dreams and common meanings. When ideological integrators as powerful as modern advertising, videos, and religious values are shared, little basis for ethnic separation remains.

Shared value socialization amounts to a great obstacle to Gandhian resistance through asceticism. The colonial outsiders in the Gandhian tradition abstained from the life-style of the colonizer not because they could not afford it or did not appreciate it, but as an act of defiance and spiritual strength. Simplicity of clothing, food, and style of life asserted opposition to alien exploitation while it disciplined its followers and symbolically united all the oppressed, both rich and poor. Can the apartheid opposition adopt similar strategies of abstention?

So far, only minor attempts at attitudinal reeducation have been made by the political movements. Calls to avoid ostentatious Christmas celebrations when there was little to celebrate went largely unheeded, as sales figures for the Black consumer market indicate. Some successful consumer boycotts occurred, as did the destruction of township liquor outlets. However, these were in response to company behavior or specific complaints rather than as ends in themselves. Moves by

Black Consciousness adherents to re-create an African communal tradition of cooperative sharing foundered due to the
pervasiveness of capitalist exposure. In a society in which conspicuous consumption is the only avenue left in which at least
a few Blacks can excel, appeals for voluntary abstention by the
masses assume a high political awareness. Paradoxically, it is
the apolitical Zionist Christian Church with its five million
members that comes closest to practicing Gandhian ideals,
though for nonpolitical reasons. Their members neither
drink nor smoke, and they donate generously to the church.
On entering Moria City at their annual Easter gathering, the
women leave such worldly luxuries as jewellery and lipstick at
the gate for safekeeping, while the men wear simple khaki
suits with the silver star of their faith.

Unlike Orwell's highly regimented conformity, consumer
capitalism manages to draw under its spell precisely those who
can least afford the peddled commodities. Instead of envy and
hatred of those who are responsible for the relative deprivation, hope lingers on that apolitical adjustments will have private rewards. It is wrong to assume that poverty immunizes
people against consumerist temptations. On the contrary, for
those who feel deprived these pseudo-gratifications have a
special appeal. Within the vast manipulative scope of consumer capitalism, revolutions are not made by an aspiring
proletariat, however much Marxist theory may glorify this historical vanguard of change. Those who have achieved some
satisfaction, not the impoverished, feel the psychological poverty of consumerism.[40] In most Western countries urbanized
professionals, teachers, and other members of the intelligentsia, but hardly the members of workers unions or labor parties, espouse radical views. Only blind faith can reiterate the
Marxian vision of a proletarian democracy: "By virtue of the
unique combination of an elaborate colonial political structure
and an advanced capitalist economy South Africa may be the
scene of the first proletarian revolution."[41] It is precisely because deprived colonial populations everywhere attempted to
modernize their newly liberated societies by emulating their
former oppressors that no qualitative transformation of post-

colonial society took place. If the proletariat has nowhere else succeeded in establishing a credible alternative, why should South Africa become the exception?

On the other hand, those who engineered a successful upheaval in the age of techniques of mind management and consumer manipulation lived outside the scope of those techniques. In the traditional societies of the Third World, peasants (as in Zimbabwe) who are not yet part of a modern economy or religious sects who are ideologically insulated from Hollywood seduction (as in Islamic fundamentalism) can resist such pervasive manipulation. The urban sector of Blacks in South Africa, however, is particularly susceptible to the "culture industry." With cultural traditions and family cohesion disrupted, and an imported Christianity serving as a poor guide for the construction of meaning, that group is not as shielded as, for example, Indian South Africans were, at least in the past. The "progress" of "the Indians," despite intense antagonisms, would have been inconceivable without the cultural insulation of an internalized traditional code of conduct.

In short, if an advanced South African capitalism has its way, it will replace liberation movements with sales. Can it succeed? How is the message communicated in racial poverty? Does it aim at normative integration, politicized compliance, or depoliticized acceptance of the status quo?

Radio South Africa, with a one-million-watt shortwave transmitter complex and broadcasts in European as well as several African languages (Chichewa, Lozi, Tsonga, Swahili) is said to draw about as many listeners as the BBC on the continent. Independent observers note the comparatively unemotional language of the newscasts, which gives the station an aura of objectivity and professionalism.[42] In this tone Black Africa, especially Zimbabwe and other front-line states, are mainly portrayed as a massive problem area while the Republic figures as an island of prosperity and goodwill. This development in the interests of all is threatened by misguided terrorists under orders from foreign powers. The criminalization of all forms of active resistance to a legitimate South

African government forms the main ideological thrust of the broadcasts. There is little doubt that this technocratic legitimation of South Africa as the most effective guarantee of development in the region has gained some credibility in Black Africa, at the expense of moral rejection of a racial pariah regime.

The popular tabloids in the Black townships focus mostly on disasters, crime, sex, and sport. The well-known formula used everywhere else is presented here: the world is a jungle. Media coverage of independent African states, for example, has greatly undermined confidence in Black rule. Presented with the statement in the Hanf survey "Whites are strict but they are honest and fair—we would not be happier under our own people," 62 percent disagreed in 1977, 65 percent in 1981, and 54 percent in 1984 in the Transvaal.[43] While the youth unrest has a generally politicizing effect, in the older generation it produces doubts about the wisdom of political protest. By reinforcing readers' concerns and manufacturing additional anxiety, the media bind their audience to the solutions they present. The message in the South African media seems to be that only the strong and law-abiding citizen can survive unharmed.

Yet many political stories portray the victims sympathetically, unlike the media in Orwell's censored world. For one thing, use of strong language and outrage about discrimination add to the media's political credibility. Indeed, South Africa proves what a Canadian commentator observed about more benign conditions: "Orwell reckoned without capitalism's confounding capacity to avoid confrontation by merchandising it."[44] Orwell himself is marketed in South Africa. The state-controlled broadcasting corporation, SABC, for example, invited critics of the government to debate on nationwide television whether Orwell's predictions apply to South Africa. In this way, the new manipulative technocracy celebrates its difference from the old totalitarian intimidation. In Orwell's system, the victims knew their fate. In the sophisticated new order of technocratic liberation the victims are expected to frolic in their false freedom.

There are virtually no independent Black-owned media—
and if any were to emerge they could easily be suppressed.
Black-run but White-owned outlets provide a fig-leaf for effective ideological control. This endeavor, however, is compromised by the circulation battle of the major papers. In order to enhance their appeal to Black readers most English
Sunday papers now publish an "extra" cover section, sold only
in the respective Black group areas. These specialized "ex-
tras," aimed at the literate Indian, Colored, and African middle classes, cannot ignore the political concerns of readers if
they wish to remain competitive. These interacting interests,
then, constitute some of the limits of depoliticization. Politics
cannot be declared taboo in Black South Africa, for politics is
far too important in a divided society to be banned altogether.
The system can silence outspoken critics but it cannot prevent
political discourse in the ruling group from spilling over into
the subordinates' realm.

The 1983 referendum debate about the new constitution
exposed this dialectic of depoliticization. The very act of exclusion of Blacks from the constitutional arrangement included them more than ever in an explosion of political debate across the color bar. The intended relegation of Africans
to "Black affairs" only resulted in a repoliticized controversy
about "joint affairs." It made patent nonsense of the Prohibi-
tion of Political Interference Act. When people can switch
channels from "Black" to "White" entertainment and politics,
newspapers and television in South Africa help to break down
ideological iron curtains, as West German media have in East
Germany. In the end, the logic of the evidence or the appeal
of the entertainment triumphs over ideological intent or artificially decreed divisions.

In summary, then, the ethnic state faces a constant dilemma
regarding the politicization of its subjects. It needs to shape
the ruling constituency into a body of loyal supporters but also
to induce in the excluded groups a state of cooperative acquiescence. This leads to a double standard concerning permissible activities, which further politicizes those operating under
restrictions. The political debates among the ruling section

percolate down into the realm of supposed acquiescence. South African Blacks find themselves in the role of passive and bemused onlookers to a White struggle over how they should best be subjugated.

Unlike the Orwellian anti-utopia, the South African regime cannot expect thought-control to succeed, despite censorship and many restrictions on media freedom. The successful ideological regimentation and internalized self-deception of a Winston Smith are the characteristics of a totalitarian-revolutionary regime. The authoritarian-corporate South African ruling elite does not aim at being loved, merely at being obeyed. Ideological mobilization of the population along Nazi or Stalinist lines meets insurmountable barriers in an ethnically divided state. For one, such grand attempts at ideological manipulation are always inclusive, forging a false unity out of antagonistic parts. Apartheid, however, is exclusive. Since a color-blind nationalistic unity would threaten the ethnic minority in power, its policy cannot be other than fragmentizing. Also, in such a situation the ruling group lacks any all-inclusive ideology that could be remotely attractive or even acceptable to the ethnically defined outsiders. Notions of a pluralistic coexistence of the segments or common interest in affluence and growth are continually shattered by the unequal realities and daily experiences of the majority population.

A security effort against an outside threat (e.g., communism) could operate as a common ideological denominator, like the sporadic government-sponsored bombardments of its own population in *1984*. Pretoria has thus had a decided interest in exaggerating "the total onslaught" for internal mobilization, just as the African National Congress is eager to magnify its capacity for a revolutionary overthrow for the sake of external credibility and sponsorship. The widely publicized trials of political activists not only aim at intimidating potential emulators but, above all, at lending credence to exhortations for vigilance and sacrifice on the part of a complacent White population. Unlike many other nationalist conflicts, in South Africa the dominant group is ideologically heterogeneous. Its

major unifying bond lies in preserving affluence and privilege, not doctrinal purity.

Most Afrikaners additionally share a desire to preserve a
distinct national community. This perception of an ethnic
identity different from that of other Europeans paradoxically
makes nationalist Afrikaners more inclined to recognize African nationalism as a force with which an accommodation has
to be reached in order to ensure the peaceful survival of Afrikanerdom. The ruling elite, morally stigmatized and ideologically confused about appropriate strategies and associated
values, has become obsessed with devising ways to outmaneu-
ver its adversaries. If the end can be achieved, whether by
military destabilization or by peace accords, the means will
seem justified.

However, as far as the Black population is concerned the
formula of unity through combating "terrorism" contains major flaws. For them, the outside enemy is associated with liberation. Despite the all-out criminalization of violent resistance, the exile movements are widely perceived as fighting a
worthy cause with different means. Even in Durban, the center of Inkatha support, where at one time 54 percent of workers named Buthelezi as their first choice for leader,[45] the support for the ANC is growing. The question was asked in
Durban: "If the ANC were to come in secretly asking people
to help it and work with it, what would happen?" In 1981, 49
percent replied that most or a large number of people would
try to help it. In 1984, 56 percent indicated the same.[46] Kenneth Grundy, in a thorough analysis of Blacks in the South
African army, concluded that although the material induce-
ments to enlist seem sufficient, "something crucial is missing."
Grundy identifies this component as a deep enough "stake in
a contemporary or even a foreseeable White-ruled South Africa to risk their lives and their social standing among peers
by opposing fellow Blacks committed to smashing the repressive arrangements."[47] Many participants believed that the
1983 extension of voting rights to Coloreds and Indians was
primarily motivated by the need for a general conscription.

"No draft without vote" became an accepted principle among Nationalists. Whether the drafted accept the symbolic participation in the separate tricameral parliamentary system by Coloreds and Indians as fulfilling this goal remains doubtful.

Since power in the ethnic state manifestly does not originate in democratic consent, other rationalizing ideologies must be used to make power legitimate. Political power in South Africa justifies itself by its utilitarian *ends*, rather than by its *origin* ("people's sovereignty"). The "common good" and "public interest" have been translated into a distinct "development ideology" in recent years. The legitimation for White overlordship now stands on the type of authority relationship that is the most bearable and benign form: technical expertise. "Competent authority" is not a racially exclusive category. By accepting parity in pay scales for identical Black and White qualifications at the professional level (teachers, doctors), the system has replaced racial privilege with privileged knowledge. It has diffused the crucial elite discontent. However, the access to credentials remains grossly unequal. The barriers to expertise are much higher for Blacks, due to impoverished family backgrounds compounded by lower state expenditure on the separate Black educational system. Despite some progress in this area, the nominal switch from race to competency leaves the ruling race with most of the qualifications, while the unqualified are left to blame themselves for their lot. The extraordinarily high value that Blacks place on education as the way out of misery reflects the success of this technocratic ideology. The equally strong White insistence on separate educational facilities ensures that the advantages of the dominant race remain intact even if the rationale for domination changes to nonracial expertise.

Legitimacy Reconsidered

In most social science writing on social revolutions, illegitimacy of the regime is awarded the key explanatory role. Chalmers Johnson and Ted Gurr contend that no ruler can consistently ignore the popular notions of justice and fairness

without being swept away by mass rejection.[48] In this function-
alist tradition, only superficially enhanced by conflict theories,
consensual support of the basic rules still constitutes the normal order, to be interrupted by periods of strife caused by
relative deprivation (Gurr) or loss of legitimacy (Johnson).
State executives and revolutionaries vie for endorsement by
the masses. Revolutions occur when state agencies fail at the
task of ensuring the basic loyalty of the populace.[49] Marxist
writers in other traditions adopt an equally voluntaristic focus.
In the arena of social conflict that is embodied in the state, the
organized coercion of the dominant faction will inevitably be
overwhelmed and reversed by strong class forces hitherto
suppressed.

The South African example serves to caution against such
simplistic assumptions. Legitimacy may be much overrated as
the determinant for stability or strife. Modern regimes can
ignore popular feeling as long as they have the support of
strategically placed key groups. As Theda Skocpol rightly
stressed: "Even after great loss of legitimacy has occurred, a
state can remain quite stable—and certainly invulnerable to
internal mass-based revolts—especially if its coercive organizations remain coherent and effective."[50] Since the South African state never possessed legitimacy in the eyes of its subordinates, it was not exposed to the danger of a politicizing loss
of legitimacy.

Political analysts should profit from the lessons from the
South African example by abandoning the notion of the centrality of legitimacy. Instead of focusing on an illusionary normative consensus in an ethnic state on the hand and coercion
on the other, they ought to explore the changing scope of
manipulative capacities of political authority. Above all, the
integrating objective conditions of dependency and co-optation must be understood. This "manufactured legitimacy"
from above differs qualitatively from the loyalties engendered
by supportive belief from below. But it cannot be equated with
outright repression, nor is this situation without integrative
meaning for its victims. Inasmuch as the result is pragmatic
acquiescence, the South African state has achieved its ends.

The crucial coherence and effectiveness of organized coercion were guaranteed in the past by the ethnic mobilization of the dominant group, the very principle that determines the illegitimacy of the state. However, due to the priorities of a modern economy and the manpower needs of the state, this past ethnic exclusiveness is being eroded through co-optation. With it the cohesion and motivation of the dominant group have become fragmented as well. Its decisive legitimacy is being defined differently by different sections. The technocrats in the present administration are attempting to rouse themselves from the economic and moral coma that racial domination implies. In this ruling-class "legitimation crisis" many feel uneasy if not embarrassed about their institutionalized racialism, and they also see its unworkability. Even the National Party leaders now consider *apartheid* a dirty word—while implementing a multiracial neoapartheid. The support for the reform image in the constitutional referendum confirms the desire for a more widely acceptable legitimacy without loss of control.

In this transition from an overtly ethnic state to a superficially multiethnic polity based on class alliances, the South African system increasingly attempts to incorporate the politically unincorporated urban Blacks economically with consumer substitutes, as well as ideologically. They hope to avert a potential crisis by replacing collective goals with individual hopes for advancement through education or material rewards. Moral legitimacy of a political order in the sense of identification with worthy institutions becomes less important in this scheme. An excluded population learns to live with institutionalized illegitimacy. This perspective may be closer to Huxley's *Brave New World*, which hinges on conditioning, than to Orwell's *1984*, which is based on intimidation.

Coercion and intimidation alone prove insufficient to explain majority compliance. Nor can ideological manipulation account for the differences between compliance and resistance. Both coercion and ideological control may succeed in eradicating, in large parts of the population, not only the capacity to resist but the very desire to do so. Social theorists from Orwell to Marcuse have described the results of these cognitive and emotional mutations. In the apt formulation of Austin Turk: "In the minds of people, social life as it is becomes social life as it ought to be."[51]

Yet the Western success with these efforts to reduce people to various states of depoliticized compliance is not easily replicated in an apartheid state, because of its illegitimacy. For South African Blacks, even at the most depoliticized level, life is not "as it ought to be." Compliance without consent characterizes their situation, even though the legitimating consent proves superfluous under conditions of dependency.

But dependency is never one-sided. The powerless do have some power, due to their rulers' dependency on Black labor and consumption. The legitimacy of Pretoria internationally and even the fragile cohesion of the dominant group are influenced by the behavior of the subordinates. Therefore, the rulers cannot be indifferent to the fate of the underdogs. Above all, the breakdown of compliance increases the costs of domination. The victims, however, have hardly begun to exploit the cleavages among their rulers. Without a full grasp of their powers of manipulation, the activists either continue with the sterile protest politics of the past or place their hopes on the self-defeating efforts of violence. Both work for manipulative integration. The first precondition for an effective challenge lies in exact knowledge of how the system works rather than in a false diagnosis of its eclipse. Liberal laments about state brutality obfuscate the reasons for compliance and resistance no less than do illusions, inspired by the apolitical ideal of legitimacy, about consensual conflict management.

6

Industrial Relations, Unions, and Employment

The Welfare State

EUROPEAN SOCIETIES have defused a lingering class conflict and, in the end, incorporated threatening, discontented masses into legitimated state structures in three ways: welfare state measures; *embourgeoisement*; and trade union rights.

Welfare state measures provide a safety net for the victims of laissez-faire growth. The extent of this state intervention depends on the political pressure, exercised through and created by working-class parties' universal franchise. In the absence of Black political enfranchisement in South Africa, such a solution can hardly be expected; there, the conservative Progressive Federal Party is widely considered to be on the radical left. Moreover, current South African policy aims at reducing economic state intervention in favor of a free-market policy. Given the massive backlog of necessary welfare state measures for some 80 percent of the population, the present South African state does not command the resources to provide a safety net for all without cutting deeply into the wealth of the White section and engaging in a politically highly controversial redistribution. For education alone it has been calculated, for example, that "if the 1980 expenditure of R 1.169 per White child had been spent on all population groups, about 13 percent of GDP and 38 percent of total government expenditure would have been spent on schooling alone."[1] Will the White electorate tolerate a far lower, minimal but equal public

INDUSTRIAL RELATIONS AND EMPLOYMENT 171

Increases in Real Personal Income per Capita, 1960–1980

	1960–65	1965–70	1970–75	1975–80
African	11.8%	23.5%	28.6%	3.3%
Asian	27.7	29.6	36.9	10.8
Colored	20.5	25.5	29.8	1.0
White	17.8	22.4	8.8	-4.4
All Groups	14.6	21.7	13.0	-4.8

SOURCE: Bureau of Market Research at the University of South Africa (UNISA), as reported in SAIRR, *Race Relations Survey 1984*, p. 242. Figures exclude Transkei, Bophuthatswana, Venda, Ciskei (TBVS).

expenditure level with the option to purchase higher standards privately? Charles Simkins has pointed out the irony of a state trying to manipulate its constituency into purchasing social services in the marketplace when they expect an increase in living standards from free-enterprise policies.[2] A sophisticated social democratic party which could reconcile the aspirations of the oppressed with legitimation of the capitalist order is nowhere in sight in South Africa.

Welfare benefits and equal social services require economic growth. In the literature on South Africa, perhaps no single topic has been as exhaustively debated as the relationship between expanding capitalism and continued racialism. Proponents of the so-called Oppenheimer thesis that growth inevitably leads to the breakdown of apartheid are contradicted by "revisionists" arguing that capitalism benefited from and strengthened the inequality of the racial order.[3] In a comprehensive survey of the debate about the relationship between economic growth and political change, Stanley Greenberg concludes that growth "brings no necessary improvement in living standards or decline in income inequalities."[4] This widespread notion is empirically incorrect. During the boom years of the sixties and early seventies, Black real incomes increased faster than those of their rulers. The same UNISA study, however, showed that in 1980 per capita income of Africans was 9.9 percent of that of Whites, while the corresponding figures for Coloreds and Indians were 21.3 percent and 30 percent respectively. Greenberg bases his conclusion on the intrusion of capital-intensive technologies that cause structural unemployment and on a greater wage differential between the settled urban Black working class and the labor surpluses bottled up in the reserves: "It is now apparent that the state has lent a new formality to the policy of class differentiation: influx control is to be maintained and unemployment channelled to the Homelands."[5] This assessment is undoubtedly correct for the pre-1985 period.

However, it is obvious too that influx control cannot be maintained effectively. Control of labor mobility broke down due to rural poverty.[6] The presence of the Cape Flat squatters, with an estimated influx of a hundred "illegal" work-seekers daily, signals the bankruptcy of traditional bureaucratic labor regulation, as do the uncounted numbers of illegal workers on the Rand and the shantytowns stacked against the fences of the greater Durban municipality. Considering the proximity and interwoven boundaries of White city areas and African territories in Natal, the administrative separation of the two parts of a single economy never did make sense, as the Buthlezi Commission amply proved. The formal abolition of the Colored Labor Preference Area in the Western Cape and the plans to build a huge new Black township in Khayelitsha also indicate the downfall of racial labor control in the Cape.

This situation, as opposed to the blueprints of policy planners, also permits the theoretically shut-out surplus labor to participate in the spoils of growth. Without the remittances of migrants in the urban centers, the reserves would be even poorer. Without the manifold forms of participation of "illegals" in an informal economy at the periphery of growth centers, massive poverty and starvation would occur. Thus it was not only the urban Blacks who benefited from rapid wage advances in the 1970s. The implications of economic growth disperse throughout a society that can no longer be partitioned, following a dual economy model, into a modernized and a traditional sector. In the absence of a substantial universal welfare scheme, economic expansion is essential for the very survival of the poor.

Calculations of employment projections by A. Roukens de

Lange indicate an "explosive growth of Black unemployment over the coming decades," due to an increasingly capital-intensive economy with a declining or negative employment generation. The number of Blacks in formal-sector employment as a percentage of the labor force is calculated to drop from 61.5 percent in 1980 to 52.8 percent in 1990, 45.1 percent in 2000, and 39.3 percent in 2010.[7] Creation of jobs for the peripheral sector (unemployed, subsistence agriculture, informal sector) will take place mostly in cities. Even if the new regional development schemes are more successful than previous attempts, growth will take place in and around the four metropolitan centers that account for 75 percent of manufacturing output at present. Farming output in the Black areas can be expected to increase only if the population pressure on the land is reduced. Development of village settlements seems to be one promising route, together with greater mechanization through farming cooperatives.

Given the estimate of 5 million unemployed in 2000, if the quality of life in the urban areas is to be preserved the government will have to abandon influx control enforced by limiting a costly public housing stock. It will have to provide cheaper site and service schemes in metropolitan areas rather than let unplanned squatter camps mushroom in the vicinity. If rural work-seekers were able gradually to build their own structures economically without bureaucratic impediments (registrations, surveys) and, most important, with an assurance of secure tenure on sufficient state-provided land in reasonable proximity to basic services (education, health) a constructive urbanization policy would be in place.

It seems that at least some sections of the business sector have now realized the futility and immorality of influx control and say so publicly. Under the pressure of costs in a recessionary economy, the head of the Urban Foundation now urges:

> We must stop regarding urbanization as an evil to be averted at all costs. Black urbanization is now inevitable and irreversible. It is necessary for economic development and critical for successful rural development. Authoritative sources indicate that ur-

banization promotes production opportunities, increases consumption, generates high income levels and offers chances of providing educational, social and cultural opportunities at a lower cost than in rural areas.[8]

But even if such warnings are heeded in spite of the Whites' fear of being swamped, it is unlikely that any South African government, of whatever outlook, can easily muster the massive resources that made European welfare schemes feasible at the start of industrialization. Yet without a gradual redistribution of the wealth amassed in an artificial White economy, stability is unlikely. Blacks can be expected to use their political power, above all, for those economic ends. Only in an expanding economy can the aspirations of all segments reasonably be met.

Embourgeoisement and Labor Stratification

Welfare-state measures would not have sufficed to defuse the European class conflict without a development that has been labeled the *embourgeoisement* of large sections of the working class. In North America in particular, this spread of purchasing power to a broad middle class stimulated growth and investment. Are similar trends foreseeable in South Africa?

The impediments to expansion of the number of the Black bourgeoisie have been probed in the discussion of the co-optation policy. Embourgeoisement of Blacks simply lacks a bourgeoisie. Capitalist outlets for Black entrepreneurs are severely limited. New opportunities for Black businessmen arose with the partial privatization of the official township liquor trade, previously operated by various administration boards. But since the tenders were contingent on sufficient funds, Whites captured their share by forming associations with Blacks. In any case, only a few hundred outlets and licenses were involved. With a barrage of laws the state has clamped down on the informal sector of Black economic activity instead of encouraging it, and has severely frustrated the emergence of a petty bourgeoisie. For example, a Black minibus taxi service of about 60,000 operators nationwide developed as a reaction to the inconvenience of the group areas and the slow, dangerous, and inconvenient bus and train service. Under pressure of the more influential bus lobby, the government drafted the Road Transportation Amendment Bill, which aimed at wiping out the unlicensed minibus trade.

Past limitations on urban business owners confined each enterprise to one trading site in the township of the owners' legal residence. The owners also had to manage their own store and trade was limited to specified essential goods. Most township businesses therefore still consist of small grocery stores, butcher shops, or coal yards rather than large supermarkets. Given the lack of adjoining infrastructure—dirt roads with no drainage and no electricity are common—Black buyers inevitably prefer the glamorous shopping atmosphere of the central business districts, from which Black enterprises were barred. The lack of capital and collateral, due to restrictions in land rights in the townships, made it difficult for entrepreneurs to expand. Even the most enterprising township retailers lack the links to manufacturing that make it possible for the chain stores to sell at preferential rates.

The opening of the Central Business Districts (CBD's) to Black trading (but not residence) results from the fait accompli of entrenched White monopolies. As the Durban *Sunday Tribune* (26 February 1984) rightly commented: "In the years since the Act [Group Areas Act] was first passed a new pattern of trading has taken root. Large and lucrative shopping centres have opened in suburbs in main cities and chainstores have established themselves firmly in these centres. To re-open CBD's now to all groups is to make little more than a gesture in terms of real opportunities for competitive trading." In any case, many of the African traders cannot afford the high rents in the White areas and have to enter into arrangements with White owners where the Black becomes yet again the junior partner.

Above all, the continuing gross income disparity keeps most of the purchasing power in the hands of the White minority and militates against embourgeoisement.

While real wage rates of Blacks rose faster than those of any

Racial Per Capita Incomes and Disparity Ratios

	Income Per Capita (Constant July 1984 Rand)					Disparity Ratio White to Other				
	1946/47	1960	1970	1975	1980	1946/47	1960	1970	1975	1980
White	4,218	5,139	7,373	8,946	8,501	—	—	—	—	—
Colored	674	810	1,226	1,540	1,619	6:3	6:3	6:0	5:8	5:3
Indian	990	897	1,443	1,998	2,165	4:3	5:7	5:1	4:5	3:9
Black	398	433	490	717	657	10:6	11:9	15:0	12:5	12:9

SOURCE: M. McGrath, *South Africa Foundation News* (December 1984).

of the other groups, particularly between 1970 and 1975, the disparity rates still indicate an extreme racial hierarchy in disposable income. In order to assess the effects of the income disparity on attitudes and embourgeoisement we must return to the labor hierarchy and break down the Black component into its constituent parts.

The figures reflect an obvious practice: well above the various Black labor designations ranks the Colored and Indian labor supply, which receives preferential treatment. In a strong urbanized middle class, particularly among the Indians, capitalist growth found a reservoir of skills and motivation. These groups increasingly fill the technical middle-management and professional positions left open by the depleted White sector. Although the majority of middle-group members belong to the working class, differential treatment, particularly the fact that many African workers receive orders from Indian supervisors, militates against class solidarity. In the Schlemmer survey that tested images of employers among 550 Black production workers the following item was endorsed by 96 percent of the sample: "[Employers] favor Indians or Coloreds over Black people."[9] Here the ingrained racialism of South African industrial relations and the perceived racial bias of employers add resentment to an already volatile situation. The managerial structures of most firms reflect the hierarchy in the wider society: Whites at the top, Indians or Coloreds at the level of middle management, and Black Africans at the bottom. In the whole of Natal one is hard put to find an African supervising an Indian employee, let alone a

White. Paternalistic high-handedness rather than democratic consultation characterizes most industrial relations on the shop floor. Africans' resentment of Indian competitors and the concomitant erosion of race relations outside the workplace have not been sufficiently taken into account. Managerial racialism erodes identification with work and contributes directly to societal instability by reinforcing a dichotomous world-view among the Black employees. Far from experiencing rewards for merit, leading to embourgeoisement, Black employees are reminded daily that an African never gives orders and never rises above members of other groups.

In this sense the term *labor aristocracy* for the Black urban insiders is hardly apt. They are a privileged stratum only in their greater degree of security regarding housing, residence rights, and access to jobs. Their increasing dissatisfaction and anger is tempered only by their dependency and political pragmatism.

The third place in the labor hierarchy is occupied by legally recruited migrant workers. They constitute approximately 60 percent of the urban male work force, and the percentage has been growing. Separated for long periods from their families in the rural areas, their remittances have become crucial for the survival of their kin. Some decades ago, migrant work supplemented subsistence farming; it is now its precondition. The impoverishment of the reserves has deepened to such an extent that virtually all able men must attempt to enter wage labor in order to have any hope of later surviving with their families in a rural area. Without the infusion of migrant earnings, the rural economy would collapse. Since migrants legally remain outsiders in the urban labor market, their political militancy is softened by severe insecurity. Many migrants are prime targets for forms of escapism, from religious cults to drugs and other forms of inward-directed aggression. Since they depend on the chiefs for land allocation and security in old age, the frustration of the dislocated can hardly afford to show itself on their homeground. On the other hand, most migrants still have the security of a rural home to fall back on temporarily, if need be. This security makes the hostel dwellers on the East Rand more ready to join unions and engage in risky strikes than the inhabitants of Soweto, in which community organizations prevail. It was the insurance of an intact subsistence realm that in the past hundred years permitted semi-peasant workers on the railways, on the docks, and in the mines to quit individually or en masse when working conditions deteriorated. With this option increasingly narrowed, migrants are forced into either acquiescence or union protection.

The common union membership of permanent residents and migrants militates against attempts to play off one side against the other. The separation of the rights of urban dwellers from those of rural migrants nevertheless figures prominently in the design of government planners. Large employers, on the other hand, particularly some mining houses, would like to keep the migrant-workers system (at least of non–South African migrants), to save on housing and other social costs associated with family settlement near the workplace.

Finally, at the bottom of the hierarchy can be found the fourth group: those who are permanently locked out of the wage economy and also do not have a piece of land to plough. With increased population density in the rural slums, together with overstocking, drought, and soil erosion, up to half of the rural inhabitants in many districts no longer have the traditional option of subsistence agriculture. This landless and unemployed segment constitutes the marginal stratum made permanent when South Africa changed from a labor-absorbing to a labor-extruding economy. These displaced *lumpenproletarians* fill the backyards of townships and the illegal squatter camps that encircle the urban places of vain hope like a Black ring.

How many of these desperate work-seekers take the road to an ANC recruitment camp across the border? The little empirical research that exists on the world-view of squatters seems to point in another direction. In their survey of squatters, Lawrence Schlemmer and Valerie Möller found that some 80 percent of the migrants adapt to the stresses of their

situation with an attitude of acquiescence. They resign themselves to bleak conditions through one of three response patterns: (1) conformists rationalize their situation by either
lowering their aspirations or inflating actual progress; (2) re-
treatists cope with the trials of everyday life by engaging in
fantasies of returning to rural homes; and (3) alienated migrants overcome initial intense dissatisfaction by escaping into
passive despair, perceiving themselves as hopelessly locked
into a life of never-ending drudgery.[10] All three types adapt
to their degradation rather than seeking to change it through
political militancy.

As has already been discussed, South African propagandists
often interpret the relative acquiescence of their ethnic outsiders as loyalty or even contentment. However, an important
distinction must be drawn between normative identification
with and factual, realistic acceptance of circumstances. In the
first case, we find a fully indoctrinated subordinate class; in
the second instance, people acquiesce because they have no
alternative. The latter syndrome explains the relative hegemony of the dominant group in South Africa.[11] And yet, state
policies can only guarantee a top layer of order in society. It is
the routinization of everyday life in the struggle for survival
that absorbs all energies so that the state does not need legitimacy or ideology to elicit compliance. Only when basic needs
are satisfied can wider political interests come to the fore.

Trade Unions and Arbitration

The issue of trade union rights depoliticized the European
class conflict. Confining the struggle to the economic realm
kept the antagonisms from spilling over into the political
sphere and undermining the system as a whole. In fact, the
conciliation and arbitration machinery for settling industrial
disputes, short of strikes and lockouts, bound the parties to
working with the existing institutions. This European model
of co-optation policy also underlies the legalization of Black
trade unions in the wake of the Wiehan Commission recommendations in South Africa. More and more employers are

coming to realize that unions normally contribute to labor peace rather than destabilize industrial relations.

However, the South African reformist business community has on the whole displayed a remarkable shortsightedness, blatantly ignoring the experiences of Western countries. Schemes such as the much-praised co-determination policy of West Germany and the Japanese model of split wages and profit-sharing schemes have yet to be seriously discussed in South Africa, where the Anglo adversary principle predominates. Behind the debate about the Wiehan Commission recommendation, the demand for union registration, and the role of industrial councils lie two models of labor relations, which may be labeled the American and the British system.

In the United States, industrial conflict became privatized. Government remained on the sidelines, channeling disputes to quasi-judicial bodies. Legislation merely established the machinery for determining bargaining units and fair labor practices, and limited the use of injunctions against unions. Labor acts mostly aimed at upholding rights rather than prescribing how disputes should be settled.[12] Mediation remained voluntary. An essentially laissez-faire policy on labor relations left unions and employers on their own to come to terms with each other, notwithstanding a high level of strikes and lockouts. Strong but localized unions and decentralized bargaining corresponded with weak employer organizations.

The British model involves an elaborate labor code, with government enforcing libel laws, granting injunctions for wild-cat strikes, and filing damage suits against non-complying unions, which can be decertified. The machinery of mandatory conciliation, compulsory delay of work stoppages, and government-supervised strike votes works only because of traditional British adherence to "the law." The system is respected by both antagonists because both view it as the least costly and most appropriate way to settle disputes. It may even increase the number of conflicts to be arbitrated. But the process of regulated bargaining is accepted because it is perceived as legitimate by both employers and unions.

South Africa has adopted most aspects of the British system

of a sophisticated labor code without the political climate needed to make it work smoothly. Distrust of governmental control and interference in union affairs creates a decisive credibility gap. One cause of South Africa's "legitimation crisis" is her proclamation of industrial democracy without having first established political democracy—which preceded economic conflict regulation in all Western states.

Contrary to the recommendations of the Wiehan Commission, the American model of recognition and bargaining is not legally enforceable in South Africa. In 1981, the Report of the Commission of Inquiry into Labor Legislation concluded that voluntarism in recognizing representative unions may not suffice to overcome employer hostility. It therefore recommended that non-recognition should be actionable before the Industrial Court as an unfair labor practice and that after a judgment a strike over recognition would be permissible. The same procedure was recommended if an employer failed to bargain in good faith. However, the government rejected these recommendations, insisting that all recognition should be completely voluntary. Without recognition requirements entrenched in law, even if the demonstration of representativeness of a union by secret ballot is met the antagonists are forced into a power contest with strikes and lockouts as the weapons. As long as arbitration merely exercises moral pressure, urges reason, or "mediates" without enforcement, the system, ironically, promotes confrontation, the very outcome it was set up to prevent.

Instead of channeling industrial disputes into labor courts that minimize the effects of conflicts, the government (in the form of the Minister for Manpower) has frequently bowed to employer pressure to intervene in settlements that might favor labor. By changing the terms of reference of conciliation boards to exclude judgments on unfair labor practices, the Minister has on several occasions prevented the conciliation machinery from confirming dismissals as unfair according to a substantial number of precedents. Even the *Financial Mail* complained: "He is intruding into the sphere of employer/employee relations and contradicting the Manpower Department's frequently stated aim that industrial relations are best served if labor and management are left to govern their own affairs."[13] This voice of the industry clearly fears that the number of strikes will increase as the credibility of conciliation boards is undermined by their granting of favors to individual employers.

Moreover, the Industrial Court has tended to confine itself to ruling on the legality rather than on the unfairness of dismissal. But legal actions by employers at the same time frequently coincided with unfair labor practices that have become entrenched in South African labor law. For this reason, emerging unions preferred legal action to the alternative of striking. However, by tending to give preference to the legality of strike action without considering the unfair practices that may have precipitated the "illegal" strikes, the courts have undermined the credibility that led to their acceptance by the unions. Thus the primary objective, labor peace, was placed behind formalistic contractual interpretations of managerial prerogatives, and the boards virtually abdicated their rule-creating function.

By establishing equal political rights, the universal franchise, paradoxically, depoliticized the Western population. That is, it gave the masses the illusion of political participation without altering the basic power structure. In fact, the extension of citizenship rights in the bourgeois revolutions of Western societies stabilized existing domination by removing the sting of formal inequality and exclusion. South Africa lacks the atmosphere of depoliticized consensus about the basic legitimacy of the state. In the absence of political democracy, economic democracy can only be a vehicle to gain entry into the political kingdom. In this process stable labor relations are the first victim on a long list.

For example, the 1981 strikes over the use of pension contributions would have been unlikely to occur had Black employees, through their authentic representatives, had any say in how their pension funds were administered; the traditional view of pension contributions to be available as savings in times of unemployment reflected the distrust of Black workers in government-regulated insurance plans. Pension contri-

Trade Union Membership, 1969–1984
(in thousands)

	Registered Unions				Unregistered Unions	Total
	African	Colored/Asian	White	Total	Mostly African	
1969	—	182	405	587	16	603
1980	57	304	447	808	166	975
1983	469	330	474	1,274	272	1,546
1984	578	338	470	1,386	230	1,616

SOURCE: *South African Labour Bulletin* 10:6 (May 1985): 78; H.J.J. Reynders, Chairman of National Manpower Commission (telex).

butions now restrict workers' mobility by locking them into unsatisfactory employment unless they are prepared to forfeit the accumulated benefits.

Even in firms with scientific color-blind management, societal perceptions constantly intrude. For example, Black personnel managers, appointed to communicate instructions down to workers, often have little opportunity to convey the true situation upward. Many feel constrained to say only what they think their superiors want to hear. In an unequal society, easy equality in industrial management is impossible. It does not make for a neutral enterprise situation, even if more sophisticated management techniques try to foster "scientific" administration, regardless of color. In the end, Black industrial-relations managers find themselves distrusted both by the Black worker whom, contrary to expectations, they cannot favor in their professional capacity, and by their boards for failing to cope with problems that are beyond their control. Intended as buffers, Black managers may well turn out to hinder industrial peace, as long as they operate in an overall racially structured environment.

The rapidly growing Black unions face extraordinary problems at this stage even apart from employer hostility. Only about 600,000 Blacks are members of registered unions, and an estimated 230,000 are paid-up members of unregistered unions. The total comprises about 15 percent of "economically active" Blacks or about 32 percent of all union members (40 percent Whites, 28 percent Coloreds and Asians) in 1984.

In some homelands the position of unions is particularly tenuous. Most homelands (except KwaZulu) have enacted their own labor legislation. This deviation from South African practice can be partially explained by underdeveloped rural areas' difficulties in attracting investment. The promise of low labor rates and a tightly controlled work force is seen as drawing firms into the homelands. In addition, the homeland administrations feel politically weak and therefore threatened by an autonomous politicized union movement.

Attempts at militant action are undermined by the size of the surplus labor pool and by employee retrenchments in a recession, as well as by the peculiarities of work organization. The strikes threatened by the National Union of Mineworkers (NUM), for example, are continuously thwarted by two factors. First, union members are drawn largely from surface employees, while underground workers are represented in the union in smaller numbers. This division also corresponds to a large extent to the cleavage between permanent employees, some living with their families on mine property, and migrant laborers, most of whom are non–South Africans. Traditionally, the Chamber has dealt with wildcat strikes by firing the workers and sending them back to the rural areas, where replacements were recruited. Fired miners could expect to be recruited again eventually. Moreover, with the number of unemployed Black workers building up in South Africa's own rural backyard, foreign migrants can no longer be sure to be considered by the Chamber's recruiting organization, The Employment Bureau of Africa (TEBA). The scale of new recruitment is kept down mainly by the cost of training new recruits.

In light of the archaic working conditions in the mines, the new Black union was particularly successful in challenging the master-servant relationship. "Picannins" no longer carry around the master's satchel containing his food, clothes, Afrikaans newspaper, and comics. Instead of White miners being last to go down the mine and first to go off-shift, they too now sometimes stand in the queue. White miners are more careful in ordering around Blacks because they can expect resistance. Industrial strike activity in general has fluctuated widely since

Race Relations at the Rock Face

Cyril Ramaphosa, General Secretary, National Union of Mineworkers:
    The relationship between Black and White miners at the rock face is influenced by what happens in the wider society where the White man is boss and his word is a command that must be obeyed. Tensions rise and violence erupts. Assaults at the rock face are common and are usually perpetrated by the White miner. After each assault the Black miner is found guilty and discharged.

    Shaft stewards on two mines met and deliberated over this problem and decided that the only solution would be physical resistance by every Black miner to violent attacks by White miners. They announced the strategy at a members' meeting and stated that whenever a Black miner was attacked by a White miner he should fight back and make sure that he hit harder and won the fight and if he did not win he should summon the help of other Black miners. The following day an assault took place between a Black and a White miner. The White miner who had started the attack was shocked to see the Black miner fighting back. The Black miner won the fight and nobody was dismissed.

    Assaults have ceased at that mine. After that fight, which was publicized, the membership soared and the system was dealt a good blow. The strategy is spreading to other mines.

1974, when national statistics became available. There was a sharp increase in strike activity in 1984–1985, fuelled by the general township politicization but simultaneously dampened by the dramatic economic downturn.

    Despite all the handicaps, the unions run highly successful organizational drives. At present, most of the Black unions steer clear of overtly partisan political involvement. Conflicting loyalties of their members, as well as different priorities in establishing organizational goals, account for this abstinence. In actual bargaining clout the union movement supersedes all the loosely organized political groupings, with the possible exception of Inkatha. The new unions, especially the Federation of South African Trade Unions, had initially set themselves

Strikes, 1974–1984

Year	Number of Strikes	Workers Involved	Total Days Lost
1974	384	59,244	98,583
1975	274	23,306	18,709
1976	245	28,013	59,861
1977	90	15,304	15,471
1978	106	14,160	10,558
1979	101	22,803	67,099
1980	207	61,785	174,614
1981	342	92,842	226,554
1982	394	141,571	365,337
1983	336	64,469	124,596
1984	469	181,942	379,712

SOURCE: *National Manpower Commission Report*, Pretoria (Government Printer, 1984), pp. 372–73; SAIRR, *Race Relations Survey 1984* (1985), p. 328.

apart from the long-established tradition of popular protest politics in South Africa. Despite a relatively successful two-day protest in the Rand in the autumn of 1984, several unions were reluctant to join calls for organizational unity. Others, like FOSATU, considered their very abstinence from community politics the most appropriate *political* stance. Instead, they focused on building distinct democratic workers' organizations with their own identity and autonomy that are not submerged in an all-class alliance.

This position has been adopted for several reasons. First, if the fledgling unions were to involve themselves in risky political adventures, they would make themselves doubly vulnerable to being crushed by the combined might of the state and capital. Only organizational strength wards off this threat. Second, since the membership is divided on political strategies and allegiances (like the rest of the Black community), adopting a partisan position *as a union* would jeopardize their organizational unity. Instead, members are encouraged to take political stances individually. And, third, while always part of the wider struggle, the unions perceive as their first priority their own distinct organizational build-up, because they want to ensure, as Joe Foster put it, "that the popular movement is not hijacked by elements who will in the end have no option but to turn against their worker supporters."[14]

The FOSATU leaders realize the present weakness of workers' organization and the overwhelming power of an internationally connected opponent in the form of vast South African capital concentrations. On the other hand, they seem to have little understanding of embourgeoisement, which has so effectively blunted workers' militancy in Western states. The FOSATU general secretary speaks of "the State's complete inability to effect reform" and categorically states that "attempts to 'buy off' the major part of the working class will fail."[15]

It is doubtful whether FOSATU's denial of the relevance of community politics can be maintained. Foster calls "the community an empty and misleading political category" altogether.[16] But since workers are not only affected by their situation at their workplace but are often frustrated by the lack of proper housing and of schooling for their children, and the general poverty of township life, such civic affairs will inevitably politicize exclusive workers' organizations.

In addition, the political movements make a conscious effort to use the unions. In an interview Joe Slovo reasserted the ANC's leadership role over the union movement: "It depends on us having the capacity of injecting the right kind of politics and thinking into the working class." Slovo stressed that "on its own the trade union movement does not spontaneously generate revolutionary politics." Whether the South African workers need the "guidance" of the exiles in recognizing their true interests or whether they are capable of shaping their own autonomous lobby, even if this takes a reformist turn, lies at the core of the debate.

In this respect the growing international assistance sought and available to South African unions can be both helpful and divisive. The distinguishing criterion remains the clear control over the funds by the recipient. In some cases, FOSATU complained that foreign union money had been used to fight international political battles. Funds had been allocated to "prop up non-existent unions and create disunity . . . for particular political purposes rather than to assist in the development of unions."[17] The veiled reference is to the South African Council of Trade Unions (SACTU), the ANC–affiliated and banned predecessor of the current nonracial union movement. Its possible revival in South Africa as a separate organization has been discussed but not implemented ever since Black unionization was legalized. SACTU in exile still claims to be the authentic voice of South African workers and attempts to channel all foreign union contact and assistance through its offices. This stance has caused bitter disputes in the British union and anti-apartheid movement, which tends to lean toward the ANC/SACTU position. The major social-democratic European union organizations, on the other hand, have long established increasingly closer direct links with their emerging South African counterparts.

As Lenin warned in "What Is to Be Done?" trade unions stabilize capitalism. By participating in collective bargaining as partners in market transactions unions transform political conflicts into economic conflicts. In South Africa, however, this "economism" is overshadowed by the unresolved political issue. Trade unions in South Africa cannot channel discontent as long as economic bargaining is inevitably politicized by the exclusion of Black workers from equal citizenship rights.

The temporary identification of business with government in the constitutional debate further politicized labor conflicts. Since business is perceived as a cunning ally of Pretoria, and the government confirms this view by standing by as an ever-ready guardian with terrorism laws to be applied against union leaders, only a change at the political center will be seen as capable of achieving improvements at the plant level. With more limited government intervention in labor disputes, archaic labor relations would have encouraged syndicalist, plant-based industrial conflicts, mainly about bread-and-butter issues like those in the United States during the first half of this century. But given the overlapping private and public spheres and the absence of meaningful influence in either realm, Black unions will have to stress the need for a large

cohesive organization to maximize pressure. This is likely to
lead to an emphasis on unity and adherence to doctrine as the
cohesive bond that overshadows occupational differences. It
seems likely to be on the labor front through open and hidden
industrial action as well as through consumer boycotts that the
South African state will face its most serious challenge and
where ultimately the politicization of ethnicity will show its
most severe effects.

Organizational unity of the entire movement remains as
elusive as ever, although a new umbrella federation (COSA-
TU) emerged in 1985. Hitherto divisive issues include: (1)
registered vs. unregistered unions; (2) industrial organization
vs. general unions; (3) outside funds vs. membership financing; (4) the role of Whites in leadership positions; and (5),
above all, the strategy of confronting state and capital through
political action. The differences among the various union
groups can best be understood not by classifying the organizations according to these issues but by viewing the issues
themselves as phases of political cleavages in Black politics.
The three fundamental splits among Blacks—independent
reformists, boycott alliances with UDF/ANC affiliations, and
"socialist," Black Consciousness unions—are mirrored in the
debate over union unity.

Reformists
To the "unity unions" belong the numerically strongest FO-
SATU grouping, with nine affiliates, and initially the Black
Consciousness–oriented Council of Unions of South Africa
(CUSA) group with eleven affiliates (including at one stage
the National Union of Mineworkers), and a host of other
independent unions such as the General Workers Union,
Food and Canning Workers Union, Commercial Catering and
Allied Workers Union, and Cape Town Municipal Workers
Union. Among them, they represent about 70 percent of all
paid-up African union members. FOSATU unions in particular, with a highly professional nonracial leadership including
many Whites in senior positions, have gained some impressive
victories in a relatively high number of strikes and bargaining

encounters. FOSATU relies on a strong democratic consultative shopfloor organization so that the leadership never falls out of touch with the members despite the high degree of legal bureaucratic professionalism, including the use of outside lawyers. Most unions in this group began early to use to their advantage provisions of registration such as the industrial council system, recognition agreements with stopgap facilities, and other negotiated organizational assistance from employers. They also built up links with the International Confederation of Free Trade Unions (ICFTU), which assists with training and funding. FOSATU unions eschew mere protest politics in favor of effective, politically independent workers' organizations. However, on an ad hoc basis they join political stay-aways when participation is clearly mandated by the membership.

The distance of the new unions from political organizations is best expressed by Cyril Ramaphosa, the general secretary of the National Union of Mineworkers: "We have chosen not to be closely allied to any organization with political objectives. But we do support any actions we feel warrant support from our membership. But we want to do it as an independent agent, if we have to support any organization, but not as part of them. Our priority is to extend our organization and build trade union unity, and take up issues that affect us as mineworkers, as well as other political issues."[18]

The attitude of reformist unions to disinvestment is, pragmatically, ambiguous but is generally economistic rather than moralistic. Spelling out FOSATU's official policy on disinvestment, Joe Foster, the general secretary, said it was "not in favor" of the withdrawal of foreign companies from South Africa at this stage. FOSATU would "wholeheartedly" support total disinvestment, including the withdrawal of foreign companies operating in South Africa, if it could be given the assurance that this would bring about the changes desired by workers; however, it had reservations about whether these changes would be brought about by disinvestment alone. But, said Foster, FOSATU might call for their withdrawal in future if this came to be "in the interest of workers."[19]

Piroshaw Camay, of the smaller and less centralized CUSA, similarly asserted that CUSA's members would, if forced to make a decision, accept job loss in the interests of liberation, since there is poverty already. "However, CUSA does not support the withdrawal of present investment."[20] A CUSA resolution notes that there should be no *new* foreign investment, particularly in apartheid structures, that is, homelands. The unions welcome the pressure the disinvestment campaign is said to have placed on the government, but ultimately strive for a workers' movement that is strong enough to "set the terms of foreign investment," insisting that the machinery and factories "presently in South Africa will be retained in South Africa to the ultimate benefit of all."[21]

Boycott Alliances

The second group, the UDF-affiliated "community unions" such as the South African Allied Workers Union (SAAWU) and the General Allied Workers' Union (GAWU), owe their appeal to their direct involvement in political and community issues. They take up "popular struggles" and mass mobilization in addition to wage demands and unfair labor practices. Most of these unions were initially unregistered, preferring recognition arrangements with individual employers to being soiled by the state-regulated bargaining system.

Above all, these "boycott unions" enroll members from various industries and favor general workers' organizations, in contrast to the FOSATU ideal of one union per industry. This involves them in frequent demarcation disputes with rival unions who try to organize in the same branch. The principle has proved most effective in areas where the community virtually all work for the same factory, as in Port Elizabeth's motor industry. But the principle weakens the union in the dormitory township on the Rand, where most people work in different sectors. Organization by community also leads to neglect of other racial groups, so that, for example, in Port Elizabeth Colored workers from other areas did not feel bound by the strike calls of exclusively African community unions.

Critics charge the community unions with an easy leadership militancy that often cannot be backed up by a verifiable paid-up membership that would be willing and able to pay for the sacrifices expected. By failing to consult with other organizations, these unions are said to espouse elitist political goals that jeopardize the welfare of the very people they claim to represent. This has led to clashes between FOSATU members and UDF affiliates who, in some instances, called FOSATU members "scabs" because they failed to join strikes in the Eastern Cape.

The community unions have borne the brunt of state repression, particularly in the Ciskei. Ciskei's Minister of Manpower, Chief Lent Magoma, threatened that workers who "misbehaved" and who were involved in either strike action or union activity would be marked as unreliable and probably never get employment again. He added that "punishment camps on military lines would be established for those workers who broke their contracts for no valid reason," a suggestion supported by Mr. Jack Roos, director of the Cape Chamber of Industries.[22]

Black Consciousness Unions

Finally, there are nine smaller unions, belonging to the Black Consciousness–oriented Azanian Confederation of Trade Unions (AZACTU). This label was originally carried by some affiliates of the CUSA group, who temporarily moved into the "unity camp." Although all three groupings subscribe to the notion of nonracialism, the BC group insists on the principle of Black leadership, since Black workers make up the bulk of the membership. In contrast to pragmatic or tactical compromises, AZACTU representatives stress "principled unity for the sake of the eventual emancipation of the Black working class."[23] When AZACTU participated in the FOSATU-sponsored unity talks it insisted that they could do so only on a footing of equality. "If this is the case then there must be a new beginning and all previous decisions must be suspended."

Such demands, as well as some unions' reluctance to provide membership verification, account for the initial failure to form a super-federation, despite the promising groundwork laid in several unity meetings. However, union politics and differing ideological stances express leadership priorities and may not always correspond with a probably much more unified attitude of the rank-and-file.

On the other hand, a new feature of strikes since 1985 was their coordination in industrywide action by rival unions. Despite the threats of layoffs in a recession, several sympathy strikes also occurred, making a new solidarity. Different unions have actively organized their members in support of consumer boycotts, particularly in the Eastern Cape. Just as the Jameson Raid at the turn of the century, Hermann Giliomee has aptly pointed out, drew rival Afrikaners into a common militancy during the Boer War, so the 1985 emergency and police repression stimulated new levels of cooperation among rival Black unions; at the same time, however, the antagonisms between perceived collaborators (Inkatha) and extra-institutional activists (UDF/ANC) deepened.

The Congress of South African Trade Unions (COSATU), the "super-federation" that finally emerged in December 1985 after four years of acrimonious unity talks, reflects the common ground between reformist and more overtly political community unions: nonracialism; industrial unionism with one union per industry, implying the dissolution or merger of General Workers unions; worker control; representation on the basis of paid-up membership and cooperation at a national level. The greater impatience, brought about by the state of emergency, resulted in a much more political and pro-ANC stance of the new body than had been expressed by FOSATU executives. Nevertheless, it would be incorrect to consider COSATU a "new front" for the ANC, as Buthelezi has charged. Under the influence of its UDF sympathizers, COSATU uses ANC symbols and rhetoric ("nationalize mining and other key monopolies") but is loath to lose its independence and have a political movement call the shots, even under a future African government. A revival of the ANC affiliate SACTU in South Africa would be bitterly resented. While the ANC has paid tribute to the organizational unity, it cannot claim credit for it. As in the resistance in the townships, the ANC represents widespread sentiments, but as an underground and exile organization the ANC has little influence in mobilizing and directing the course of events. Many variations of ANC aspirations spring up under different auspices with similar goals to the ANC but without any organizational linkage to them.

It is indicative that the old, recurring division in Black politics also plagued the new union federation. The multiracialism of COSATU, in which a quarter of the secretaries-general of the newly affiliated unions are White, prevented CUSA and other Black consciousness unions from joining. They are more likely to merge into a rival union than to give up the principle of Black leadership by throwing in their lot with COSATU.

Despite these divisions, the ever more effective trade union organizations will pose the real challenge for government and business alike. Coordinated civil disobedience and a general political strike now no longer seems a dream, but, given the right trigger, a real possibility. Effective consumer boycotts, mainly due to union participation, proved the strength of concerted action. Consumer boycotts politicize and discipline the apolitical. The benefits of this far outweigh the damage to White shopowners. For the success of the revolution it is the consciousness-raising that counts, not the lessons taught to the opponent. It is in this attitude change that the unions have made perhaps their greatest contribution to social change so far. Its mass membership no longer see themselves as helpless victims. Whether through supportive judgments by the Industrial Court initiated by unions, through informal negotiations at plant level, or through strike action, the unions have proven that the politically rightless do have power if they decide to use it.

The unions and Inkatha are the only legal semi-political Black mass organizations that work within state institutions to alter the system. Both are allowed to hold mass meetings and even courted by a state that severely restricts its boycotting political protest opposition. But unlike Inkatha, the unions have not damaged their credibility through their acting within the framework of state institutions and regulations. In-katha is seen as a moderate co-optable ally, albeit with a price; the unions are perceived as a class antagonist whose demands would inevitably transform the system.

The state of the unions comes closest to providing an empirical example, a kind of microcosm, of what would happen if free nonracial incorporation were to be allowed in the political realm. Far from the monolithic unity that racists assume on the basis of color and orthodox Marxists on the basis of class interests, individuals and groups interpret and organize their reality in accordance with many other conflicting loyalties and ideologies.

The same predictions can also be made concerning the effects of a well-established resistance movement such as the ANC. Forced underground and into exile, it cannot be a normal political party but merely a broadly based alliance of opposition. Once this strategic solidarity disintegrates, when apartheid is dismantled, the various ideological strands within the alliance will come into conflict, brought out by the necessity of forming concrete answers to concrete problems. In the past, these splits were avoided by repression. Hence, the common-front approach of obstructionist protest gained priority in the absence of legal involvement. However, just as the unions—once they were legalized and faced with pragmatic challenges in the economic realm—split, realigned, and merged into competing, autonomous interest goupings, so the various ideological groupings in the political arena will be in permanent flux, once freedom of political participation has been restored. Especially if a system of proportional voting guarantees all minority interests a fair representation, polarized blocs will be avoided and pragmatic coalitions of several parties become a necessity.

7

A Plural
or a Common Society?

SEVERAL FACTORS UNIQUE to the South African situation suggest that the dream of a relatively democratic society has a better chance of being realized in an integrated South Africa than elsewhere. The reasons for this realistic optimism are not those of classical liberalism. Rather, it hinges on feasible policy changes that make the crude choice of "dominate or be dominated" obsolete. Taking the comparative lessons into account, it can be demonstrated that in South Africa ethnicity and democracy may prove far more compatible than a primordial perspective can envisage.

When Nationalist Afrikanerdom insists on group rights for itself it means right as a *racial* group. Apart from Whites, however, few South Africans desire legislated protection of their racial identity. Politicized Colored and Indian South Africans, irrespective of party affiliation, advocate a common nonracial citizenship in a polity that supports individual merit as the criterion of privilege. Politicized Africans agree: from its inception, the African National Congress has promoted the irrelevance of color and the eradication of ethnic divisiveness among Blacks. The imposed racial classifications lie at the heart of South Africa's illegitimacy.

It is ironic that it is the minority that perpetuates a racial allocation of power; this would be in the direct interest of the racial majority, but they, quite remarkably, adhere to merit-based individualism. The group that would most benefit from its long-term position of advantage nonetheless rejects nonracial meritocracy. Comparative race-relations research has frequently discovered that when members of groups encounter one another in new situations, the boundaries between them are likely to be overcome if they compete on an individual basis with one another; conversely, the boundaries will be strengthened if they compete as groups.[1] Since the minority Whites are losing this group contest on demographic and economic grounds, nonracial, individual (i.e., non-group) competition would be their best assurance of future security.

Moreover, for cultural, economic, and political reasons South Africa cannot be lumped together with other pluralist societies. As long as the negative lessons of divided societies elsewhere are mechanically and uncritically applied to a forcibly segmented South Africa, its unique potential is overlooked and the analogy remains ahistorical.

Religion and Resistance

Religion, for example, has hardly been a cause of friction in South Africa, because of insufficient power attached to it for it to become politicized. The peaceful coexistence of all major Christian denominations, in addition to small pockets of Hinduism, Islam, and Judaism, demonstrates that religion as such does not poison intergroup relations. It is the privilege and exclusion for which culture has become a marker that has made *culture* a term of ill repute in South Africa.

It would be wrong to deny the importance of racial perceptions after a long period of enforced racialism: group feelings are an empirical reality and cannot be legislated out of existence or wished away by a narrow, old-fashioned liberalism.[2] As long as group rights are instituted not at the expense of but in addition to individual rights, a moral claim for such voluntary collective entities can also be upheld.

Societies where racial divisions coincide with cultural differences are unlikely to eradicate racial divisions. Differences in religion or language reinforce visibility. Cultural heritage maintenance then becomes at the same time a perpetuation of racial group cognition. In South Africa, however—fortunately—races and cultures overlap greatly. Most people in the

urban sector speak one of the official languages, the major
Christian churches have members of more than one racial
group, and the educated of all racial groups share a common
cultural outlook and aspirations. This allows class divisions
that cut across racial boundaries. Where the Shiite Moslem in
Lebanon considers American consumer culture an evil empire whose promises and vices corrupt the believer and dis-
tract from the real purpose of life, many South African Blacks
would like to share in capitalist affluence. Like Afrikaner nationalism, which used the state to seize its share of wealth from
English imperialism, so Black nationalism, on the whole, aims
at capturing capitalism for its own benefit rather than over-
throwing it. Moreover, the assumption of shared Christian
ideology under which this conflict is fought holds the opponents within certain humanitarian bounds. Even implacable
opponents of the government grant its sincere Christianity.[3]

When popular spokespersons for the oppressed affirm the
common Christianity of the oppressors, they cannot be seen
as a dehumanized personal enemy to be eliminated with callous ruthlessness—as happens in religious violence from Bel-
fast to Lebanon, India, and Sri Lanka. The racial outsider
remains simultaneously a Christian insider who must be enlightened, cajoled, or even threatened but who cannot be
destroyed.

Given this widespread religious sentiment among Blacks,
the White portrayal of the resistance as "communism" lacks
credibility. But equally doubtful is the Marxist insistence that
capitalism alone is the motivating force behind White policy.
Whatever economic motives are at work, they have to be reconciled with widely practiced religious customs among the
Afrikaners.

Nevertheless, comparisons with religiously inspired resistance, be it Iran or Poland, hardly apply. Thus Allister Sparks'
assertion emphasizes only one aspect: "Nowhere else, not even
in Poland, is religion such a pervasively important factor in
the politics of a nation."[4] Unlike in Poland, in South Africa
religious practice is fragmented among dozens of competing
denominations. The predominant Protestant tradition, be it

Church Membership according to Race (1980 Census)

Church	Whites	Coloreds	Asians	Africans	Total
Ned. Geref.	37.4%	26.0%	0.5%	6.5%	14.0%
Geref.	2.8	–	–	–	0.5
Ned. Herv.	5.4	–	–	–	1.0
Anglican	10.1	13.5	1.1	4.7	6.5
Methodist	9.1	5.4	0.5	9.2	8.5
Presbyterian	2.8	3.7	0.1	4.1	3.7
Congregational	–	6.5	–	1.2	1.5
Lutheran	–	3.7	0.1	4.1	3.2
Roman Catholic	8.7	10.1	2.6	9.9	7.6
Apostolic Faith Mission	22.8	1.9	–	0.7	1.2
Full Gospel	–	–	2.8	–	0.1
Independent African	–	4.5	–	29.3	20.4
Other churches	12.8	15.6	4.7	6.3	8.4
SUBTOTAL	91.8	87.0	12.5	74.1	76.6
Jewish	2.6	–	–	–	0.5
Hindu	–	–	62.4	–	2.1
Islam	–	6.3	18.8	–	1.3
Other	0.6	1.2	1.5	0.6	0.7
SUBTOTAL	3.2	7.5	82.6	0.6	4.5
Unknown/None	5.0	5.5	4.9	25.3	18.7
TOTAL (thousands)	4,528	2,613	821	16,924	24,886

SOURCE: HSRC Investigation into Intergroup Relations, Main Committee Report, *The South African Society: Reality and Future Prospects* (Pretoria: HSRC, 1985), p. 36.

of the Anglican, Calvinist, or Lutheran variety, lacks the pervasive coherence and emotional symbolism that make central Catholicism such a disciplinary force. In Poland, the church provides the alternative meaning to an opposing party doctrine. It is an act of opposition to be active in the church movement. South Africa, on the other hand, prides itself on being a Christian state. Black religious activism, therefore, reaffirms the common bond even when the specific policy is called in question. In the South African context, Black theology implies reform, not revolution. Liberation theology has different implications in different situations. In South Africa it stresses the brotherhood of man, denouncing the policy of apartheid as heresy.

The churches provide a platform and shelter for protest.

But religiously inspired protest pleads for repentance, mercy toward the victims, and a return by the powerholders to the true value of the faith. Praying together to the same God, be it for rain or the dismantling of apartheid, binds the rulers and the ruled, in a situation unique in the annals of contemporary oppression. Thus a front-line state president waits for miracles: "I am not a prophet, but I am a praying man; I believe in God. I can't see him allowing that [apartheid] situation to go on."[5] The internal leader of a guerrilla movement equally expects divine intervention: "I have no power, but the Almighty God has. South Africa can be as dishonest and clever as they want and try to blind the whole world. The world was made by the Almighty. He will see to it that Namibia will be free."[6]

On the other hand, the same baptism does not necessarily prevent Christian brothers from going to war against each other, as history has amply demonstrated. The South African Kairos theologians have perceptively observed: "There we sit in the same Church while outside Christian policemen and soldiers are beating up and killing Christian children or torturing Christian prisoners to death while yet other Christians stand by and weakly plead for peace" ("The Kairos Document," unauthored and undated). From this moral sensitivity can also flow active resistance and civil disobedience. A minority of South African church people now invoke the doctrine of "just war" against a "tyrannical" government that is increasingly considered "in principle irreformable."

Other Blacks, however, pray for different goals. The rapid growth of the "Zionist" church movement—grossly neglected in the political literature on South Africa—offers the best example of how the poor give meaning to poverty and invent new mechanisms to cope. More than 30 percent of all Black South Africans now claim membership in one of the many sects of independent African churches that combine Christian rituals with ancestral traditions. Where leadership opportunities are blocked in most spheres, the sects offer religious entrepreneurs a domain of their own. Both the leaders and the followers profit materially from their religion. The strict puritanical rules—no drinking, gambling, gossiping, smoking, sexual promiscuity—give Zionists, recognizable by their silver star and dress code, preferential employment chances. Greater than average savings are ensured by discouraging leisure activities, even soccer playing. These savings are shared to a large extent. No member of the small groups feels left alone in a crisis. The rituals of healing place the needy in a circle of touching, caring fellows and make up for the lack of costly Western medicine. Yet it would be wrong to view the mass movement as a mere mutual aid society. Like the spreading cults in Western societies, the disciplined enclaves provide community, a sanctuary from abuse, and a temporary refuge from outside hostility. Menial tasks are sanctified and bestowed with meaning. By viewing the world around them with pity, "God's troops" strengthen their self-esteem. The moral absolutes elevate their followers from a downtrodden existence into a position of superiority, with a monopoly on truth and salvation. This ideological institution seldom tolerates competing loyalties. All the experts agree that the Zionists avoid political commitment. "These gentle, peace-loving people are not engaged in a crusade of social reform. They are not intent on moving the earth by social upheaval. Nor are they the least interested in bringing about political change. At one time the Ethiopian churches aligned themselves with the aims of African nationalism, but Zionists have never espoused any political cause."[7] Kiernan probably means an oppositional political cause; surprisingly, the massive church endorses the White rulers as legitimate political authority.

In his annual 1985 Easter sermon before one and a half million followers, Bishop Lekganyane of the Zionist Christian Church—a man whom Botha had addressed as "Your Grace" and assured "of our highest regard"—spoke of lack of Christian love as the source of many ills. He concluded with a plea for love and protection of the visitors: "Lord, we pray that You keep our State President, Mrs. Botha and us all, safe from harm. Amen."[8] Most Black political activists and intellectuals ignore or underplay mass expressions of "false consciousness." In the writings of Ezekiel Mphahlele, for example, the hope is expressed that African religion could substitute for the ideological hold that Christianity has acquired over the African mind. Ancestor worship, Mphahlele hoped, could assist Blacks to "snap out of the trance into which we were thrown by Western education."[9] In fact, however, a fundamentalist religious dynasty has successfully synthesized traditional beliefs and colonial Christianity into a far more enduring brand of status quo support than the unfulfilled promise of mainstream Christian equality has ever been. If the ANC leadership wants to win mass support it may be better advised to work on the Zionist Christian Church hierarchy than to dismiss this enormous group as a relic of political underdevelopment.

Critics of South African liberalism lament that its fatal attitude of nonviolent reconciliation has infected African nationalism.[10] By fighting a rearguard action against the excesses of apartheid, by stressing interracial mediation and the adoption of Black clients, White liberals, say their critics, lubricate the racial order. If the charge were true in its one-sidedness, however, it would apply much better to the churches and, now, to Black Christians.

Significantly, even the anarchistic destruction of property by Soweto's enraged youngsters is sometimes justified by references to God and biblical precedents: "If everything is to be destroyed, then let us destroy and not exempt a single thing. Let us not lose God's support by doing injustice; that is doing harm to some and securing others, whereas they are all on the same elevation of guiltiness. Let us not be like King Saul, who infringed by securing King Hagat whereas ordained to exterminate everything by God. We are Africans and brothers in love, and ought to share the pains and bitterness and the fruits of joy."[11]

The slow pseudo-reform policies of Pretoria, however, increasingly erode that Christian goodwill toward an enemy. Many of the politicized township youngsters are now ready to kill instead of following Tutu's or Lekganyane's advice.[12] The ANC's new policy of being less scrupulous about avoiding soft, civilian targets exemplifies the growing militarization of group relations. If the technocrats in power cannot effectively control their security forces, both sides will resort to brutality. State violence inspires civilian violence, not, as intended, civilian intimidation. However, as the events in Northern Ireland and Lebanon demonstrate, societies can adjust almost permanently to a stable level of violence, a "violent equilibrium," albeit at great cost to the quality of life of all.

The distinct possibility does exist that the often predicted bloodbath in South Africa may turn out to be a Black one. Given the ruthlessness of indoctrinated security forces and vigilante commandos who could use their superior firepower without restraint in the future, worse atrocities cannot be excluded. However, such a course would clearly destroy the foundations of an advanced economy that relies on at least a minimal level of labor peace and workers' identification with productive tasks. Increased state repression would destroy an economy that relies on voluntary participation.

Economic Interdependence

The historical advantages of racial privilege have accumulated for Whites such a pool of educational advantage, skills, mobility, and collective attitudes that in any nonracial, industrial setting individuals of this group would inevitably be disproportionately represented in the upper stratum. This results from the long-term shortage of and great demand for higher qualifications. While the unskilled poor Whites of the 1920s and 1930s, migrating to the cities and competing with cheaper African labor, had to rely on racial state protection, their urbanized, graduating Afrikaner counterparts of the 1980s can safely market their knowledge of computers or business administration or their professional expertise without preferential racial treatment. Even a gradual Africanization of the civil service through attrition or an affirmative action program in the private sector would pose little threat in the foreseeable future to the White monopoly of expertise. Only the dwindling White working class (mostly mine workers), the lower echelons of the apartheid bureaucracy, and a few other marginal groups in state employment would be adversely affected by a nonracial policy of equality of opportunity. Much of this loss of racial privilege, in any case, would be only in the realm of status reduction.

Even the often frustrated conservative Afrikaner farmers could adjust. Capital-intensive farming methods have lowered the demand for African labor. The recent history of Zimbabwe demonstrates that under majority rule a White mechanized farming sector can profitably coexist with increasingly productive traditional agriculture as long as state policy realistically adjusts subsidies and price guarantees to the advantage of both. Use of apartheid for labor control and job reservation has become outdated. With manufacturing capital's growing interest in using a stable, skilled, and productive labor force instead of the traditional migrant labor, it is no longer economic considerations, but political ones, that perpetuate neoapartheid.

The most crucial form of apartheid, the restriction of Black labor mobility, is now collapsing, a process with far-reaching implications for sociopolitical relations in general. In 1979, the Riekert Commission recommended the reconstruction of labor control away from the direct coercion by police raids in the streets to the indirect mechanism of fines for employers of "illegals." However, the ascendant business interests refused to accept self-policing and continued to employ "illegal" workers. As a second form of restriction the Commission envisaged control of accommodation through construction of urban housing; however, the funds were diverted into the Bantustans and few new houses were built. With the legalization of migration to cities dependent upon unavailable housing, rural workers bypassed the official checkpoints, settling in mushrooming squatter camps outside urban centers. This situation forced the government to abandon the provision of formal housing as a condition of employment. Instead it began to concentrate on site and service supply schemes to at least channel the labor force into regulated settlements under the guise of orderly urbanization. The final breakdown of labor control occurred in the Bantustans. Tribal Labour Bureaus, manned by African officials, were supposed to endorse willing migrants on the basis of employers' requisitions and call-in cards. This Africanization of control foundered on a mixture of corruption, incompetence, and administrative mismanagement. Since the plan ignored large sections of the impoverished rural population, these people had little reason to wait when employers in the cities hired first and had the worker's status legalized by the rural authorities later. Thus the rapid growth of a more permanent urban working class under fewer restrictions on selling their labor anywhere, organizing in unions, owning property, living with their families, and developing an informal economy has now become an officially recognized fait accompli.

The threat to White security has, then, been redefined. From concerns about being overwhelmed by cheap labor, a consolidated, urbanized Afrikanerdom now considers the instability of an advanced economy to be its greatest threat, for only a collapsed economy would devalue White skills. The likelihood of such a collapse hinges on the unresolved political question. The escalating costs of apartheid make the slide into permanent economic stagnation and instability à la Lebanon a real possibility. This potential for structural crisis undermines the technocratic hope of buying off dissent, for successful co-optation largely depends on an expanding economy. Inability to pay the costs of the Verwoerdian ideological blueprints forces the ruling technocrats to consider political concessions in order to contain resistance. But such a reform policy develops its own dynamic that may well escape the control of technocratic planners who have to react to unpredictable responses from below.

The technocratic vision of racial reform is bound for ultimate failure if it continues to underestimate the need for acceptable political incorporation—in other words, for the genuine abolition of apartheid. The rhetorical commitment to the elimination of racial discrimination rings false in a society in which a racial minority maintains ultimate control. Thus the transfer of political power, not merely multiracial power-sharing or the abolition of material discrimination, becomes the issue.

The political solution is said to depend on negotiations between representative leaders of opposing racial groups. A reasonable compromise worked out in a national convention would, it is hoped, establish a system of power-sharing that would constitutionally guarantee the rights of minorities. A consociational grand coalition of mutually suspicious camps, both liberals and nationalists agree, would prevent an escalation of bloodshed. The exiled ANC too, for reasons of its own, is sometimes quoted as "willing to discuss and negotiate specific mechanisms to protect White rights."[13] Envisaged, obviously, is a Zimbabwe-style solution, in which guarantees of racial representation could ease Whites into a transition to genuine racial compromise.

This vision, which could be called the consociation or national convention prospect of a future South Africa, is not without serious problems. The fundamental flaw lies in its emphasis on race. Since power-sharing between mobilized groups always amounts to a compromise, it will inevitably fall short of Black expectations of full rights and will simultaneously be perceived by the right-wing minority as a sell-out of White rights. This erodes the middle ground of compromising reformists in favor of extremists on both ends of the spectrum. A negotiated racial compromise, if it ever comes about, will reinforce racial group boundaries on both sides; racial claims and racial competition will be constitutionally entrenched. Under such an arrangement racial minority members are likely to lose in the long run, since they depend on the concessions of the majority.

In a nonracial society dependent on competition between individuals, on the other hand, achievement replaces ascribed minority status as the criterion for the allocation of scarce resources. Under a system in which Whites would vote for Black candidates and Blacks vote for White candidates because of their ideological outlook or personal attributes, minority members would fare better than under a system of racial group rights. To be sure, such an ideal, color-blind system of voting seems out of the question in South Africa today, where racial stereotypes are inculcated from early childhood on both sides, although the predominantly conservative, genuinely nonracial outlook of most Blacks makes it more likely that they would be inclined to support competent White candidates than that the more skeptical and prejudiced White electorate would endorse qualified Blacks as their representatives. Therefore, multiracial political activity in joint political parties has to precede any color-blind voting system. The repeal of the Political Interference Act, which forbade cross-racial politics, is an encouraging sign. Equally hopeful are talks about the eventual de-ethnicization of the ruling National Party, by allowing non-Whites to become members, although at present this remains a pipedream. Nonetheless, an urban, consumerist electorate in an industrial society with no institutionalized racial or ethnic differences holds far better prospects of stability and legitimacy than a fragile coexistence based on racial group rights.

A consociational strategy of negotiated racial group compromises can work in a preindustrial political culture in which the group leaders can command the unquestioned loyalty of their followers, but in a modern economy, mass higher education and divergent interests have politicized the urban population to a high degree. Many will refuse to follow "leaders," however real and genuine, in dubious compromises. Except in some rural areas, the concept of *leaders* becomes questionable. Black urban representatives in South Africa act merely as articulators of grievances, spokespersons of divergent interests, rather than leaders of monolithic communities. Just as the notion of leadership has to be revised, particularly in the absence of free and representative elections, so the concept of community needs revision. The current view imposes a preindustrial notion of kinship bonds or, worse, racial similarities on atomized, heterogeneous populations. Incorporation into a common political system can, however, no longer be based on putative innate primordial or racial ties. The only legitimate institutionalization of group rights possible can take place on the basis of individual, voluntary self-association. Rights and influence of minority political parties, for example, can be guaranteed through proportional representation—or even overrepresentation—as well as veto rights. This seems the only legitimate compromise between a Westminster system of winner-take-all and the consociational model of power-sharing. Relative group autonomy in cultural matters, as long as group membership is determined by the individuals concerned, also represents a legitimate demand in light of fears of permanent majority domination or threats to group existence.

Consociational theory is preoccupied with electoral systems and the problem of forging a working relationship between semi-autonomous ethnic segments in traditional societies. None of the consociational writers, including Lijphart, has yet addressed the different requirements for consociationalism in an interdependent advanced industrial society. How can its major class actors as well as unorganized economic interest groups be brought into a working relationship? This would seem, of necessity, to be different from the political system of power-sharing and to be based on novel organizational principles. Here the model of industrial bargaining with binding arbitration seems more feasible than veto rights or sham coalitions.

The Western democratic tradition offers no legitimate alternative to the universal franchise on all civic matters—at all levels of government, one-person-one-vote, on a common voters' roll of all adult citizens regardless of personal qualifications (save insanity or the forfeiting of civil rights by a conviction by independent courts). This system of democracy, despite its many deficiencies, has proven the most workable mechanism for the representation and reconciliation of conflicting interests. Any system that restricts rights or separates Black political rights from White political rights is bound to fail, as are all the quaint proposals of a qualified or weighted franchise. Even less realistic in an industrial economy is the periodic enthusiasm for partition, even if the partition were "just." The massive population transfer implied or explicit in these blueprints echoes the fascist and Stalinist deportations in the name of totalitarian dreams. Partition is no solution for the country's race relations, because ethnicity in South Africa cannot be territorialized.

Analogies between a gradual, incremental introduction of the universal franchise in Western Europe and North America and a similar process in South Africa ignore a crucial difference. It is impossible to emulate nineteenth-century "solutions" a hundred years later in another part of the world. History does not repeat itself. As part of a global system, South Africa is not immunized against political progress elsewhere; it moves in tandem with world events. Therefore the notion that South Africa cannot be expected to introduce democracy overnight but can well be expected to move from feudalism to an enlightened absolutism overlooks a hundred years of political development.

Only universal franchise can grant South Africa long-term internal stability and international legitimacy. South African business is beginning to heed that message. Economic citizenship through unionization cannot work without genuine political democratization as well. Local and international capital in South Africa can ill afford to let the country slide into racial warfare. It is greatly in the interests of business to use its clout to ensure fundamental deracialization. And a precondition for serious deracialization must be a massive public reeducation effort, primarily of Whites in the civil service. Their ideological confusion, vested interests, and anxiety about the future block fundamental progress.

The colonial solution of a White departure does not apply to South Africa, since it is not a colonial problem. Whites are there to stay in significant numbers, although emigration may well increase again when the crisis escalates. Racist intransigence can sabotage even majority rule. Worse, it can jeopardize a reasonable transition, to the detriment of all.

If the nature of the post-apartheid society could be convincingly clarified, apocalyptic fantasies and illusions would give way to realistic hope. A justified belief in a secure future can in itself free energies submerged by a stubborn determination merely to hold out. Unfortunately, the Freedom Charter is as vague as the liberal designs for a national convention in specifying the vital details of post-apartheid security. However, once a nonracial vision with concrete merits grips the imagination of Whites and Blacks alike, its difficult implementation will have begun. Better than moral indignation, blind belief in coercive power, or illusionary racial deals, a creative political realism will free South Africa from its moral paralysis. Instead of the continued liberal exhortations that South Africans will "suffer the future," a more effective approach could show convincingly that they can *enjoy* the future, provided nonracial policies are adopted.[14]

In summary, it may be argued that, fortunately, little *cultural distance* separates the urbanized population groups in South Africa. They are, however, separated by a gulf of *social distance*. The latter is maintained both by legal means and, largely as a result, by customary barriers of employment and educational differentials. Since social distance diminishes with the provision of equal opportunities in an integrated economy, the relatively weak South African cultural cleavages do not form the obstacle to democratic majoritarianism they do in genuinely plural societies. Furthermore, the South African binding economic interdependence does not exist in the typically plural societies of semi-industrialized Lebanon, Cyprus, Nigeria, Sudan, and Sri Lanka; all these states have relatively autonomous segmental economies. Even ethnic competition in industrial settings does not provide sufficient counter-evidence to this interdependence. The ethnic voting in Belgium or Northern Ireland stems from historical identities as well as material advantages tied to ethnicity. The economic unification of Europe or the demise of Quebec nationalism, on the other hand, shows how ethnic sentiment declines when it impedes economic advantages and symbolic needs are fulfilled differently.

The pluralist analogy therefore misleads rather than enlightens in the South African situation. This is not to deny the importance of racial perceptions in certain periods but to emphasize the situational nature of racial boundary maintenance. It cannot be assumed to apply inevitably under all circumstances, at least not when it has become dysfunctional.

A racial group alone cannot form a moral community, contrary to Samuel Huntington's claim that "racial communities also have moral claims and rights."[15] Nobody would recognize such claims, for example, for an association of criminals. Racial group rights could only rest on cultural distinctions that happen to coincide with phenotype, or because of restitution programs due to past discrimination. Historically and comparatively viewed, racial groups also persist on their own when certain occupations coincide with physical characteristics, but as this racial division of labor breaks down in a modern economy, the functional basis for racial groupings disappears. In the absence of endogamy rules and other religious barriers, color becomes an artificial and invidious boundary. This is the situation in South Africa. When Blacks and Whites share aspirations, Hollywood soap operas and leisure activities, jokes, tastes, and sacred texts (as is particularly true of White and Brown Afrikaners), a constitution built on false group identities perpetuates offensive racialism under the guise of ethnicity. When no cleavage exists between groups in meaning and belief, their political separation lacks any moral or cultural basis. The intense ideological battles within the Black apartheid opposition also go to prove the weakness of the bond of color or even of common oppression. According to all empirical evidence, if a free election were held in South Africa tomorrow, the Whites would be astonished by the diversity of Black voting.[16] These surveys suggest that a free political contest under universal franchise would still result in one of the more conservative governments in Africa, in which radical socialist demands on the left would compete with Black and White conservative groups on the right, with the government determined by a broad center of social-democratic and liberal voters in shifting coalitions. The White racist projection of ideological solidarity on the basis of color simply overlooks the wide range of outlooks among their putative antagonists. Institutionalizing color in a power-sharing arrangement based on the apartheid designations would induce people to uphold the color differences only so long as there were rights attached to the distinctions.

Compromise, the virtue of consociationalism, can be institutionalized as long as it is not done in a racial version. Consociationalism is not identical with accommodation in the sense of convergence of policy preferences. On the contrary, divergent sectors accept, in light of the costlier alternatives, common rules that permit them to pursue antagonistic interests peacefully. Consociationalism amounts to an institutionalized truce; it is neither the reconciliation of differences nor the capitulation of one party to another, but a compromise for coexistence. Inasmuch as consociationalism gives formal recognition to racial segments, it perpetuates an invidious division. However, there is nothing offensive in the institutionalization of religious or linguistic ethnicity. Their maintenance constitutes a worthy end in itself, but it is the *eradication* of racial divisions in an interdependent society that should be the primary goal. Thus racially based consociationalism can indeed ensure the perpetuation of, rather than the solution to, strife.

It is necessary, then, to consider not only the *degree* of pluralism but the *kind*. The question to be asked is, "Consociationalism for what?" While consociationalism may be both practicable and desirable under conditions of religious ethnicity, it could make matters worse in a racially divided society. Here democratic majoritarianism, not the unstable multiracial compromise, could in the long run generate a nonracial society.

The multiracial consociational model, as interpreted by nationalist Afrikanerdom, would freeze racial boundaries in order for one group to retain, at the very least, group power over its own affairs. At present, new bodies administering illusionary "own affairs" spawn as fast as new multiracial institutions regulating "common affairs." From a liberal perspective, racial power-sharing can only be justified as a transitional device to ease in nonracialism and lessen the danger of a right-wing backlash on the way. And from a Marxist viewpoint the entire question of racial power-sharing and ethnic rivalry in South Africa is seen as a giant smokescreen that detracts from the real issue: What kind of economic system should South Africa adopt? As long as ethnicity and racial integration are the primary items on the national agenda, they overshadow alternatives to free enterprise policies. While racial sharing is debated, free enterprise continues as the apparently natural order of accumulation. In this sense, anger against racialism serves capitalism well. The immediate debasement by racial discrimination leaves no energy and vision for class exploitation. Even Lijphart admits: "When ethnic or religious segments are the most prominent collective actors in a plural society, class interests will have little chance to be articulated and promoted."[17]

It has been said that the dreams of paradise are the seeds of totalitarianism. Milan Kundera has warned about glorifying the alternative utopia: "People like to say: Revolution is beautiful, it is only the terror arising from it which is evil. But this is not true. The evil is already present in the beautiful, hell is already contained in the dream of paradise and if we wish to understand the essence of hell we must examine the essence of the paradise from which it originated. It is extremely easy to condemn gulags, but to reject the totalitarian poesy which leads to the gulag by way of paradise is as difficult as ever."[18]

However, African nationalism can hardly be accused of dreaming about a paradise. Its alternative society is far more modest: it aims at the realization of bourgeois freedoms, not socialism. The Freedom Charter's terms resemble the old-fashioned values of liberal democracies. They lack the ideological zeal of the classless society and the fascist rule of the master race. The Freedom Charter is a pluralist document: "national groups" coexisting in equality, with mutual tolerance. Ironically, even the "radical" Charter, the core blueprint of the apartheid opposition, flirts with group rights by stating in its second clause: "All national groups shall have equal rights!" Indeed, as the many socialist critics of the Congress alliance have pointed out, its very principle of organization corresponds to the official race classification. The current degradation is so deep that mere group equality, with eventual abolition of apartheid, is perceived as paradise. This is both the strength and the weakness of the nonracial forces. Without the ideological certainty of an alternative eschatology, African nationalism is an unlikely victim of a totalitarian temptation. A goal of mere formal equality with the ruling minority lacks the revolutionary inspiration of dreams of true utopias. In the liberal modesty of the nonracial opposition lie its justness and moral promise. It is because the officially differentiated segments in South Africa are so much alike in their aspirations that the ruling minority fears losing control, not because, as the minority asserts, the majority is different.

8

Policy
Implications

Constitutional Alternatives

THERE ARE THREE MAIN ARGUMENTS for the urgency of fundamental sociopolitical change in South Africa. First, exclusion of the Black majority from the central governmental institutions not only violates democratic principles but also increases the costs of racial domination for the ruling minority. When these costs begin to outweigh the benefits, the minority in power can be expected to seek political alternatives, short of full abdication of political control. Second, a reversal of political power through the defeat of the ruling sector cannot be envisaged in South Africa in the foreseeable future. In fact, neither side is likely to defeat the other, short of mutual destruction. Even if a unilateral victory were possible, the price would be so high that the political value of the victory would be, at best, dubious. Therefore, third, in this stalemate power-sharing stands as the only alternative to continued instability. An early anticipation of the costs for both sides of an escalating antagonism provides the most convincing rationale for alternative constitutional proposals.

Only if these arguments are accepted is it meaningful to talk about constitutional conflict regulation. Constitutions reflect rather than alter power relationships. Just as bargaining procedures in the industrial sphere are accepted by employers and unions, the institutionalized rules in politics are observed because all competing groups stand to benefit from compliance.

It follows from the above that neither the unilateral designs of an ethnic technocracy nor preference for an unmodified one-person-one-vote, winner-take-all system without minority protection has a chance of relatively peaceful realization. Genuine power-sharing is a second-best alternative from the view of committed partisans on both extremes, but clearly the only realistic alternative to escalating strife.

While a nonracial system of government remains the ideal, the existing prejudices and vested interests must be taken into account. Therefore pragmatic provisions for obtainable interim improvements should be sought, with the expectation that in this way further changes will be initiated. Political change constitutes an ongoing process and not a one-time solution. At this point, the task seems to be to alter the political status quo in the preferred direction rather than waiting for an opportunity to institute utopia. At the very least, a real political learning process can be initiated and can lay the foundations for future compromises.

A realistic power-sharing system will take cognizance of the diversity in South Africa. The justifiable anxieties of cultural minorities about domination will be taken into account. Therefore, unlike the present policy of assigned racial classification, the politics of multiculturalism should allow all individuals to choose their cultural group affiliation. This free choice of identity constitutes the decisive difference between genuine deracialization and the existing practice.

In South Africa, models of political power-sharing by groups (as opposed to individual representation) cover a wide range: the elite cartel of consociationalism; a federated, regionally based democracy; a corporate federation in which ethnicity is not territorialized; or a confederation, with sovereign cooperating units under an umbrella organization. Almost all these proposals suffer from the structural weakness that they intend to institutionalize a share of political power for the currently constituted four racial groups.[1] Race is falsely equated with ethnicity. In addition, most proposals aim at making the untenable African rural-urban distinction constitutional or perpetuating the existence of homelands under the guise of consolidated, larger federal units. While the reality of ethnic homogeneity and the present homeland bureaucracies with all their concomitant vested interests must be taken into account, their political reintegration into the South African state remains an obvious economic imperative. There is no need to test public opinion within Transkei, Bophuthatswana, Venda, and Ciskei (TBVC) regarding the maintenance of their unrecognized independence, since the population was originally lured into losing their South African citizenship by collaborating elites. However, the TBVC administrative structures could well be maintained as a necessary regional bureaucracy, as long as the economic development imperatives of the total region are not subjected to ethnic considerations.

A crucial difference exists between state cohesion in South Africa and resolution of ethnic conflicts in other parts of the world. In Catalonia or Sri Lanka, in Quebec or Nigeria, rebellious nationalists demand secession or greater regional autonomy. In South Africa, the exact opposite is the case: Black nationalism aims at a unitary state. It is the minority in power that advocates secessionist policies. Because of this state strategy of fragmentation and, of course, the prospect of a reversal of power by the numerical racial majority, the disfranchised have always demanded a centralist rather than a federal state. Regional, ethnicity-based decision-making has become so discredited in South Africa and is so much associated with status quo conservatism that it is almost considered undemocratic. Genuine democracy, in the eyes of radical South African democrats, requires strong centralist government intervention to bring regional disparities in line with a political formula that guarantees greater equality. Regionalism is so closely tied to ethnicity that institutionalizing the one is viewed as perpetuating the other. To aid tribalism under the cloak of decentralized decision-making is the last policy Black nationalism in power would like to pursue.

Yet what forms the core of socialist policies in other parts of the world should not be dismissed out-of-hand as reactionary in South Africa. Even Lenin and Stalin recognized and insti-

tutionalized the different nationalities in the Soviet constitution, albeit in a powerless assembly. More important, modern
forms of federalism have been adopted by the most progressive forces in Western democracies, from Australia to Canada
and from West Germany to the United States. In South Africa
as elsewhere, democratic, nonracial participation in political
decision-making by the optimal number of equally enfran-
chised citizens suggests decentralized government. Anxiety
about majority domination can be alleviated by a high degree
of minority autonomy. Freedom of movement of all citizens
among regions remains a precondition, as does revenue-sharing and the equalization of regional economic disparities. The
lack of secessionist tendencies (except among some Afrikaner
ideologues) clearly augurs well for a cohesive federal state, not
as a compromise between disintegrating segments but as a
more democratic form of political organization.

Thus, the power-sharing model that can best reconcile the
conflicting interests with an optimal chance of democratic
conflict regulation is a federal system. Therefore the constitutional question is better posed as, what kind of federalism
should be considered? A regionally based federalism constitutes the most common type, but there is also the possibility
of *corporate federalism* (a term coined by C. Friedrich), in which
groups of persons rather than territories are granted rights
and powers. Most South African analysts who favor the territorial devolution of power hope to sidestep the overall numerical ratios. They advocate that the regions not be strictly proportionally represented in the central parliament as they are
in the United States Congress. However, any geographic federation would only gain legitimacy if the regions were represented according to their population size, although new federal units would not have to be approximately equal in
population or geographic size. Economic interdependence
and historical allegiances seem the most obvious criteria for
determining boundaries of eight or ten new provinces instead
of the present four. Scattered homelands would then merge
into newly delineated compact regions or provinces.

Friedrich's corporate federation, based on freely chosen

group membership, on the other hand, would solve the problem of the interspersed nature of group settlements. It is a design that appeals to Afrikaner Nationalists insofar as it would leave them constitutionally "master in their own house," even if the houses are amidst many more kraals and townships. A corporate racial/ethnic federation, however, has little chance of acceptance by the ANC, although the group may revise its traditional insistence on a central state. There are reports to the effect that "Mbeki indicated to the Commons Committee that while the ANC would not consider a race federation based on units such as 'Bantustans' and racially defined Group Areas, it might be prepared to talk about a geographic federation within the context of a nonracial and democratic unitary South Africa."[2]

Reaching a compromise between the two positions would be a matter of constitutional engineering in negotiations. For example, in a federal South Africa, the powers of two assemblies could balance each other: a lower house, elected on the basis of universal franchise, and an upper house in which regions or *self-defined* cultural/ethnic groups would be represented. If the lower house were elected by all adults on a common voters' roll and the upper house elected or appointed by the constituent groups qua groups or regions, such a federation would closely resemble many democratic states (West Germany, the United States) where majorities in the two houses are needed to pass legislation. Indeed, as Forsyth argues: "It is precisely the great merit of the federal state, properly conceived, that it integrates *both* the group *and* the individual into one and the same political order."[3] Those who do not want to align themselves with any ethnic group could follow the Yugoslav model, which allows people to classify themselves simply as Yugoslavs, sitting alongside the ethnic/national groupings.

The obvious question to be asked here is why there should not be solely an individual incorporation into a unitary state according to the Westminster system, with no constitutional regional or group representation? Afrikaner nationalism views Westminster voting in the South African context as actually being undemocratic. The weight of numbers would not allow meaningful self-determination of minorities. Such fears are justified if one accepts the assumption that all Blacks would want to join a counter African nationalism or even a counter Black racism. It falsely projects the Afrikaner perception of attempted group domination, based on race, onto their opponent and ignores the vast ideological differences among the disfranchised. But given the experience of ethnic mobilization and the concomitant suppression of minorities in many other societies, these anxieties have to be taken seriously. They are legitimate fears that go deeper than the desire to maintain privilege. The often-quoted guarantees of constitutions alone are not sufficient safeguards. As the *Economist* has expressed the South African predicament of concerned conservatives: "The issue for South Africa's critics is not abhorrence of Apartheid, but the extent to which genuine reform can be brought about without a lurch into civil war, economic chaos and an authoritarianism of the Black nationalist left instead of the White Afrikaner right."[4]

Liberalism has for the most part failed to recognize the legitimate aspects of mobilized ethnicity, by associating ethnicity solely with unfair advantage or the height of irrationality. But insofar as ethnicity expresses cultural distinctiveness and the quest for individual identity through group membership, it may fulfill desires that liberalism ignores. People do not necessarily want to be all the same. If it is part of human nature to seek differentiation from other members of the species, then cultural ethnicity satisfies a deep-seated need. Cultural ethnicity only becomes problematic if it is transformed into economic and political ethnicity for the advantage of its members at the expense of outsiders. This benign definition of ethnicity is, however, difficult to extol in South Africa, due to its tainted history.

There would be little disagreement about the right to retain a preferred language or practice a specific religion. In practical terms cultural group autonomy means, for example, that the state does not interfere with the educational preferences or language rights of any sizable group. It also means that the state should proportionately subsidize private religious or language education while maintaining a public school system of equal standards for all communities.

A cultural federalism could ensure that the Freedom Charter's declared right of all people to "develop their own folk culture and customs" could be meaningfully implemented. For example, instead of the two European official languages being uniformly imposed everywhere it would be practical to give a regional language equal status in a particular area. Thus, in Natal, Zulu and English could be the official languages, while Xhosa would have the same status in the Eastern Cape and Sotho in the new federal units in the Transvaal. There would be no need to have a second official language in regions such as Western Cape and Orange Free State, where the overwhelming majority speak Afrikaans, while in the melting pot of the Pretoria-Witwatersrand-Vaal (PWV) area a multilingual policy would apply as far as practicable. The confusion of the great variety of home languages is mitigated by the high percentage of bilingualism or multilingualism in South Africa, particularly among urban Blacks. Virtually all adult permanent township residents speak one of the European languages. The 26.9 percent of Africans in the urban areas who cannot speak either English or Afrikaans are mostly migrant workers. On the other hand, only 11 percent of Indians, 8 percent of Whites, and 5 percent of Coloreds can speak an African language.

An important precondition for genuine multiculturalism would be the compulsory teaching of the second language in the area schools, linked to bilingualism or even trilingualism as a prerequisite for civil service careers. Such a policy would reward multilingual Blacks more frequently. At the same time the learning of an African language by Whites, Coloreds, and Indians would truly "Africanize" the society and foster communication and understanding among the different ethnic segments in future generations. Black writers, both in translation and in the original, could be as much a standard part of school syllabuses in all communities as is von Wyk Louw or Paton.

Home Languages in the RSA, according to the 1980 Census (5% Sample)

Language	Whites	Coloreds	Indians	Africans	Total
Afrikaans	2,581,080	2,251,860	15,500	77,320	4,925,760
English	1,763,220	324,360	698,940	29,120	2,815,640
Dutch	11,740	–	–	–	11,740
German	40,240	–	–	–	40,240
Greek	16,780	–	–	–	16,780
Italian	16,600	–	–	–	16,600
Portuguese	57,080	–	–	–	57,080
French	6,340	–	–	–	6,340
Tamil	–	–	24,720	–	24,720
Hindi	–	–	25,900	–	25,900
Telegu	–	–	4,000	–	4,000
Gujarati	–	–	25,120	–	25,120
Urdu	–	–	13,280	–	13,280
Chinese	–	–	2,700	–	2,700
Xhosa	–	8,440	–	2,870,920	2,879,360
Zulu	–	5,580	–	6,058,900	6,064,480
Swazi	–	1,060	–	649,540	650,600
Southern Ndebele	–	440	–	289,220	289,660
Northern Ndebele	–	100	–	170,120	170,220
Northern Sotho	–	2,440	–	2,429,180	2,431,620
Southern Sotho	–	5,320	–	1,872,520	1,877,840
Tswana	–	9,300	–	1,346,360	1,355,660
Tsonga	–	1,180	–	886,960	888,140
Venda	–	40	–	169,700	169,740
Other	35,020	2,660	11,160	73,900	122,740
Total	4,528,100	2,612,780	821,320	16,923,760	24,886,020

SOURCE: Adapted from HSRC, Main Committee Investigation into Intergroup Relations, *The South African Society: Realities and Future Prospects* (Pretoria: HSRC, 1985), no page number. These South African statistics do not include the "independent" homelands: the figures for Xhosa, Sotho, and Venda speakers should be considerably higher.

The gigantic task of constitution-making would be to abolish the economic and political inequities historically associated with ethnicity.

Implications of the Group Areas Act

The Group Areas Act constitutes the most far-reaching legacy of the Verwoerdian dream. Long after all apartheid laws are repealed, the factual resettlement in racially homogeneous localities will persist. Neighborhood schools will mean predominantly racial schools. Leisure activities and normal social contact will take place largely within ethnically similar communities. In light of these unalterable social facts, the question arises as to how the initial injustice and lingering bitterness from the Act can be accommodated. How should a democratic election take the racial structures into account? Should a nonracial policy reverse the legacy through deliberate ethnic scrambling, or should it concentrate on a course of equalizing the infrastructure and services of vastly unequal neighborhoods?

The Federal Republic of Germany paid substantial compensation to the surviving victims of Nazism. The Canadian government symbolically acknowledged its guilt over the wartime expropriation and relocation of Japanese-Canadians. In this vein, the South African government could at least accept financial responsibility for the losses of victims of the Group Areas Act. While confiscated properties of Coloreds, Asians, and Africans were "compensated" at the discretion of officials, they were in most cases immediately sold to White bidders for a much higher real market value. It is this difference between compensation paid and actual market value, recorded in subsequent sales and available in the deeds of land registers, that could, together with accrued interests, form the basis of an easily administrable monetary settlement. Such a gesture would not even take into account the psychological anguish suffered by the past racist expropriation.

Surprisingly, none of the Indian or Colored political parties have so far made financial restitution for Group Area losses part of their platform. While all these parties advocate the abolition of the Group Areas Act, this demand overlooks that many relocated victims and their children have become accustomed to their new environment and do not want to move again. But they do resent the losses incurred and the past easy enrichment by White municipalities at their expense. Since the White municipal authorities were the main beneficiaries of the Act, a special restitution tax, levied upon those authorities and added to White area property taxes, would be the morally most justifiable way to finance the scheme. If individual compensation is not considered feasible, then the municipal upgrading of services and infrastructure in the generally inferior non-White areas through these special taxes could be made a priority.

Indeed, the ethnic residential pattern created under the Act is likely to persist for a long time, even with the restoration to individuals of the right to choose where they wish to live. In this case, the class differences between affluent and poor neighborhoods are likely to be accentuated. The Black middle class will gradually move out and the "have-nots" will be left among themselves in their racially homogeneous ghettoes compared to the racially mixed better areas. Few Whites, Indians, or Coloreds will be moving into the Guguletos, Sowetos, or Umlazis, which will even more strongly develop into rundown East Side quarters across the railway track, serving as quarters for impoverished rural newcomers in search of scarce jobs. If the multiracial "haves" want to avoid the seething discontent of the ghettoes spilling over into their affluent areas in the form of ubiquitous crime, as in Rio, Detroit, or Lagos, they had better make the townships sufficiently attractive to allow for a civilized life to replace depressed hopelessness.

How? Not following the American model, in which municipal expenditures on a suburb or city area depend on the taxes raised in it, but, perhaps, using the Canadian and European example of metropolitan financing. Here taxes collected *at large* are spent generally according to need, and the richer areas subsidize the poorer sections of the city. Another model would raise funds through levies upon employers (according to the numbers of Black employees), since the firms benefit most from the Black dormitories. However, this scheme would discourage labor-intensive production and would inevitably lead to further replacements through mechanization and, hence, unemployment.

While the financing of the Black areas has to be allocated according to the resources raised *at large*, political representation is optimally ensured in its opposite—a ward system. In such a system all neighborhoods or designated areas of a metropolitan region (wards) are guaranteed representation on the councils. In theory, a Black person could run for office in a predominantly White ward and vice versa, although in practice most representatives would be respected residents of their ward. Ward candidates could run individually or, more likely, as members of political parties, operating across ward boundaries. More than in an election at large, a ward system would minimize the dependency of the weaker parts on the goodwill of the more powerful sectors, because of guaranteed direct representation. At the same time, a ward system would ensure that minority ethnic groups be represented, since their vote in their residential area could not be "swamped" by majority ethnics in a winner-take-all system.

It would be wise to allow for several rather than one ward representative on the municipal/regional council, to be elected by proportional voting. In this way, several political groupings within a constituency could vie for their share and expect to be represented rather than fall by the wayside as would be the case in the Westminster system. In order to avoid unwieldy councils, it would therefore be wise to delineate relatively large wards represented by several different delegates, rather than small ones each represented by only one person. Similar rules would apply to numerically equal-sized rural constituencies, which will inevitably be more ethnically heterogeneous.

Local councils cannot substitute for central political representation. But democratically elected grass-roots representatives at the local level could initially also act in an indirect election of a regional and central parliament. All ward councillors could elect a regional and central assembly from among themselves, according to proportional representation of whatever groupings emerge. Presumably, the greater rationality of elected ward representatives would also ensure a more competent central assembly, minimizing the chances of electing demagogues as a result of the screening of their peers. Above all, the indirect voting in a proportional system would reflect the ethnic and/or ideological composition of the country: no minority or area would remain unrepresented. If such a system were to be backed by the consociational prescriptions of veto rights for minorities in existential matters as well as required representation on all administrative bodies, an optimal and widely legitimate democratic system would emerge.

In all likelihood most representatives would be Blacks. But by all accounts these new delegates would also primarily reflect the predominantly moderate social-democratic and religious outlook of their constituency. The majority of these representative spokespersons would have no difficulty forming coalitions with like-minded members of other ethnic groups, and most would already be members of nonracial parties.

It would be a fatal mistake on the part of the present rulers to manipulate representation through fiscal, ethnic, or numerical gerrymandering. Neither the taxes paid nor the ethnic composition of a district can serve as a legitimate criterion for its voting strength. Head-counts of residents or registration of voters alone guarantees legitimacy. That such equal counting of adult persons for a one-person-one-equal-vote system will necessarily overlap to a large extent with existing residential patterns of ethnic homogeneity is a result of the Group Areas Act. It would be prudent to ensure that the delineation of constituencies is carried out by a multiracial body of representatives or judges who enjoy the highest reputations for impartiality.

Constituency representation by a numerically approximately equal number of wards differs in fundamental respects from the government's proposal for regional government. It is not based on discredited urban Black councils or other racially homogeneous bodies, but on a nonracial universal franchise that does not institutionalize enforced racial categories, yet the ethnic composition of an area will be likely to be fairly reflected in the representation. It also eliminates the racial distinction between "own" and "general" affairs, so central to the 1983 constitution. Instead, legitimate area interests come to the fore. These are articulated by whoever the majority of residents thinks can represent them best, as in all Western democracies.

Security and Group Rights

Constitutional group rights and a Bill of Individual Rights alone do not guarantee justice. At best, they proclaim an intention. What is crucial is whether, and how, stated rights can be enforced against violators. In the last analysis constitutional rights reflect power relations. Security remains a bottom line, and security mostly emanates from control over armed force.

A sovereign state is usually characterized as exercising the monopoly of force in its territory. However, there are many examples of a soveriegn state permitting the self-policing of areas under its control. If it were agreed upon that the police forces were to be locally recruited and employed, they would also reflect the dominant ethnic composition of the population in each area. This is already practiced widely, with the exception that the overall control remains in Afrikaner hands. This situation would have to change, making a more autonomous community police. The necessary coordination between the different forces in a metropolitan area under the ultimate control of the elected regional administration would pose few problems.

As far as the military is concerned, however, ethnic units could facilitate a Lebanization of South Africa. The army must owe its allegiance to the state rather than to its communal segments if the state is not to disintegrate in a crisis. Here the Zimbabwean example of a racially integrated army could serve as a model. As long as the military is not the domain of one ethnic group but proportionally represents all population groups, perhaps even deliberately overrepresenting minorities, it can hardly be used to suppress one sector without the risk of disintegration. The inevitable institutional socialization into an integrated, small, but efficient professional military of high standards—perhaps backed up by auxiliary volunteer commandos in each area under professional control—can be expected to override sectional or racial loyalties. This is clearly true for Black soldiers and policemen in the present system, where the army ethic has proven stronger than racial solidarity. In fact, Black policemen are considered far more ruthless than Whites, because of the constant hidden suspicion of disloyalty to their White masters. Their ostracism and renegade status in the townships may in fact reinforce this attitude, rather than leading them to "turn the guns around," as the ANC advises.

More radical proposals, such as to leave military control in White hands as an ultimate safeguard for handing over political power to a majority government, fail to recognize the legitimate claim of a sovereign government that it cannot tolerate a potentially or openly hostile counter-force in its midst. However, should it be agreed upon, the Afrikaners could hardly expect a more generous compromise than such a hard security assurance as ethnically controlled armies in return for abandoning ultimate political control.

Besides such negotiated security provisions, territorially based jurisdictions for Afrikaners ("White Bantustans") amount to anachronistic dreams in an interdependent economy. Gush Enumins (the fanatic settlers in Israel), be they on the Westbank or in the Orange Free State, cause problems for peaceful coexistence more than they lessen opposition to it. If racist ideologues would like to purchase their own land and work it without using Black labor, there is, however, nothing that should stop such ancient flights of utopia. These enclaves may help to neutralize the potential terror of hard-core racists beyond the control of any government, let alone of reasoned persuasion. If some rural Afrikaners wish to imitate Hutterite colonies or other communes of alternative life-styles, so be it. Private communes of racist escapists from a threatening reality will inevitably fade into insignificance as long as they are not publicly sanctioned by special legal status.

However, a strong case may be made for state recognition of collective cultural rights. Cultural self-determination is not bound to a territorial base. Indeed, the United Nations' *Study on the Rights of Persons Belonging to Ethnic, Religious, and Linguistic Minorities* lists a wide range of rights that could fall under the rubric "cultural, religious, and language" autonomy.[5] The most crucial would be educational policy, that is, the right to establish denominational schools. The observance of religious or customary holidays and the right to use the minority language in official communications are other examples of desirable public ethnic recognition. One could also ask why should there not be an exclusively Zulu, Afrikaans, Islamic, or Hindu television station and broadcasting facility in place of the state-regulated uniform institution, espousing a correct line of official propaganda, that exists from Pretoria to Cairo at present? As long as such multiculturalism is supported by a large enough constituency and does not infringe on the common, overriding individual citizenship rights of its adherents, the diversity of "meaning-conferring activities" can only enrich the whole society.

Such cultural self-determination in a new nonracial South Africa can emulate various legal forms and precedents. The PFP proposals of corporate "cultural councils," represented in an upper house, is the most widely known. The bodies could also be modeled in part upon the self-governing professional societies in the medical and legal fields. Their self-regulatory existence rests on the assumption of a special competency of its members. So cultural or religious autonomy could be justified on the basis of special interests and knowledge unique to members of a religion or ethnicity. The widely supported self-government of Native people in North America provides another model of legitimate collective self-determination. Natives try to break out of the welfare colonialism by reclaiming their aboriginal land base and first-nation status. Those examples of legitimate cultural self-expression in South Africa, however, are inextricably tied to two prerequisites: (1) that group boundaries and membership are no longer imposed, but self-chosen; and (2) that no unequal political power and economic privilege are publicly bound up with private ethnicity and heritage maintenance.

Addressing Economic and Status Grievances

Comparative evidence from other divided societies points to the importance of relative economic equality for harmonious intergroup relations. The inequality that exists in South Africa could be redressed at the political level through proportional revenue-sharing and equalization payments for less developed regions or institutional sectors, including affirmative action programs to compensate for past inequities. Unequal development does not present an insurmountable obstacle in a growing economy. In the same way that class conflicts were reduced in progressive West European countries through institutionalized bargaining and compulsory arbitration resulting in ever fewer strikes and lockouts, conflicts about material privileges could be settled without escalating violence. The chances of political violence, however, are much greater when economic and ethnic group cleavages converge. When material inequality crosscuts ethnic cleavages, the common material interests override ethnic loyalties.

Attaining stability requires that the massive Black unemployment and rural poverty be tackled through public works programs and tax incentives for job creation. The recession, if it forces the government to cut its spending on apartheid parallel administrations and Namibia in favor of pressing needs such as housing and Black education, could be a blessing in disguise. In addition, government policy could, for example, pressure the private sector to integrate training, promotion, and job opportunities, by refusing to grant government contracts to firms that do not comply with a stipulated labor code. The present constitution does not require that "general affairs" be administered by a mainly White civil service alone. Attrition of the Afrikaner monopoly could allow qualified Blacks to move into management positions in the vast parastatals and thereby set an example to the private sector.

The gradual Africanization of the higher echelons of the civil service—the pilots of South African Airways, medical staff at hospitals, faculty positions in universities—seems particularly crucial. Role stereotypes would be contradicted in the eyes of a prejudiced public, and the application of criteria of merit demonstrated to Black youth skeptical of career chances.

Other legitimacy implications can best be demonstrated with the example of the judiciary. Hugh Corder, in his analysis of forty years (1910–1950) of interpretations of conflicting rules and judicial precedents by judges of the South African Appeals Court, found a strong commitment to the legislative policy and ideology of the ruling group.[6] The study shows that the expectation of the judiciary serving as a guardian of justice for the disfranchised is misplaced. While the judges adopted a generally liberal line on matters of personal freedom, they upheld the state whenever the status quo was threatened. The law constrains authority and makes administrative action more predictable; it seldom acts as a trail-blazer.

Yet there is room for judicial discretion. If judges transcend their social background and ideological ties with the established order, as happens occasionally, they can advance the cause of justice even within the narrow confines of the South African system. By reinterpreting the rights of urban Blacks (Rikhoto) or insisting on due process, judges have on occasion made inroads upon an authoritarian administration. Contradictions between the democratic legitimation needs of an executive state and the sense of necessary control among the dominant segments lend themselves to far greater exploitation than a conservative judiciary is willing to perceive. Above all, the racial and ideological disparity in sentences for offenders (mostly as handed down by regional magistrates who are dependent civil servants) proves a strong political bias for the South African legal system. That persons on the political right receive far milder sentences for "terrorist" offenses than those on the left and that infractions by Whites against Blacks are generally treated more leniently than vice versa constitutes an embarrassing indictment of the system of justice.[7] John Dugard has emphasized that there has never been a Black judge appointed and that Blacks represent only a tiny percentage of the membership of the four Bar Councils. "It would not be too speculative, therefore, to portray the over-whelming majority of our judicial officers as White Protestant males of conservative outlook, who support the present polit-ical/racial status quo (and often the National Party Govern-ment), and who have little personal contact with members of the other racial groups, except at the master-servant level."[8] Improved training of these judicial officers or their exposure to prison conditions, necessary as these steps may be, can hardly result in changes in an institution that has executed more than 150 Blacks for rape since 1911 but has never sen-tenced to death, let alone executed, a single White for the rape of a Black woman, though such rapes are far more frequent.

Only a partial Africanization of the judiciary can achieve the balance and legitimacy so crucial for the credibility of the legal system. While Black judges would labor under corresponding personality biases due to their social background, at least they could be expected to be familiar with the situation of the ma-jority of offenders and could perhaps restore the balance in the disparity in sentencing. Paradoxically, questioning the very apolitical objectivity and neutrality that judges flaunt as their trademark would be a prerequisite of their true justice. Only when judges become conscious of their political role (as Blacks can be expected to be) do they begin to work for change in the system.

Moreover, because the symbols of dominance—the laws and everyday conduct—are left unchanged, the slow reform from above is perceived by its intended beneficiaries not as libera-tion but manipulation. One of the fallacies embraced by an ethnic technocracy is the assumption that it can solve the racial problem by budgetary means alone. More township housing, better Black educational facilities, and higher wages, neces-sary as they may be for stability, do not eliminate discontent. What matters is the meaning given to these initiatives by the recipient, not by the donors. A government cannot manufac-ture meaning in order to engineer mass loyalty. Reform from above is increasingly held suspect unless it clearly has been instituted under pressure from below. Since such "weakness" is the last thing the establishment wishes to admit, many well-intended concessions have failed in their impact even before they are implemented. The work of the Urban Foundation, for example, is constantly suspected of being part of the grand apartheid design of merely pacifying the urban insiders.

The Pretoria government consistently underestimates the status frustrations and symbolic grievances of the highly politicized Black middle class, on whose true incorporation any accommodation is dependent. Pretoria has yet to issue a much-needed statement of intent that will spell out the process of deracialization clearly. In the volatile social climate of South Africa, an untrained bureaucracy and police display attitudes of supremacy as rigidly as ever in daily encounters, whereas all over the world other police forces and social service personnel undergo lengthy professional sensitivity training in intercultural relations.

Addressing Educational Grievances

As is well known, South Africa uses segregated educational institutions at all levels for its four racial groups, regardless of shared languages and cultures. This is in keeping with the forced separation of groups in residential areas and in political rights. The intellectual undercurrents of apartheid in the curriculum, particularly in history textbooks, have been amply documented.[9] Poverty is assumed to be the natural state for Blacks. Giving little emphasis to precolonial Africa, the texts mainly describe events in Afrikaner history. Blacks are portrayed as posing problems for the Whites. This colonial and Eurocentric bias presents world history in terms of competing nationalisms. The apartheid indoctrination, however, is no longer based on theories of biological racism, but on the more insidious myth that Whites settled in an empty land, that Black underdevelopment is self-inflicted, and that the conquerors amply deserve their spoils. Added to this is an exaggerated emphasis on cultural differences among Blacks that are said to necessitate separate institutional facilities.

The gross inequality in education merely reflects the larger inequality in life chances. The materially impoverished backgrounds of Black students also severely handicap them in the competition with Whites, as do the many legal barriers. The vastly higher school drop-out rates for Blacks further indicate the vast economic gap between Blacks and Whites. At least 30 percent of Black pupils do not go beyond four years of schooling, and 50 percent drop out at the end of primary school. The educational system does little to compensate for the societal inequality but, rather, reinforces it by a differential allocation of resources along racial lines. The per capita expenditure for Black students is one-tenth that for Whites. As a consequence, teacher-student ratios are much higher in the poorly equipped Black schools than in the vastly better facilities for the other groups. In Black schools, the average teacher-pupil ratio is 1:41, compared to 1:19 for White schools. Class sizes of up to 63 for primary school and 43 at secondary level are common in certain areas.[10]

However, the racial groups are no longer taught different curricula. At the end of secondary school Black students undergo a written examination similar to that given in White schools. Requirements for matriculation exemption are standardized. Blacks, however, take the tests in their second language. Instruction for the first four years is in one of the Black languages, after which, almost without exception, English is adopted. This is done at the behest of the Blacks themselves, who demand to be judged by universal standards. To them, an education in Afrikaans or in their vernacular constitutes an obstacle to the universal credibility expected of education. However, the lower budgets, unqualified teachers, and second-language instruction combine to ensure a much higher failure rate for Blacks than Whites despite similar syllabi. Of 75,000 Blacks sitting for the matriculation examination in 1984, only 50.1 percent passed and only 11.5 percent passed with matriculation exemption.[11]

At the same time, better education ranks first among Black aspirations, especially among parents. Educational credentials are seen as the only feasible key to a better life and at least minimal status in a society in which most other routes for advancement are blocked. The state has had to respond to the

Levels of Education by Racial Group (1980)

	Whites	Blacks
None	15.7%	48.20%
- Std 6	15.1	37.50
Std 6	9.0	6.20
Std 7	6.1	3.00
Std 8	16.9	3.00
Std 9	5.1	0.90
Std 10	19.5	0.80
Diploma + Std 9, 10	8.4	0.35
University degree	4.2	0.05

SOURCE: Adapted from *Financial Mail* (1 February 1985): 53.

political frustrations expressed by Blacks in educational institutions as well as to the economy's need for a more skilled work force. This second factor now dominates the debate over education. It is no longer possible to restrict Blacks to roles as hewers of wood and drawers of water, as the old "Bantu education" policy had planned. The new demand for a work force trained in vocational and technical skills, which the White sector alone can no longer fill, has altered educational priorities. In addition, the strategy of co-opting the relatively privileged urban sector into the system implies higher education for a future Black middle class, who have been envisaged as a bulwark against the rural poor and as a stabilizer of free enterprise against socialist visions.

Both expectations have thus far failed to materialize. The expected depoliticized defense of the status quo by relatively privileged Black students turned into the most politicized and long-lasting school unrest the society has ever experienced. Grievances about authoritarian learning conditions[12] were combined with the much deeper resentment against being second-class citizens and having no future under the new constitution and in the stagnating economy. The prime objects of co-optation, urban educated Blacks with much-sought-after residence and work rights, have turned out to be the most militant rejecters of the imposed racial order and inferior status. Promises of material benefits have so far been unsuccessful in diffusing the feelings of symbolic deprivation.

Projections of Matriculation Passes, 1980 and 2000

	1980		2000	
Whites	49,239	52.5%	43,700	31.0%
Coloreds	7,226	7.7	11,700	8.3
Asians	4,819	5.1	7,700	5.5
Blacks	32,535	34.7	77,900	55.2

SOURCE: Adapted from Charles Simkins, "Society," p. 114.

   This trend toward militancy continues despite increased expenditures on Black education. Unit costs (excluding capital
expenditure) in 1984/85, of R 156 per Black student, R 498
per Colored, R 711 per Indian, and R 1,211 per White student, still show vast discrepancies, but the educational budget
for the first time surpassed military expenditures. Much of
this money, of course, is wasted on duplication of segregated
facilities. Salaries of teachers with the same qualifications,
however, were equalized—but only 24 percent of the total
Black teacher corps of 120,650 in 1982 met the minimum requirements for senior certificates plus professional training.
Most Black teachers were severely underqualified or had no
professional training at all.
   The contradiction in educational policy lies in the economic
need for trained people, which undermines the restrictive
purposes for which the education has been provided. While
the number of White students has remained effectively the
same, in line with the declining White population ratio, the
number of Black students at the various educational institutions has increased rapidly. This increase has not been confined to primary levels. The number of Black students at sec-
ondary-level educational institutions between 1978 and 1983
increased from 467,000 to 678,500, and at tertiary level, from
19,900 to 44,300. The appearance of Black university gradu-
ates in such sizable numbers in the job market is a new phenomenon and distinguishes the South African economy from
its counterparts elsewhere in Africa. An educated class of this
size can no longer accept a lack of political rights even if they
are bribed heavily to do so. It is precisely the achievement of
material equality that enables people to tackle the issues of

political and social inequality. The South African educational system has yet to find an answer to this predicament.

The establishment has diagnosed a crisis of education in South Africa. Various commission reports, notably that of the de Lange Panel, have addressed the crisis no longer in terms of ideological content or curriculum but mainly in organizational terms. Now dominating the debate is how scarce resources should be allocated among the racial groups and how educational administration should be organized most effectively.

The government tends to ignore the political underpinnings of the conflict in education as well as the conflict at large and instead to treat the antagonisms as a management problem. In contrast to this social engineering approach, most Black spokespersons focus on conflicting *interests*. They probe how competing claims can be reconciled through institutionalized *bargaining* and explore how the parties can be *empowered* to participate meaningfully in the bargaining process according to mutually acceptable procedures that bestow *legitimacy* on the policy. The government, however, adopts *manipulation* as its principal technique. It *imposes* solutions. This management perspective basically denies that there are conflicts of interests. The government assumes that attending to the interests of the dominant party also benefits its adversary. Using this assumption, it concentrates on removing obstacles ("agitators") to an unquestioned goal of maintaining consensus. At the same time this educational policy aims at *fragmenting* resistance and *co-opting* useful allies; however, the slightest provocation triggers coercion. While manipulative management of conflict may succeed for a while due to superior resources, it lacks legitimacy and increases costs of domination compared with political incorporation achieved through universal franchise and equal citizenship.

Without equal or integrated schooling, except in private schools, little success can be expected in combating Black educational disadvantages and improving interracial understanding. Currently popular approaches abroad, such as interracial team teaching, peer group teaching, and the buddy system in the United States and Canada, presuppose racially mixed classrooms. The same is true for the private and voluntary "brother-sister program" to facilitate the success of foreign students in West German universities. In South Africa, the latter would quickly be dismissed as unnatural and tokenistic, while no institutional structures exist in which the former could take place in any meaningful way. In this respect it should be most worthwhile to observe the effects private schools in South Africa have on human relations.

In the meantime, public schools aiming at improved interracial contact may do something by promoting meetings between different racial schools for noncompetitive sports activities or in collaboration on projects of mutual interest, to permit experiences of shared goal achievement. Hiring Black teachers to teach White students may prove more valuable in altering stereotypes than Whites teaching Blacks. Youth leadership camps drawing students from a range of schools may also have at least limited success in changing attitudes. All these initiatives are hampered by an overall structural context that would quickly dismiss these efforts as technicist reformism; yet even when the structures change, a revamping of traditional attitudes and interpersonal networks will be needed. Finally, those willing to establish private scholarships could "adopt" a Black student. Larger business enterprises could adopt Black schools in their area and ensure that their facilities are upgraded. Every scholarship that foreign institutions provide, and every foreign treacher who is sent into Black schools, contributes to the equalization of life chances. More than the financial assistance, the direct contact and the expectations and obligations created would make at least a small improvement over the present anonymous hopelessness.

The Style of Accommodation

The consensus that the current South African constitution aims for will always be the result of concessions, not negotiations. Consultation is not identical to bargaining. Since conflict regulation is based on the goodwill of the ruling party, any

concession smacks of paternalism. "It has already been decided to involve Black Local Authorities," declared P. W.
Botha, announcing at the same time a new forum "set up for
them" as proof of a major break from previous policy.[13] Such
unilateral decrees lack the legitimacy that would make them
work. A more effective procedure would be to ask a representative adversary which mechanism its side prefers, and then
bargain about a mutually acceptable compromise or, in the
event of a deadlock, a mutually acceptable arbitration.

If the talks are not to be hopeless from the start, clarity
about the negotiating process seems crucial. Several tested
principles and procedures for successful negotiations are
available. First, negotiations aimed at results rather than mere
posturing would have to begin with *informal contacts* between
the major and most extreme antagonists. Thus, in South Africa the ANC and the government would have to clear contentious issues informally before they were aired formally on a
public platform. Van Zyl Slabbert's warning is apt: "Public re-
jections and postures create additional obstacles for effective
behind-the-scenes horse-trading."[14] Once a minimal consensus emerged and a potential compromise was envisaged, all
other interest groups that could jeopardize an accord must be
brought into the negotiating process. This two-stage approach
seems necessary to protect the credibility of the central parties. If, for example, Pretoria were to attempt to negotiate
seriously with Inkatha first, in the hope that this would then
circumvent the ANC/UDF organizations, Inkatha would be
easily outradicalized and lose legitimacy. Buthelezi's reluctance to yield to Pretoria's vague overtures without firm guarantees about the government's intent demonstrates his grasp
of this principle. The two-stage approach does not imply
lesser importance of center parties or undue recognition of
more radical groups; it merely accepts that the middle groups
can be accommodated within the parameters set by the extreme antagonists without complicating the initial bargaining
by introducing the inevitable leadership competition for
greatest internal legitimacy. It is hard to imagine a more ridic-
ulous statement than the feigned confusion by government

spokesmen: "Among all the competing Black groups, we do not know with whom to negotiate."[15]

Obviously, if both parties are interested in reaching a compromise they will set few preconditions for talks. All too often, before the negotiations have even started, the antagonists list nonnegotiable issues that amount to a virtual negation of the possibility of policy compromises. As long as Pretoria demands that the ANC renounce guerrilla warfare and the ANC in turn insists that all apartheid laws be repealed as preconditions for negotiation, no talks will take place. All contentious items must be on the agenda if any real bargaining is to take place.

It would be helpful if the antagonists were to agree on a mutually trusted third party to chair, mediate the negotiations, and generally act as go-between. However, even if this third party had great legitimacy it would be unlikely to acquire the power of creating binding arbitration. The government in power would erode its claim to sovereignty if it were to agree to such a rational mechanism for conflict regulation. However, once agreement has been fully reached, an outside power can guarantee compliance with the accord through specified incentives and sanctions.

It is of vital importance that the parties to the compromise be able to guarantee the compliance of their constituencies. Only if the government can secure right-wing adherence to the new rules will those rules acquire meaning. Similarly, only if the opposition movements are able to discipline their followers can a new regime achieve stability. Paradoxically, that should give Pretoria a vested interest in having a strong opponent and widely acclaimed Black leadership, rather than a weak and fragmented opposition—the aim of current government policy. The chaos of leaderless and frustrated resistance proves counterproductive to peaceful conflict regulation.

All leaders must be permitted political freedom even if they refuse to profess a humiliating allegiance to the constitutional rules in whose making they had no part. Only if all persons who claim a following can participate freely in the democratic competition can their representativeness be established and the disruption they threaten be contained by mutually binding rules.

The informal contacts of elites in non-governmental institutions facilitate successful accommodation. If elite accommodation is confined to the political realm, without social contact within crucial support groups (universities, professional and business organizations, unions, churches, army, voluntary associations, service clubs, etc.), a deeply politicized distrust is the likely consequence.

The arduous process of reaching an accommodation often proves as important as the ultimate result. This means that racial legislation should be included as part of the agenda for negotiations. Political accommodation is dependent on voluntary social integration. Leaders in a power-sharing arrangement cannot be expected to exercise moderation unless institutional support structures create mutual trust. Although South Africa has made advances in reintegrating segregated institutions, in practice the presence of Blacks is merely token. It is unrealistic to demand that government commit itself beforehand to abolishing apartheid, as the ANC expects. But a public statement of regret about past injustices, an acknowledgment of the need to offer compensation, with an assurance of intent, could ease the situation, as could a temporary ANC truce to test government's intention. In this way both sides could save face and not submit to conditions that amount to prior surrender.

In the wake of criticism of the constitution, Pretoria tentatively began to set up a consultative Black forum or multiracial state council. But it remains an unconventional convention, insofar as the Nationalist administration now tries to solicit Black opinion from outside the established political institutions. The problem is that the few so-called moderate spokespersons approached fear that being seen talking to government will compromise them in the eyes of their own radicalized constituency. Dialogue outside the public spotlight facilitates frank exchanges without the need of posturing, as has been argued, and clarifies the contentious issues as well as the controversial areas of potential compromise. However, an ongoing secret dialogue alienates those excluded and may well discredit the Black participants. Without an open mandate to negotiate, the Black leaders and their presumed followers alike rely on trust. The brokers must constantly renew this fragile relationship by extremist rhetoric that does not necessarily forward the negotiations. The whole process favors the dominant group, which deals individually with those who speak for Blacks and can exploit cleavages and different strategies. The greatest danger of such secret elites and alliances is that an illusionary consensus may emerge whose acceptability has not been tested in open discussion.

In such a situation, few prospects exist for a traditional consociational elite-cartel. Formation of a grand elite coalition of divided segments depends on the grass-roots followers' acceptance of controversial alliances and disappointing compromises. In a traditional hierarchy the leader can rely on unquestioned acceptance of decisions. An attitude of apolitical deference to leaders fosters a fatalistic tolerance of disappointments. Politicization changes this picture. Politicized resentment generally favors the group advocates who demand the unobtainable ultimate, rather than compromising moderates. Extreme demands for sacrifices and the promise of further struggle, with their promised psychological rewards of purity and self-esteem, appeal to the disenchanted. The promises of meager spoils by reformers seldom match the excitement of anticipating utopia. Besides, the South African government has repeatedly discredited moderate counterelites by ignoring their requests.

Consociationalism developed successfully before industrialization in Switzerland, the Netherlands, and Austria, while it failed in Germany because an atomizing and politicizing industrialization had preceded national unification. This wresting of people from their traditional subcultures and thrusting them into the mix of an industrial society changes their experiences and outlooks to such an extent that preindustrial, consociational policy-making is no longer possible. A more democratic means of representation of interests must be found to replace the past reliance on traditional leaders. While any system of mutual group guarantees thus remains a second-best option for the antagonists in a no-win situation, even its chances of success in South Africa recede further the longer a genuine power-sharing compromise is delayed.

The vital question of political prisoners shows how far establishment thinking remains from contemplating real negotiations with a comparatively modest leadership in its jails for acts of sabotage committed twenty-five years ago. Although the liberal opposition and business ritualistically call for the release of all authentic leaders and their inclusion in negotiations, they do not employ whatever clout they have to see that Pretoria complies. This reinforces Pretoria's hard-line stance. Black opinion does not yet figure in these calculations. Instead of using Mandela's release as a gesture of reconciliation and show of goodwill, the government adopts, in the words of a senior official, "a position of high moral ground." The mainstream English sector, worried about marketing and image, pragmatically advocates an even more callous emulation of Russian practices: "He [Botha] should seize the opportunity of Nelson Mandela's illness—before the man dies in prison and all hell breaks loose—and ship him out of the country on a one-way ticket to medical treatment abroad."[16] The government continues to criminalize its major opponent. It equates the ANC with the PLO or with the IRA, with which even the British Labour Party would not speak. However, the false analogy overlooks that the ANC represents the majority sentiment of the population in South Africa. Because it is not an extremist fringe group, it has not yet practiced unrestrained terrorism against White civilians, although a few such incidents have occurred. By rejecting early negotiations as weakness, Pretoria merely incites its opponents to bomb their way to the negotiating table. As many examples in history have proven, those who stubbornly refuse to share power finally end up losing all power.

Reeducating the White Constituency

Many observers doubt that the delicate process of genuine bargaining will succeed in an authoritarian political culture: "White South Africans are too deeply socialized to accept racial dominance rather than inter-racial balancing, reciprocity and cooperation as the normal mode of social and political transactions. The whole principle of accommodating White interests to Black demands (however limited these might be) is alien to the political culture and basic style in White politics."[17] Any ingrained authoritarian and paternalistic habits in White politics can, however, be unlearned. Evidence indicates that soon after apartheid measures have been repealed, many Whites who had expressed opposition will agree with the change. Law-abiding deference to legitimate authority molds White attitudes. Such a hope no longer counts as idealistic optimism when the benefits of genuine bargaining outweigh those of racial dominance. To be sure, sociologists have identified the phenomenon of "cultural lag"—the slowness of adjustment to conflicting objective demands. But using the modern sophisticated techniques of mass manipulation, a political reorientation could be achieved relatively quickly today.

If the neutralization of conflict potential is indeed the primary goal of a technocratic government, then a massive reeducation program for its own constituency should have the highest priority. However, very little is being done in this area. In party political discourse, government spokesmen frequently reinforce traditional doctrines rather than question cherished formulas of the past. In their desire to ward off right-wing challenges they pander to conservative sentiment and portray themselves as steadfast traditionalists. Since careers are at stake in by-elections, the ruling technocrats frequently adopt a defensive stance toward the ideologues. They, as an opposition, can outdo the government in their extremist rhetoric. While in this predicament a certain amount of double-talk can be expected from the ruling party, the deception does backfire by reinforcing traditional views.

As a result, and despite an official departure from tradi-

POLICY IMPLICATIONS 245

tional apartheid ideology, substantial numbers of Whites still endorse the Verwoerdian setup. If the Human Science Research Council's 1984 survey of White, Colored, and Indian political attitudes adequately reflects the national sentiment, the high degree of support for traditional apartheid testifies to the failure of grass-roots political reorientation. Racist indoctrination persists not only among the two right-wing parties but among the Nationalist constituency as well.

A White ideological reorientation cannot be expected unless the all-powerful media undertake deliberate reeducation. However, although the Afrikaans press in many ways explores untrodden paths, it is shackled by its ties to the National Party. To publish a Colored columnist in an Afrikaans paper or use a Black announcer on Afrikaans television is celebrated as a major breakthrough. Above all, Afrikaner audiences receive little exposure to realities of Black experiences and attitudes. Black militancy is caricatured, trivialized, or criminalized, but its causes are not portrayed. For example, instead of giving its readers a taste of Black opposition, during the constitutional debate *Rapport* refused to accept a paid UDF advertisement. The coalitions statement intended "to clarify the UDF's stand on violence" was found by editor Wimpie de Klerk to be "unacceptably sharp" and "pure propaganda." This selective reporting reinforces the false picture of harmony interrupted by minor conflicts caused by agitators with whom a strong government adequately copes.

The state-controlled electronic media embody the height of "consensus" politics, South Africa-style. Like *Pravda* or Moscow television, not once have the supposedly independent commentators ever found it necessary to criticize the government in power. While opposition views are given regular airing in news bulletins as far as necessary to create an aura of impartial fairness, it is television that is clearly the most powerful ideological weapon of the state. In the White referendum in the autumn of 1983, television was massively used to promote a "yes" vote, the size of which surprised even its managers. Television has not, however, been called into service to politically reeducate White South Africans to deracialization.

Afrikaans-Speaking Whites' and English-Speaking Whites' (1,024), Coloreds' (1,242), and Indians' (1,406) Attitudes toward Seven Fundamental Apartheid Structures in March 1984

Apartheid Structure and Population Group	Respondents' Attitudes (%)				
	In Favor	Neutral	Opposed	Uncertain or Do Not Know	Total*
Mixed Marriages Act					
Afrikaans-speaking	78.9	3.8	16.6	0.8	100.1
English-speaking	41.3	15.2	41.3	2.2	100.0
Coloreds	24.6	19.3	45.2	10.8	99.9
Indians	26.9	21.8	47.8	3.6	100.1
Immorality Act					
Afrikaans-speaking	81.3	4.9	13.4	0.4	100.0
English-speaking	37.8	16.5	41.0	4.7	100.0
Coloreds	23.4	16.8	47.4	12.4	100.0
Indians	23.0	22.9	49.4	4.7	100.0
Group Areas Act					
Afrikaans-speaking	76.8	6.1	16.1	1.1	100.1
English-speaking	42.4	15.5	38.4	3.7	100.0
Coloreds	22.8	13.6	54.3	9.4	100.1
Indians	24.9	20.6	51.7	2.8	100.0
Separate Education					
Afrikaans-speaking	90.2	4.2	5.1	0.6	100.1
English-speaking	55.4	13.1	28.3	3.2	100.0
Coloreds	21.1	12.8	56.9	9.2	100.0
Indians	27.8	16.5	52.3	3.5	100.1
Separate Amenities					
Afrikaans-speaking	84.9	5.3	8.1	1.7	100.0
English-speaking	50.5	16.8	30.1	2.7	100.1
Coloreds	10.9	14.1	66.4	8.6	100.0
Indians	19.1	17.9	58.3	4.5	100.0
Black Homelands					
Afrikaans-speaking	89.6	2.6	4.2	3.6	100.0
English-speaking	60.3	10.8	19.7	9.1	99.9
Coloreds	27.1	15.3	37.2	20.4	100.0
Indians	30.0	22.4	33.8	13.9	100.1
Separate Voters' Rolls					
Afrikaans-speaking	92.1	2.6	2.5	2.8	100.0
English-speaking	64.3	11.1	17.7	6.9	100.0
Coloreds	17.7	12.2	53.2	17.0	100.1
Indians	24.5	18.3	45.9	11.3	100.0

*Totals do not always equal 100%, due to rounding.
SOURCE: Human Science Research Council, Institute for Sociological and Demographic Research, Pretoria. Surveys in subsequent years of heightened unrest showed a substantial increase of Whites who believe that the pace of reform is too slow and that political power-sharing is inevitable.

Out of fear of disturbing the ethnic sentiments of a prejudiced audience, the manipulators of consciousness have merely reinforced the status quo. Generally unimaginative and parochial television programs are carefully screened to omit any nonracial political alternatives. What filters through as normal human contact from foreign productions remains of the sterile Hollywood variety, or, at most, reaches the standards of the popular Bill Cosby comedies. The cultural boycott of South Africa by foreign academics, producers, and actors paradoxically aids Pretoria's censorship.

Finally, the reeducation of the ruling constituency cannot be achieved without a radical revision of the school curriculum. A realistic historical account of conquest and colonization should be substituted for the current Afrikaner ethnocentrism. The image of Blacks as pawns and victims in imperial power games must be supplemented with insights into the nature of resistance and the causes for counter-mobilization. Professional, intergroup-oriented teacher training could eliminate the parochial focus on group traditions and "master symbols."

According to Johanna du Preez, a communications lecturer at the University of South Africa, the myths promoted by the biased textbooks include: authority ought not to be questioned; Afrikaners have a special relationship with God; as an isolated and afflicted minority, the Afrikaner is threatened and has to rely on military ingenuity; South Africa as the economic leader on the continent has a God-given development task to fulfill.[18] Leonard Thompson's seminal *Political Mythology of Apartheid* traced the historical background of those powerful collective fables as the Covenant and laid bare their function in the mobilization of the *volk*. Although much of the ethnic fervor has waned, it has not been replaced with a critical education, aimed at individual autonomy in making sense of a bewildering reality. Instead rote learning and spoon-feeding remain the norm, resulting all too often in "intellectual parrots" full of information but geared toward conformity.

Conclusion:
Prospects for an
Evolutionary Transition

DESPITE THE FORMIDABLE OBSTACLES, on various levels, to a fundamental transition, there are reasons to hope for a more peaceful resolution in South Africa than in other divided societies. This realistic hope is founded in four distinct features of the South African conflict. First, economic interdependence in a resource-rich country gives all groups a stake in accommodation. Unlike the Middle Eastern situation, the South African conflict is not fundamentally over values, but over privilege and power. These material and political interests are open to compromise, unlike religious definitions of absolute truth. Race constitutes an invidious distinction that can be discarded when it becomes dysfunctional.

Second, South Africa does not represent a colonial conflict, which can only be solved by the departure or defeat of an alien conqueror; African nationalism recognizes Afrikaner nationalism, and vice versa. The terms of coexistence, not the domination of one over the other, are the points of contention.

Third, despite the militant rhetoric, the ideological differences between Black and White are not as rigid as the color classification suggests. Common Christian values and a common Westernized consumerism engender similar aspirations. The two main organized Black opposition movements, the ANC and Inkatha, do not espouse socialism.[1]

Finally, an ethnic technocracy has begun to perceive the rising costs of apartheid domination and is engaged in modifying its control through reform. Even a Conservative Party in power could only delay but not resist a powerful capitalism that now insists on changes in stabilization policies. These reforms develop their own dynamic and have unintended consequences outside planned control.

Liberation in the emotional sense it is not. But technocratic reform accumulates small-scale changes that may in the end make liberation considerably different from the way it is traditionally perceived. Under the pressure of unionized and politicized subjects, the counter-revolution from above may well ameliorate the political alienation by hastening deracialization and political incorporation.

Technocratic liberation aims at eliminating the status inconsistencies of formalized racial classification by replacing it with class stratification. If successful, that action would increase the intra-group conflicts and further minimize the racial distinctions, particularly between Whites, Indians, and Coloreds. A class system would bring South Africa nominally in line with other Western societies. Only dogmatists can maintain that such progress is not worthwhile when compared with the system of apartheid. Whether South Africa's social engineering will achieve its end still hangs in the balance. Much depends on the choices of political leadership on both sides. Neither accommodation nor escalating confrontation is inevitable.

A widespread myth has it that the future will essentially be a continuation of the past: just as the Sharpeville emergency and the 1976/77 upheaval were eventually brought under control, so the revolt of the mid 1980s will abate.[2] This cyclic theory of "unrest," in which violent "tremors" with different "epicenters" shake the country like natural disasters, overlooks at least six distinct differences between the 1980s revolt and the Soweto upheaval nine years earlier. First, many more adults are now involved alongside the township youth. Second, the revolt has penetrated into the countryside, with little-known locations in the Cape and Orange Free State becoming centers of violent protest. Third, the widespread and continuous upheaval has necessitated the use of the military and of emergency legislation to combat the revolt. Fourth, the 1980s revolt has a more political and revolutionary thrust. Endemic general frustration has exacerbated specific grievances. Organized internal dissent has fused with externally based efforts, whereas in 1976/77 the ANC was surprised by the militancy of the students, which it tried to harness only afterward. Fifth, the 1980s revolt exposed Black class divisions by making the nascent African middle class the prime target. It occurred during a severe fiscal crisis of the state that eroded the cooptation policy of the urban insiders. As one analyst observed: "A lumpenproletariat, the unemployed and unemployable, seem now to be the driving force behind the unrest."[3] And, sixth, in contrast to 1976/77, powerful labor organizations now exist that can give the revolt organizational clout and political muscle. Coercive military power cannot secure individual productivity or prevent consumer and industrial action.

In sum, there is a new quality to the opposition that technocratic planning could not anticipate. It has exposed the limits of manipulability for important sections of the Black population. For them, the socialization for patience has ended. Fanonesque notions of cleansing through confrontation, of exorcizing colonial degradation through martyrdom, have emerged. The barbarous wrath unleashed against in-group members deflects resentment against the unassailable outgroup. The ANC has in consequence experienced a dramatic influx of recruits. Its diplomatic defeat at Nkomati turned into a psychological victory at home. There is no longer any possibility of leaving the movement out of political reform; the success of reform, as well as township stability, now depends on the legalization and incorporation of the ANC.

This greatly changed situation demands far-reaching responses both by the state and by the employers. It has undermined past efforts at depoliticization by technocratic reformers. The attempt at gradual African political inclusion via ethnic states and third- or second-tier local administrative institutions will have to be abandoned in favor of central state representation. Incorporation cannot be confined to powerless local-level politics and meaningless "own affairs." These questions will be raised at the political center that technocratic reform had hoped to neutralize and depoliticize through manipulative consensus politics. In short, the conflict has moved beyond concessions which can no longer assuage.

New formulae for stability have emerged: a common citizenship with universal franchise, though not necessarily in a winner-take-all Westminster system: proportional representation of parties, based on self-association instead of imposed racial origin; an undivided, not necessarily centralist, but federal state. It is likely that the common anti-apartheid stances of a strategically divided opposition will be replaced by an even more divisive debate about the nature of democratic socialism in South Africa.

Many analysts have noted the mutual misjudgments of the opponent's strength in South Africa. If both sides do not realize the possibility of an indefinite period of "violence without victory," negotiations are unlikely. As long as one side thinks it can neutralize its antagonist it need not be concerned about compromises. Hermann Giliomee has observed, "The most serious failing is the inability of each side to assess the other's real strength, leading to a frightful inability to embark on constructive thinking and courageous compromise."[4] Pretoria believes that it can repress or manipulate the opposition, particularly the ANC. In reality, the very act of repression has imbued the organization with an aura of mystique and purity. Imprisoned or banned, its leaders can do no wrong and are not compromised by daily controversies. Purity is the power of the powerless.

There is a similar underestimation of White intransigence on the part of foreign liberals and the international left. Naive speculations abound regarding the imminent collapse of the regime: "The isolation of the White minority could crack its willingness to resist at some unpredictable but not so distant moment."[5] Hope is based on a "general insurrection" that would sweep the minority out of power as the Shah in Iran fell unexpectedly under the pressure of street forces and a deserting army. But South Africa is not a personal autocracy that suffers from uncertain loyalties of its security apparatus. Neither the isolation of a feudal dynasty nor the religious fanaticism of its opponent characterizes the conflict; rather, an ethnically mobilized group clings to power at all costs. At the core of this determination lie the perceptions that the Afrikaner can only survive as a group, or race; that this survival must be in South Africa, as the only country he can call home; and that greater repression as well as concessions or negotiations, if necessary, but not total abdication of power, can best ensure this survival. Any collapse of the will to rule would presuppose a substantial dilution of Afrikaner group feelings into individual interest calculations. While this process of de-ethnicization has been underway ever since Afrikanerdom achieved power, the formidable legacy of mobilized ethnicity still blocks any individualistic, nonracial form of government and is likely to continue to sabotage liberal, universalistic political incorporation for a long time to come.

The intellectual ferment in Afrikanerdom has, however, never been greater. An establishment pillar, the Human Sciences Research Council in Pretoria, in 1985 released a thorough report on Intergroup Relations that flies in the face of government policy.[6] To implement these recommendations, the government would have to dismantle the Population Registration and Group Areas Act. In Stellenbosch, the academic cradle of the tribe, student representatives seek contact with their African peers in the ANC in defiance of the state. Behind the church facade of unity, intense ideological debates take place. New and thriving political journals such as *Die Suid-Afrikaan* match their best international counterparts in innovative soul-searching and sophisticated analysis.

If this ferment succeeds in stopping the escalation of violence, the state would have to change its central political paradigms in three respects: (1) it would have to agree to real power-sharing, not just concessions but negotiations with the implied recognition of African claims; (2) it would have to abandon ascribed group boundaries in favor of individual rights or rights of self-chosen groups; and (3) it would have to make a serious attempt to ameliorate the material inequalities resulting from the political imbalance. This would lead to a lowering of the White standard of living, particularly in a stagnating economy. As has frequently been pointed out, state actors react and rarely make such necessary "conceptual leaps."[7] Yet the resolve of technocratic Afrikaners to come to terms with reality must also not be underestimated. However, despite all the debate, the core of Nationalist supporters—the police and army, as well as the extreme right—will not defect for some time from traditional notions of supremacy and racial group rights. An escalation of violence thus would result in a no-win situation with ever higher costs to both sides and to the South African economy as a whole.

In this "permanent transition" the interests of South African business are most threatened. It is to this class actor that an analysis of the future must turn. In the absence of compromising possibilities between two opposing nationalisms, can business break the deadlock? A prediction about the role of business rests on two assumptions: first, that South African capital does not constitute a monolithic group with identical interests, not even in the same branches; second, that technological and sociopolitical changes have brought about new interest configurations that have fundamentally altered historical relationships between specific economic and political actors. At least three major employer groups must be distinguished: agriculture, mining, and manufacturing.[8]

White agriculture historically flourished through the political destruction of a viable African competition, an artificially cheap labor supply, generous access to state funds for irrigation and for recouping losses due to weather, and state price guarantees. Until the mechanization of farming in the 1970s, White farmers needed to "tie down" their Black labor through a feudal system of tenancy, since they were competing with more attractive urban employment. With the large-scale displacement of labor by capital-intensive farming and the growth of the tenant population, the landowners' interests shifted to elimination of the feudal legacy. Impoverished Bantustans, however, proved increasingly incapable of absorbing the surplus workers, while influx control slowed the urbanization process. White farmers split in their support for traditional apartheid. Many maize farmers in the Transvaal support the conservative ideologues after being dropped from state protection; others worry about their threatened export markets and back Botha's sham reforms; and the sugar farmers of Natal advocate political power-sharing with Buthelezi in a multiracial administration of the region, in order to stall the government's land consolidation policy.

In mining, divisions have arisen in several ways. Besides the differences in geological productivity of mines, there have been several common developments that have led to divergent responses by the mining companies. Faced with a serious strike threat in the summer of 1985, they again departed from the past unity of the chamber in wage policies. The compound system constitutes a major cause of chronic labor unrest. The high turnover costs of migrant labor, together with the shift to skill-intensive technologies, makes a higher ratio of domestic laborers who reside in family units on the mines more cost-advantageous—though still more expensive than foreign migrants. Higher Rand earnings facilitated wage increases pressed for by an increasingly stronger union. Above all, White workers have continuously lost political influence after the purge of the HNP from the Nationalist Party in the early seventies and the split of the party in 1982. The long-standing job color bar has now all but collapsed, with the last White privilege, that of blasting reservations, being removed.

Manufacturing felt the rising cost of apartheid most, but traditionally needed the restrictive color bar least. Skill shortages stifled growth. Overpaying White workers contributed to a high inflation rate. A stagnant domestic consumer market limited economies of scale, while external hostility affected expansion beyond South Africa's borders, disrupted foreign capital flows, and undermined confidence. A costly decentralization policy taxed the urban sector, but mainly benefited new investors. Above all, the political instability eroded labor relations and caused low productivity.

In the predicament of a degenerating economy and inflammable security situation, business—assuming it can act concertedly and with clout—can choose any of three options. First, it can support the government's repression in the hope of restoring law and order through coercion. Capital could even push for a reformist military dictatorship that would equally repress right-wing resistance to nonracial but capitalist incorporation. Such a stance would confirm the Marxist notions about the collusion between capital and state in coping with an organic crisis whose alternative is socialism. Restoring order by all available means is, after all, the first reaction when the security of daily routine is threatened.

However, the success of such a reaction remains doubtful, because it would increase Black alienation and international isolation. It would fall short of its promise. Even without sophisticated weapons, mass rage has the capacity to wreak havoc in an advanced industrial economy. A few youths can paralyze highways at night; they can temporarily cut the vital railway and bus links between the townships and cities; they can invade shopping centers and use arson as a weapon of general destruction. If the employed joined in deliberate industrial sabotage, the economy, though it could not be brought to a standstill, could be crippled seriously without the state or employers having effective coercive countermeasures. Sooner or later the resistance will have access to more and better weapons. Pressure to abandon all current restraints or counter-violence will likely be successful. Leadership aspirants face the choice of either getting ahead of township sentiment or being bypassed by more militant contenders. The ANC old guard, far from harvesting the fruits of unemployed rage, is in danger of following rather than leading the militancy. Much greater intraracial strife between feuding Black factions will occur. This will not be to the overall benefit of minority rule, since its scale and intensity are inevitably spilling over into the plants and unions, where harmony is needed. Once bombs go off in factories and discothéques, planes are hijacked, and public figures are assassinated, a single minor symbolic event can trigger chain reactions on both sides that none of the more responsible leadership can control. Once this threshold has been passed, negotiations for power-sharing come too late. The option then will be surrender or "victory": a fight to the death. The capital outflow, emigration, and destruction will be on such a scale that the country will have great difficulty recovering, regardless of who eventually comes out on top.

For business profits, this represents the worst scenario, although the sentiment of its managers may squarely back the forces of law and order. A modern economy simply cannot be run without a minimal identification of workers with their task, incentives for productivity, and opportunities for upward mobility—all presupposing a basic contentment with living conditions in general.

In short, an equilibrium of violence can exist in the separate service economies of Lebanon but not in an interdependent South Africa, where Blacks and Whites have to work together in the same place. A balance of high-level use of force does not allow for the operation of a technologically vulnerable, cooperative mode of production. A modern economy ceases under these conditions. South Africa would be further cut off from its global connections and commercial lifelines. The quality of life declines dramatically in a true siege economy.

To pack up and relocate elsewhere remains the option for some sectors. Major capital sectors in South Africa, however, are bound to the land by resources and structural investments that are not portable. It is these sectors (mining, real estate, local manufacturing, even commercial agriculture) that must consider the second option: to come to terms with the revolution by striking an early deal. Business could actively finance the liberation on the understanding that the basic socioeconomic structure would remain intact. African nationalist aspirations would be met by gradually replacing the Afrikaner bureaucracy, including the parastatals, with nonracial, e.g., African, control. In supporting the exchange of Afrikaner political power with African political hegemony, business would enter into a new alliance but save its major interests. Profit, after all, does not depend on color or ideology but on stability. A capitalist African Azania with international legitimacy would be the industrial powerhouse of the continent, with a large underdeveloped domestic and outside market at its doorstep.

Since the ANC, by its own definition, does not constitute a socialist movement and to all intents and purposes represents an aspiring but hitherto excluded middle class, such a historic compromise among big capital, small traders, and bureaucrats would not founder on class antagonisms. To be sure, the aspiring Black "bourgeoisie" would not be enticed to capitalism without capital, but, like Afrikaners before them, they could realistically hope to acquire their share of capital through control of the state. After all, the demand of the Freedom Charter for the nationalization of key industries is already half met, considering the large state-controlled sector of the economy that they would take over.

Another factor makes the ANC option attractive to business as a whole: the ANC could be expected to restore order in the townships. Only a widely legitimate mass organization can re-socialize youth who have increasingly been thriving on anarchy. Without such disciplining influence, a capitalist work ethic would be unlikely to prevail. Finally, the ANC in power would hold in check the growing anti-capitalist "ultra-leftist elements" (AZAPO, etc.). Since these tasks will probably involve strong-arm tactics rather than gentle democratic persuasion, business is unlikely to be much concerned about civil rights violations under the new regime. In fact, rather than support a right-wing White military it would be inclined to back nationalist Black military power to achieve stability.

Yet business is likely only to flirt with this second option. Its major deficiency lies in the fact that it provides neither direction nor prescription for how a stubborn Afrikaner hegemony can be dislodged peacefully. Capitalist cost-benefit calculations fail with power centers such as the bureaucracy and the security forces. Far from losing in a confrontation, the army, for example, gains status during war. Unlike the Israeli defense force, which functions as an integrating institution, the Afrikaner-led South African army indoctrinates its conscripts to view all Blacks as potential targets. Such entrenched interests and institutional practices are rarely swayed by rational profit calculations. In addition, business itself cannot be sure about the outcome of free political activity. It views the com-

munist elements with the ANC with unease. Would free Black
leaders calm, or incite, the townships? Can assurances about
free enterprise be trusted?

Business would have had few problems in concluding such
a deal with Buthelezi's pro-enterprise Inkatha. In Natal, the
White establishment is engineering a Zulu-dominated, multiracial administration. Buthelezi has become a powerful regional leader. However, he does not command much loyalty
among urban Blacks outside his ethnic group. He could not,
therefore, ensure stability at a national level in the face of the
growing ANC/UDF hostility toward him. Only in the event of
an ANC-Inkatha reconciliation could Buthelezi, as the leader
of the strongest ethnic group, gain more broadly based, nationwide acceptance.

Finally, open support for the ANC would harm the working
relationship with the Pretoria government, without certainty
about the success of the alternative. Hence, business will be
reluctant to play the leading role in paving the way for a takeover. Instead, it will defer to government and urge negotiations about power-sharing that are bound to fail under present government auspices. So far Pretoria has not been forced
even to contemplate serious negotiations, because it is still far
too powerful to have to concede vital terrain of control.

This scenario makes the third option more attractive for
long-term business planners: to support the unions as an alternative route to stability. Strange as it may sound, in the
unique South African situation, unions and capital have more
in common than the adversary principle suggests. The major
Black unions have kept aloof from political affiliations and
operate with a different agenda from that of the ANC or the
protesting UDF middle-class aspirants. The democratically
organized unions' main thrust is toward extracting optimal
economic benefits and improvement of working conditions
from employers for their members. Unions do not wish to
make the country ungovernable, lose foreign investments, or
expropriate all private enterprise—at least for the time being.
At present, unions are ambivalent partners of reform rather
than revolution. As Ken Owen has neatly juxtaposed: "Re-

form requires an economy that can deliver to all communities the promise of a better life in a new kind of state. If revolution requires the breakdown of administration, reform requires effectiveness. If revolution requires schools to be closed and drains to be clogged, reform requires both to be open. If revolution requires destruction of the nascent Black middle class, reform requires the expansion and protection of that middle class."[9] Unions currently oscillate occasionally but clearly tilt toward reform. Yet they are not tainted by collaboration. They enjoy high legitimacy. Above all, they are rooted in real, not questionable, organizational strength. All political tendencies defer to workers' rights.

Can business afford a union strategy? Can it overcome its traditional "boss-in-the house" stance? The dismal record on the employers' side leaves much scope for improving management-union relationships. The profits in Rand of the export sector have risen to such heights after the decline of the currency that the companies could easily afford generous wage settlements. Recalcitrant employers could be brought into line through legal action in the Industrial Court. Dealing with unions allows progressive companies to forge ahead rather than business as a whole being hamstrung by its most reactionary parts. Under free-enterprise rules, government would find it difficult to interfere in the autonomous business-union prerogatives. However, to make the relationship work, employers would have to extend their protection of union activists outside the workplace. In short, a capitalist hegemony would compete with an ethnic hegemony; an industrial citizenship would temporarily coexist with the denial of full political citizenship.

Such a situation would be bound to create major contradictions and could not last. A seat in the boardroom would hardly substitute for a place in parliament, assuming South African corporations were to adopt the German co-determination model. Even this limited co-optation of unions was fiercely resisted by German industry and only instituted through the political muscle of labor parties. Nevertheless, the theoretical possibility should not be excluded that "township socialists will

change once they administer pension funds," as one enlightened company director explained. The union strategy requires a substantial price. But in the quest for political incorporation the unions, controlled from below, represent a safer
and more manageable bet for capital than the more unpredictable political organizations, controlled from above. The
militancy of the union is unlikely to fall behind the militancy
of the political movements, which will surely attempt to use
unions for their own ends. But unions know how to manage
this through shop-floor democracy. Business, on the other
hand, can deal with union militancy on its own ground and by
rules established in genuine bargaining, rather than imposed
by government or other outside actors. Whether business will
have the foresight to cope wisely with this challenge remains
to be seen. The future of South Africa will be decided in the
interplay among the three options sketched.

The possibility exists that with the rise of costs, splits within
the heterogeneous business camp will make it impossible to
act rationally. The ability of capitalism to recognize its long-
term interest is frequently overrated. The phrase "disorganized capitalism" aptly summarizes reactions to crisis.[10] South
African business—for a long time on the margin of political
decision-making—has not yet developed a political style and
corporate culture conducive to concerted planning or lobby-
ing. It was only when political events directly intruded into
business operations and the costs of apartheid could no longer
be passed on to someone else that business accepted its political role. When the immediate crisis is over South African business would willingly retreat again into its shell. Without the
township violence and the outside pressure the reform lobby
would not have come into being. The condemnation of political violence therefore must not overlook this trigger effect
that makes the irrationality rational. Only a year before the
revolt began, South African business interests, with a few ex-
ceptions, enthusiastically backed Botha's constitutional reforms, which largely set off the new resistance. Two years earlier in the Carleton and Good Hope conferences of the
business elite with government, the new pact between advo-

cates of technocratic reform and free enterprise was formally endorsed without a single dissenting voice. The free-enterprise doctrine alone will certainly not allow Blacks to become part of an economic system where entrenched elites command the monopoly of capital and resources. It would indeed mainly depend on the clout of unions to insist tenaciously on a social democracy in continuous unspectacular struggles on many sites. Some long-term economic redistribution through profit-sharing schemes, inheritance taxes, and higher corporate rates, as well as an optimal welfare system, would inevitably have to accompany formal political equality. Such redistribution is bound to be resisted fiercely by entrenched power. However, for those who calculate rationally, there is no better option than accommodation.

Since powerful local and international capital interests are dependent on the Black alienated majority, they will, in the long term at least, choose political pacification rather than unfeasible repression. The predisposition for such a historic compromise, if necessary at the expense of an intransigent Afrikaner nationalism, no doubt exists on all sides. The continuous revolt against false reform galvanizes reforms to prevent further revolts.

With the pseudo-constitutional reforms propagated by the National Party, the process of gradual abolition of apartheid has itself become discredited. The government's offer to negotiate under preconditions and only with moderate Black leaders adds fuel to a false expectation among Blacks of seizing power rather than sharing it. How, then, can this political and constitutional stalemate be broken?

Government could pave the way for legitimate power-sharing through legislation enabling a constitutional assembly, just as free trade-union activity was allowed in the late 1970s. All adult South Africans could elect a constitutional assembly on a one-person-one-vote basis and a common voters' roll in a free political contest. This single act would restore the legitimacy of the political process and the resulting constitution, to be tested in a subsequent referendum. The nonracial voting—on the basis of proportional representation—for candidates

to the constitutional assembly would guarantee that all interests be fairly represented in this "national convention"; its
members would be vested with an unquestionable democratic
legitimacy rather than all being drawn from the existing leadership of hostile camps; the strength of each competing claim
would have been clearly demonstrated; and the likely emergence of working coalitions around constitutional agreements
would promise similar outcomes under the new legitimate
rules. Invited outside observers with specific mandates could
monitor the fairness of the electoral process, including media
time and election expenses.

All sides would save face. The ANC would not have to dis-
arm but would be hard put to reject participating peacefully
in the democratic exercise. Pretoria would still be in control
until the new constitution had passed its major tests. After all,
the government would have set the terms by initiating the process. What at present may appear as voluntary suicide for the
powerholders may prove indeed their only rational way of
survival in light of worse alternatives.

Alas, the old question returns: do ruling groups merely
react to challenges when it is too late? From Bismarck's innovative social security measures to Disraeli's land reform, conservative elites have at times anticipated the rising costs of traditional policies and initiated progressive reforms. Most often,
however, ruling groups had to be forced into defeat or compromise by the demonstrated power of their adversary. Pretoria so far refuses to negotiate seriously, because it is not yet
compelled to do so. However, many trends and forces have set
the scene for the final demise of apartheid. It may be a far less
traumatic transformation than is generally predicted. Among
the promising indicators is the mixture between pragmatic
rationality, moral bankruptcy, and ideological exhaustion
among substantial numbers of the Afrikaner technocracy.
The widening split between economic and political powerholders reinforces the confusion about appropriate strategies
in light of the force increasingly being exerted by unions,
township revolts, and external pressure. Growing numbers of
otherwise conservative Whites are becoming reconciled to a

South Africa without apartheid. It largely depends on White policy choices whether "things have to get worse before they get better." Legal deracialization alone, however, is unlikely to substitute for substantial economic transformation in combination with a new nonracial culture that would heal the deep wounds of long-term degradation and injustice. The dismantling of apartheid will have to be followed by the creation of a true social democracy if South African capitalism does not want to drown in the wake of the inevitable post-apartheid aspirations.

Appendix
Chronology of
Events in South Africa

B.C. Ancestors of the San ("Bushmen") and Khoikoi ("Hottentots") inhabit South Africa

A.D. Bantu-speaking people settle in South Africa

1488 Diaz "discovers" the Cape

1652 The Dutch East India Company sends Jan van Riebeeck to establish trading station at the Cape

1658 Slaves imported from West Africa and Asia

1778 Eastern boundary of the Cape settlement established at the Fish River

1779–1850 Clashes between the Xhosa and Afrikaners ("Boers") over the Fish River territory

1795 Britain occupies the Dutch Cape Colony

1803 Dutch regain the Cape by treaty

1806 Britain reoccupies the Cape

1815 Boer (Slagtersnek) rebellion on frontier

1816–1828 Zulu kingdom is formed by Shaka; warfare among African nations

1820 Arrival of first 5,000 British settlers

1829 University of Cape Town opens

1834 Slavery abolished by British parliament

1836 The "Great Trek": five thousand Boers ("Voortrekkers") leave the Cape Colony

1838 Boers defeat the Zulu at the battle of Blood River after massacre of Boers under Dingaan; Republic of Natal founded

1843 Natal proclaimed British colony; Voortrekkers leave

1845–1875 Under British colonial rule segregation is introduced throughout Natal

1852–1854 Britain recognizes South African Republic and Orange Free State as independent Afrikaner states

1853 "Representative government" granted to Cape Colony with qualified franchise for non-Whites

1860 Indentured laborers brought from India to Natal to work on sugar plantations

1867 Diamonds mines opened in Griqualand West

1868 Britain annexes Basutoland (Lesotho)

1870 Diamond mines opened at Kimberley; within years the diggings employ 45,000 workers

1877 Transvaal proclaimed British territory

1879 Zulu rebellion under Cetewayo; Britain occupies Zululand

1880–1881 First Boer War; Afrikaners in Transvaal regain independence

1884 Germany annexes Namibia

1886 Gold mines opened on the Witwatersrand; within a decade the mines employ 100,000; Johannesburg founded

1893 Mahatma Gandhi arrives in South Africa

1894 Natal Indian Congress founded

1895 Jameson Raid into Transvaal

1899–1902 War between Britain and the two Afrikaner Republics

1904 Chinese workers imported for the Transvaal gold mines

1906 Bambata rebellion against poll tax in Natal suppressed by British troops

1907–1913 Gandhi's first campaign of passive resistance ("Satyagraha")

1910 The Cape Colony, Transvaal, and Orange Free State join to form the Union of South Africa; the constitution of the Union preserves restrictions on Black rights in a self-governing British dominion; Louis Botha first Prime Minister

1912 African National Congress (ANC) is founded

1913 African landownership limited to reserves by Natives Land Act

1914–1919 The Union of South Africa fights alongside Britain in the First World War against Afrikaner opposition

1920 Forty thousand African miners strike

1922 General strike called, followed by imposition of martial law and official segregation

1925 Afrikaans recognized as second official language

1930 Enfranchisement of European women; Afrikaners form secret Broederbond

1936 Native Trust and Land Act increases the area of native African reserves but eliminates native African voting rights

1939–1945 South Africa joins Allies in the Second World War

1946 Sixty thousand African miners strike, closing mines; laws passed to outlaw Black strikes and to segregate union organizing

1948 D. F. Malan's National Party achieves power, codifying segregation by race (apartheid)

1949 Rioting in Durban by Africans against Indians; 142 killed, 1,087 injured

1950 Group Areas Act to establish residential segregation

1951 Legislation introduced to disfranchise Colored people in the Cape; Bantu Authorities Act establishes Bantustans

1952 ANC and South African Indian Congress initiate passive resistance against apartheid

1958 Treason trial; 20,000 march to protest the extension of pass laws to women; Verwoerd becomes Prime Minister

1960 Sharpeville massacre; Unlawful Organisations Act is passed, banning the ANC and the PAC; Pondoland uprising; state of emergency declared

1961 South Africa becomes a Republic and is expelled from Commonwealth; sabotage begins; laws passed allowing detention without trial

1964 Rivonia trial against ANC leadership under Mandela

1972–1973 One hundred thousand Black workers strike in Natal; Bantu Labor Relations Amendment Act passed in an attempt to stop the growth of the Black union movement

1975 Mozambique and Angola become independent

1976–1977 At least 575 people are killed in Soweto uprising and other townships

1980 Increasingly more sophisticated sabotage against government installations; unions are legalized

1983 United Democratic Front and National Forum formed to boycott racial tricameral parliament; Whites vote 66 percent in favor of new constitution

1984 Strikes climb to 469, involving over 180,000 workers; new constitution gives Asian and Colored peoples limited participation, with racially separate houses for Coloreds, Indians, and Whites; average 20 percent participation of registered Indian and Colored voters; South Africa and Mozambique sign peace pact at Nkomati; Bishop Desmond Tutu is awarded the Nobel Peace Prize

1985 On 21 March (25th anniversary of the Sharpeville massacre) 19 mourners are killed in a funeral procession at Langa; consistent urban resistance; state of emergency declared; currency value declines dramatically

1986 P. W. Botha offers release of Mandela in return for the freedom of two Russian dissidents; political power-sharing and common citizenship in an undivided South Africa promised; students return to school after a year's boycott

Notes

Sources listed in the bibliography are referred to here by author and title. Other citations are given as fully as access to source materials permitted.

Preface

1. Joseph Lelyveld, *Move Your Shadow* (New York: Times Books, 1985), p. 5.
2. Nadine Gordimer, "The Just Cause," *New York Review of Books* 22:17 (7 November 1985): 5.
3. (Frankfurt: Edition Suhrkamp, 1969).
4. (Berkeley: California, 1971).
5. (New Haven: Yale, 1979).

Introduction

1. For a better example of the genre see Leonard Thompson and Andrew Prior, *South African Politics*. Another "reference guide to movements, organizations and institutions" from an orthodox class perspective is Robert Davies, Dan O'Meara, and Sipho Dhlamini, *The Struggle for South Africa*, 2 vols. (London: Zed, 1984). In a preface the Mozambican Minister of Information praises this text as "firmly based on scientific analytical method" and "a reflection of the creativity unleashed by our revolution" (p. xvii).
2. Editorial, *Journal of Contemporary African Studies* 1: 1 (1981).
3. David Yudelman, *The Emergence of Modern South Africa*.
4. Stanley Greenberg, *Race and State in Capitalist Development*; "Ideological Struggles within the South African State," Proceedings of the Conference on Economic Development and Racial Domination, University of the Western Cape, Bellville (8–10 October 1984); and *Legitimating the Illegitimate*, forthcoming.

5. A point made by Wilmot G. James, "The South African State in Transition."

6. R. Johnstone, Review, *Journal of Southern African Studies* 11: 1 (October 1984).

Chapter 1. The Contradictions of Apartheid

1. In 1985, for the first time since the 1913 Land Act, the government has acknowledged the right of specific Blacks to live in a rural area outside the "homelands" and outside designated townships. In the case of the threatened removal of Driefontain and Kwa-Ngema, the Africans not only were allowed to keep the farms they acquired prior to 1913 but extra state-owned land was transferred to them as compensation for land flooded by a new dam. Here fierce resistance culminating in the killing of community leader Saul Mkhize in 1982 successfully combined with the moral pressure that resulted from the written undertaking by three Boer presidents to permit Stuurman (messenger) Ngema to keep the land in perpetuity in payment for his services to the Boer Republic.

2. According to Gerrit Viljoen, the minister in charge, those Blacks who were South African citizens and lost this status when their "homelands" became "independent" will be given the option of regaining their South African citizenship. Citizens of a "homeland" that might become independent in the future will be given the opportunity of maintaining their South African citizenship, thus holding double citizenship (Interview, *Financial Mail*, 30 August 1985, p. 66).

3. William Peterson et al., *Concepts of Ethnicity* (Cambridge, Mass.: Harvard University Press, 1982), p. 25.

4. South African Broadcasting Corporation (14 February 1985).

5. Ibid.

6. Samuel P. Huntington, "Reform and Stability in a Modernizing, Multi-Ethnic Society," p. 13.

7. Michael Banton, *Racial and Ethnic Competition* (Cambridge, Eng.: Cambridge, 1983), p. 397.

8. Sampie Terreblanche, *Sunday Times* (Johannesburg) (13 November 1983).

9. Jan Lombard, *Sunday Times* (Johannesburg) (13 November 1983).

10. James, "The South African State in Transition," p. 15.

11. See, for example, Gavin Relly, the Chairman of Anglo-American Corporation, in *Leadership* 4: 3 (1985): 18.

12. Ibid., p. 13.

13. David Yudelman, *The Emergence of Modern South Africa*.

14. Lawrence Schlemmer, *Black Workers' Attitudes*, p. 21.

15. In "Human Resources," *Leadership SA* (1984–1985): 10.

16. *SA Foundation News* (February 1985).

17. *Financial Mail* (18 January 1985).

18. Merle Lipton, *Capitalism and Apartheid* (Aldershot: Gower, 1985), p. 374. This important treatise against the neo-Marxist contention of collusion between capitalism and apartheid unfortunately was published too late to be fully included in this analysis.

Chapter 2. Ethnicity, Nationalism, and the State

1. Tom Bottomore and Patrick Goode, *Austro-Marxism* (Oxford: Clarendon, 1978), p. 107.

2. Stanley Greenberg has elaborated on the concept of an *ethnic state* in an unpublished paper, "Order and the Ethnic State" (1 March 1982). Unfortunately, Greenberg focuses mainly on labor control and neglects the psychological and security dimensions of ethnic hegemony. Nevertheless, we owe several insights to Greenberg's perceptive discussions, both in this paper and elsewhere, and particularly in his comprehensive *Race and State in Capitalist Development*.

3. Michael Banton, *Racial and Ethnic Competition* (Cambridge, Eng.: Cambridge, 1983).

4. Willem de Klerk, *The Second (R)evolution*, p. 12.

5. Clifford Geertz, "The Integrative Revolution"; Harold R. Isaacs, *The Idols of the Tribe*; P. L. van den Berghe, *The Ethnic Phenomenon*.

6. E. Laclau, *Politics and Ideology in Marxist Theory* (Verso, 1979); Robert Norton, "Ethnicity and Class," *Ethnic and Racial Studies* 7: 3 (July 1984): 426–34.

7. Edna Bonacich, "A Theory of Ethnic Antagonism: The Split Labor Market," *American Sociological Review* 37 (October 1972): 547–59; M. Hechter, "Group Formation and Cultural Division of Labor," *American Journal of Sociology* 84 (1978): 293–318.

8. Gordon Graig, "Outsiders," *New York Review of Books* (13 June 1985).

9. L. Lowenthal and N. Guterman, *Prophets of Deceit*, 2nd ed. (Palo Alto, Ca.: Pacific Books, 1970).

10. John Ogbu, *Minority Education and Caste* (New York: Academic Press, 1978), refers to this type as "autonomous" ethnic groups. However, autonomy suggests a measure of political independence that many self-reliant groups do not possess. Their strength lies more in potential than in actual political autonomy.

11. Arend Lijphart, *Democracy in Plural Societies*.

12. Legitimacy manifests itself in the widespread belief that a government exercises rightful power in its given domain. This popular consent can be gauged empirically by the degree of support such authority enjoys. Majority approval alone, however, does not necessarily constitute legitimacy. The system of political rule must also be considered morally appropriate according to less measurable evaluative criteria. Popular despotisms such as Nazi Germany may have mustered the consent of their people, but clearly remained illegitimate morally.

Legitimation denotes the process that culminates in legitimacy, although the two concepts are frequently used synonymously. Delegitimation occurs when crucial support-groups of a regime defect and change their approval into a search for political alternatives. Such a crisis of legitimacy results when a system fails to fulfill the expectations of new social groups or fails to govern effectively. A legitimation crisis exists when an elite has exhausted its moral, political, and intellectual capital. According to Jürgen Habermas, a legitimation crisis is characterized by the inability of a system to ensure mass loyalty, engender meaning, and integrate disparate interests. Other social scientists, in particular S. M. Lipset, have singled out the effectiveness of regimes—their modernizing, economic performance rather than their extra-material, normative values—as decisive for maintaining authority.

13. After ten years of continuous legal residence, foreigners are theoretically eligible for citizenship. Successful application depends on five further preconditions: command of the German language as determined by a written test, an express commitment to the democratic order of the constitution, absence of a criminal record, proof of adequate housing, and adequate financial means. Even if all these preconditions are fulfilled, the foreigner has no legal claim to citizenship, which is granted at the discretion of officials. Of all eligible foreigners approximately one percent have acquired citizenship. Only six percent say they would like to become German.

14. For a discussion of these trends in Canada see Kogila Moodley, "Canadian Multiculturalism as Ideology," *Ethnic and Racial Studies* 6: 3 (July 1983): 320-31.

15. Anya Peterson Royce, *Ethnic Identity Strategies of Diversity* (Bloomington: Indiana University Press, 1982).

16. Heribert Adam and Hermann Giliomee, *Ethnic Power Mobilized.* For a Marxist analysis of this process, particularly interethnic changes, see Dan O'Meara, *Volkskapitalisme*, and for a liberal interpretation, David Welsh, "The Political Economy of Afrikaner Nationalism."

Interestingly, among the 3,000 South Africans from all groups who earned more than R 100,000 a year in 1980, 2,212 had Afrikaans as their home language; 548, English; 98, both official languages; and 82, other mother tongues. At the same time, those in the middle-income bracket (R 15,000 or more) were predominantly English-speaking, while the lowest group reflects almost exactly the population ratio. The statistics indicate the rapid stratification that took place with state patronage in the once relatively homogeneous Afrikaner section. In the absence of state patronage, it is not surprising that only forty-seven Blacks were in the top income bracket, earning more than R 100,000 (*SA Digest,* 17 May 1985, and *The Citizen,* 11 May 1985).

17. Heribert Adam, "Racial Capitalism vs. Capitalist Nonracialism," *Ethnic and Racial Studies* 7: 2 (May 1984); Michael Savage, "An Anatomy of the South African Corporate Economy: Ownership, Control and the Interlocking Directorate."

18. Kenneth W. Grundy, *Soldiers without Politics.*

19. D. T. Moodie, *The Rise of Afrikanerdom*; André du Toit and Hermann Giliomee, *Afrikaner Political Thought, 1780–1850.*

20. Paul Brass, ed., *Ethnic Groups and the State* (New York: St. Martin's Press, 1985).

21. Leo Kuper and M. G. Smith, eds., *Pluralism in Africa.*

22. Gail M. Gerhart, *Black Power in South Africa*; Heribert Adam, "The Rise of Black Consciousness in South Africa"; Sam C. Nolutshungu, *Changing South Africa.*

23. T. Karis and G. M. Carter, eds., *From Protest to Challenge*; T. G. Karis, "Revolution in the Making: Black Politics in South Africa"; Tom Lodge, *Black Politics in South Africa.*

24. Theodor Hanf et al., *South Africa: The Chances of Peaceful Change.*

Chapter 3. Conflicts in White Politics

1. Philip H. Frankel, *Pretoria's Praetorians.*

2. *Star Weekly* (9 October 1982).

3. Ibid.

4. *New York Times* (25 July 1982).

5. For a comprehensive though often vague discussion of the military's mental map in South Africa, see Frankel, *Pretoria's Praetorians.*

6. Marinus Wiechers, *Sunday Times* (9 October 1983).

7. Peter Lambley, *The Psychology of Apartheid.*

8. *The Economist* (22 May 1982).

9. For the making of a genuine "Afrikaner liberal" see the fasci-

nating analytical autobiography by F. van Zyl Slabbert, *The Last White Parliament* (Johannesburg: Jonathan Ball, 1985).

10. *Sunday Tribune* (30 June 1985).

Chapter 4. Conflicts in Black Politics

1. *Star Weekly* (5 September 1983).
2. Quail Commission Report. For a summary see South African Institute of Race Relations, *Race Relations Survey 1980* (Johannesburg: SAIRR, 1981), pp. 404-5.
3. *Cape Times* (22 July 1983).
4. Fatima Meer, "Change in South Africa: It's Just a Mirage," *Post* (27–30 July 1983).
5. A. Rajbansi, Chairman, South African Indian Council, *The Leader* (16 September 1983).
6. R. Southall, "Buthelezi, Inkatha and the Politics of Compromise."
7. L. Schlemmer, "The Stirring Giant: Observations on the Inkatha and Other Black Political Movements in South Africa"; John Kane-Berman, "Inkatha: The Paradox of South African Politics."
8. *Financial Mail* (17 September 1982): 1382.
9. *Reality* (November 1984): 36.
10. Ibid.
11. Buthelezi, letter to O. Tambo (20 October 1984).
12. Theodor Hanf et al., *South Africa: The Chances of Peaceful Change*, pp. 318–61.
13. J. Brewer, "The Membership of Inkatha in Kwa Mashu," p. 133.
14. Buthelezi, speech, King Shaka Day, Umlazi, 28 September 1985.
15. J. M. Coetzee, "Satyagraha in Durban," *New York Review of Books* 32: 16 (24 October 1985): 12.
16. Buthelezi, speech, 28 September 1985.
17. *Weekly Mail* 1: 13 (1985).
18. *Inhlabamkhosi* (April 1984).
19. Buthelezi, speech, 28 September 1985.
20. Buthelezi, *Leadership* (June 1985): 66.
21. Ibid., p. 68.
22. Buthelezi, Business International Conference, The Plaza, New York City (7 June 1985).
23. Buthelezi, speech, 28 September 1985.
24. Ibid.
25. ANC press statement, Lusaka (16 August 1985).
26. Buthelezi, speech, 28 September 1985.

27. Buthelezi, speech, 7 June 1985.

28. Brewer, "Membership of Inkatha," p. 133.

29. R. Southall, "Buthelezi, Inkatha and the Politics of Compromise."

30. Letter of A. J. Gumede, UDF President, to Buthelezi (30 April 1984).

31. Statement to Kwa Zulu Legislature (May 1984).

32. *SA Outlook* (September 1979): 134–38.

33. Leaflet, UDF (August 1985).

34. Nelson Mandela, "In Our Lifetime," p. 247.

35. N. Sizwe, *One Azania, One Nation.*

36. Joe Slovo, "South Africa—No Middle Road," p. 147.

37. Thabo Mbeki, "The Futton Thesis: A Rejoinder," p. 609.

38. Neville Alexander, "Nation and Ethnicity in South Africa."

39. Lyban Mabaso, "In Search of National Unity," *BCMA Newsletter* (May/June 1983).

40. Editorial, *Frank Talk*, 1: 6 (February/March 1985).

41. Mabaso, "National Unity."

42. Ibid.

43. Alexander, "Nation and Ethnicity."

44. M. J. Bhengu, *Inhlabamkhosi* (April 1984): 24.

45. Herbert W. Vilakazi and Absolom L. Vilakazi, "White Intellectuals," *Frontline* (May 1985): 27–29.

46. In 1919 in Amritsar, India, the British Army under the command of General Dyer killed 349 protesting women and men and wounded 1,516 others. The deadly attack on student demonstrators by National Guardsmen at Kent State University during the Vietnam War remains a black mark on the American record.

47. Francis Wilson, *Sunday Times* (24 February 1985): 25.

48. *Sunday Tribune* (3 March 1985).

49. Johannes Rantete, *The Third Day of September*, p. 34.

50. *The Economist* (22 June 1985).

51. *Sunday Times* (16 June 1985).

52. *Financial Mail* (12 October 1984): 34.

53. John MacLennan, *Sunday Tribune* (24 February 1985).

54. Rantete, *Third Day of September*, p. 24.

55. *SA Report* (18 October 1985).

56. *Financial Mail* (12 April 1985): 59.

57. W. G. Runciman, *Relative Deprivation and Social Justice* (Berkeley: University of California Press, 1966), 12.

58. Schlemmer, *Indicator SA* 2: 4 (1985).

59. Barrington Moore, *Injustice: The Social Bases of Obedience and Revolt* (White Plains, N.Y.: M. E. Sharpe, 1978), p. 91.

60. William Raspberry, *The Washington Post* (27 March 1985).

61. SABC Commentary (4 April 1984).
62. Helen Kitchen and Michael Clough, *The United States and South Africa*, pp. 27–31.
63. Frank Wisner, "Southern Africa: An American Perspective Today," p. 474.
64. Basil Davidson, "Apartheid: A System beyond Reform."
65. *New York Times* (7 February 1982).
66. *Africa Confidential* 26: 14 (3 July 1985).
67. B. Breytenbach, *The True Confessions of an Albino Terrorist*, p. 327.
68. *The Sunday Star* (Johannesburg) (1 September 1985). Thirty-four percent favored Mandela's release if he renounced violence.
69. Breytenbach, *True Confessions*, p. 327.

Chapter 5. Compliance without Consent

1. See I. L. Horowitz, "Political Legitimacy and the Institutionalization of Crisis," *Comparative Political Studies* (1968): 45–69, who develops this theme in the cauldron context of Latin America. The "permanency" of the Nationalist regime in South Africa since 1948 supplies quite a different meaning to the concept. For a general overview of legitimation problems in different societies by eminent political scientists see Bogdan Denitch, ed., *Legitimation of Regimes* (Beverly Hills: Sage, 1979).
2. Some analysts in the Marxist tradition have freely appropriated the Weberian concept of legitimacy to elaborate Gramsci's notion of hegemony. For a recent comprehensive treatment of structural and ideological factors in this tradition see Stanley Greenberg, *Race and State in Capitalist Development*, comparing South Africa, Israel, Northern Ireland, and Alabama. Another up-to-date analysis of South Africa is Deborah Posel's "State Ideology and Legitimation: The Contemporary South African Case." See also D. Posel, "Control of Reform and Reform of Control: The South African State after 1978," unpublished ms., 1984.
3. D. T. Moodie, *The Rise of Afrikanerdom*, p. 164.
4. Hamish Dickie-Clark, "The Study of Conflict in South Africa and Northern Ireland."
5. George F. Kennan, *Foreign Affairs* (January 1971).
6. Amnesty International, *Annual Report* (London, 1983).
7. *Washington Post* (5 September 1984).
8. *Beeld* (28 September 1984).
9. Breyten Breytenbach, *The True Confessions of an Albino Terrorist*, p. 320.
10. Austin T. Turk, *Political Criminality: The Defiance and Defence of Authority* (Beverly Hills: Sage, 1982), p. 199.

11. General Johan Coetzee, Commissioner of Police, Supplement to *Financial Mail* (6 September 1985).

12. *Financial Mail* (19 April 1985).

13. *Financial Mail* (23 March 1984).

14. Nicholas Abercrombie et al., *The Dominant Ideology Thesis* (London: Allen and Unwin, 1980).

15. Barrington Moore, *Social Origins of Dictatorship and Democracy* (Harmondsworth: Penguin, 1969), p. 204.

16. John Kane-Berman, "Vote of Thanks to Alan Parton," (Johannesburg: SAIRR, 37th Alfred and Winifred Hoernlé Memorial Lecture, 1985), p. 15.

17. Austin T. Turk, *Political Criminality*, p. 162; William A. Gamson, *Power and Discontent* (Homewood, Ill.: Dorsey, 1968), pp. 135–42.

18. As is asserted by Sam Nolutshungu, *Changing South Africa*.

19. Neville Alexander, "Nation and Ethnicity in South Africa," p. 12.

20. Michael Buroway, "State and Social Revolution in South Africa."

21. Robert Davies and Dan O'Meara, "Total Strategy in Southern Africa: An Analysis of South African Regional Policy since 1978."

22. If the 1983 constitutional racial ratios of parliamentary representation were to be extended to Africans, the formula would have to be 4 (Whites): 2 (Coloreds): 1 (Indians): 16 (Africans).

23. In the Indian case, the so-called Zulu-factor is often mentioned as crucial. However, this cannot explain the even lower poll among Indians in the Transvaal, where Buthelezi's warnings to Indians not to allow themselves to be co-opted hardly carried weight. The reasons for the discrepancy could be found in historical and class factors. The members of the Transvaal Indian community are descended largely from Muslim traders and have a higher concentration of middle-class persons than the predominantly Hindu Indians in Natal, more of whom are working-class. It is indicative that the candidates of the majority party (NPP) in the Indian group (like that of the Coloreds) come from humble backgrounds while the better educated, wealthier, and politically skilled rivals of "Solidarity" surprisingly were narrowly defeated. The lack of experience and higher education in the two junior chambers, particularly in the Labor Party, will predispose them to successful manipulation by the Nationalists or tutelage by the White opposition.

24. Asked how a party could exist and grow without the support of the community's intellectuals, David Curry, the Deputy Leader of the Labor Party, shrugged and replied, "Most intellectuals have never supported us anyway in their elitist distance from the grass-roots concerns" (personal interview).

25. Dharam Singh, a lawyer active in the Natal Indian Congress, expressed the elitist resentment by the old leadership most bluntly at an NIC meeting: "How can a butcher, baker, and second-hand car dealer dictate to academics?" (*Sunday Tribune*, 31 July 1983). The (Indian) Teachers' Federation vehemently objected to such a prospect.

26. Wilmot G. James, "Class, Race, and Democracy: Nolutshungu's South Africa."

27. Ibid.

28. Theodor Hanf et al., *South Africa: The Chances of Peaceful Change*; Buthelezi Commission Report; Lawrence Schlemmer, *Black Workers' Attitudes*.

29. Schlemmer, *Black Workers' Attitudes*, p. 44.

30. *Southern Africa Report* 3: 36 (13 September 1985).

31. *Southern Africa Report* (13 September 1985), reporting on a survey by Mark Orkin in conjunction with Fatima Meer's Institute for Black Research. The validity of many South Africa opinion surveys depends on the sampling technique and the kinds of questions asked. There are vast differences in methods and political motivation, which often achieve contradictory results. Given the widespread suspicion of officialdom, a simple variable such as whether interviewers were recruited or known in the townships of the respondents will heavily influence results. Random sampling tends to produce more conservative responses, while the quota system, often used in low-budget surveys, leaves more room for interviewer bias. However, there is no doubt that at least rhetorical support for "socialism" has markedly increased—to 77 percent, in the Orkin survey, and also reported in Martin Nasser's study. The Nasser "Report on Black Employee Attitudes to Capitalism," however, was based on written responses, which created a bias toward the views of the better educated.

32. Joseph Rothschild, *Ethnopolitics* (New York: Columbia University Press, 1981), p. 14.

33. André du Toit, *Sunday Tribune* (9 October 1983).

34. *South African Digest* (24 May 1985).

35. Gus Silber, *Frontline* 4: 4 (1984).

36. *Stats* (March 1984): 37.

37. *Business Briefing* 21 (May 1984).

38. *Financial Mail* (22 February 1985).

39. *Leadership*, First Quarter (1985).

40. William Leiss, *The Limits to Satisfaction: An Essay on the Problem of Needs and Commodities* (Toronto: University of Toronto Press, 1976).

41. Buroway, "State and Social Revolution in South Africa," p. 117.

42. See D. R. Browne, *International Radio Broadcasting: The Limits of the Limitless Medium* (New York: Praeger, 1982); John C. Lawrence, *Race Propaganda and South Africa*.

43. *Indicator SA* 2: 3 (October 1984): 6.

44. Jay Scott, *Globe and Mail* (22 December 1983).

45. Schlemmer, *Black Workers' Attitudes*, p. 16.

46. *Indicator SA* 2: 3 (October 1984): 6.

47. Kenneth W. Grundy, *Soldiers without Politics*, p. 280. The British, of course, invented an effective solution to the problem of multi-ethnic armies by fostering *regimental* loyalties. The spirit of Scottish, Irish, Gurkha, and Indian troops in the service of Her Majesty equaled the motivation of nationalist armies. A similar institutional socialization to security loyalty seems to work in South Africa, and Grundy may be far too optimistic in expecting Black policemen and soldiers to defect to a cause that despises them as "lackeys of the system."

48. Chalmers Johnson, *Revolutionary Change* (Boston: Little, Brown, 1966); T. R. Gurr, *Why Men Rebel* (Princeton: Princeton University Press, 1970).

49. Jürgen Habermas, *Legitimationsprobleme im Spätkapitalismus* (Frankfurt: Suhrkamp, 1973).

50. Theda Skocpol, *State and Social Revolutions* (Cambridge, Eng.: Cambridge University Press, 1980), p. 32.

51. Turk, *Political Criminality*, p. 27.

Chapter 6. Industrial Relations, Unions, and Employment

1. A. Roukens de Lange, "Demographic Tendencies, Technological Development and the Future of Apartheid," pp. 6–7.

2. Charles Simkins, "Society."

3. For an up-to-date comprehensive overview from a liberal perspective see Merle Lipton, *Capitalism and Apartheid* (Aldershot: Gower, 1985).

4. Stanley Greenberg, "Economic Growth and Political Change: The South African Case," p. 701.

5. Ibid., p. 699.

6. Hermann Giliomee and Lawrence Schlemmer, eds., *Up against the Fences*.

7. De Lange, "Demographic Tendencies," p. 3.

8. Jan Steyn, *Sunday Times* (4 November 1984).

9. Lawrence Schlemmer, *Black Workers' Attitudes*, p. 21.

10. Lawrence Schlemmer and Valerie Möller, "Migrant Labour in South Africa."

11. Lustick and Smooha have each described a similarly engineered successful control of the Arab minority in Israel. See Ian Lustick, *Arabs in the Jewish State* (Austin: University of Texas Press, 1980); Sammy Smooha and Don Peretz, "The Arabs in Israel," *Journal of Conflict Resolution* 26: 3 (September 1982): 451–84.

12. See the Wagner Act, 1936; Norris–La Guardia Act, 1932; Taft-Hartley, 1947; and Landrum-Griffin, 1959.

13. *Financial Mail* (12 October 1984): 28.

14. Joe Foster, "The Workers' Struggle—Where Does FOSATU Stand?"

15. Ibid.

16. Ibid.

17. SAIRR, *Race Relations Survey 1984* (1985): 310.

18. *SA Labour Bulletin* 10: 4 (1985): 70.

19. *Southern Africa Report* (10 May 1985).

20. *Financial Mail Manpower Survey* (12 April 1985): 22.

21. *FOSATU Policy Statement* (April 1984); *SA Labour Bulletin* 10 (May 1985): 44.

22. *The Star* IE (10 September 1984).

23. *Work in Progress* 37 (1985): 23.

Chapter 7. A Plural or a Common Society?

1. Michael Banton, *Racial and Ethnic Competition* (Cambridge, Eng.: Cambridge, 1983), p. 12.

2. See the vast literature on ethnic conflict, of which P. van den Berghe's *The Ethnic Phenomenon* remains the best overview, albeit from an unnecessary sociobiological perspective. A traditional political-science approach to the management of ethnic conflicts in various Third World societies is employed in Donald L. Horowitz, *Ethnic Groups in Conflict* (Berkeley: California, 1985).

3. A discussion between Alan Paton and Beyers Naudé included this dialogue: "Paton: There does, however, seem to be a deepening spirituality among some Afrikaans leaders, and the President in particular. Naude: . . . if, for instance, I listen and analyze carefully those parts of addresses delivered by the President where he refers to God, to dependence on God, to the leading and guidance of God, I certainly have the impression that he does so in a very sincere way. He is not playing with words. It is his deep and sincere conviction." *Leadership SA* 3: 4 (1984): 92. Along similar lines, Tutu muses aloud: "When God says, 'Love P. W. Botha,' I say to him, 'You can't be serious God.' He then says, 'I am. The consequences of being a member of the body of Jesus Christ is that P. W. is your brother.' You have to work out what that theological position means. It means that I have to long for the very best for him." *Leadership SA* (June 1985): 16.

4. *The Star* IW (14 May 1984).

5. Kenneth Kaunda, *Financial Mail* (26 April 1985).

6. Nathaniel Mahuilili, Founder Member and Acting President of SWAPO, *Financial Mail* (5 April 1985).

7. James Kiernan, "The New Zion," *Leadership* 4: 3 (1985): 98.

8. *SA Digest* (24 May 1985).

9. E. Mphahlele, cited in Ursula Barnett, *A Vision of Order*, p. 256.

10. Paul Rich, *White Power and the Liberal Conscience* (Johannesburg: Ravan, 1984).

11. Johannes Rantete, *The Third Day of September*.

12. It is indicative and ironic that a 16 June 1985 authorization by the South African Council of Churches of a prayer for the downfall of an unjust apartheid authority was followed by a conservative outcry of protest. An outside observer would have expected establishment satisfaction that the apartheid opposition is still praying. Allan Boesak's "apartheid is heresy" theme presupposes a shared value system. On the role of the churches see: John de Gruchy and Charles Villa-Vicencio, *Apartheid Is a Heresy* (Cape Town: David Philip, 1983); Allan Boesak, *Black and Reformed* (Johannesburg: Skotaville, 1984); Desmond M. Tutu, *Hope and Suffering* (Johannesburg: Skotaville, 1983); Marjorie Hope and James Young, *The South African Churches in a Revolutionary Situation* (Maryknoll, N.Y.: Orbis Books, 1981); John W. de Gruchy, *The Church Struggle in South Africa* (Grand Rapids, Mich.: Eerdmans, 1979).

13. Oliver Tambo, quoted in *Washington Post* (25 April 1985).

14. Robert Rotberg, *Suffer the Future*.

15. Samuel P. Huntington, "Reform and Stability in a Modernizing, Multi-Ethnic Society," p. 13.

16. Theodor Hanf et al., *South Africa: The Chances of Peaceful Change*; Buthelezi Commission Report.

17. Arend Lijphart, *Power-Sharing in South Africa*.

18. Milan Kundera, *The Book of Laughter and Forgetting* (New York: Penguin, 1981), p. 234.

Chapter 8. Policy Implications

1. Murray Forsyth, *Federalism and the Future of South Africa*, p. 19.

2. *Africa Confidential* 26: 22 (30 October 1985).

3. Forsyth, *Federalism*, p. 9.

4. *Economist* (15 December 1984).

5. Francesco Caportori, *Study on the Rights of Persons belonging to Ethnic, Religious, and Linguistic Minorities*.

6. Hugh Corder, *Justice at Work*.

7. For evidence see the various submissions by "Lawyers for Human Rights," based at Witwatersrand University, and also *The Star* IE (5 November 1984): 15.

8. Dugard, *Sunday Tribune* (27 Junuary 1985).

9. Leonard Thompson, *The Political Mythology of Apartheid* (New Haven: Yale, 1985).

10. SAIRR, *Race Relations Survey 1984*, p. 650.

11. Ibid., p. 665.

12. The banned Congress of South African Students (COSAS) demanded the recognition of democratically elected student representative councils (SRC's), the scrapping of age-limit restrictions, an end to excessive corporal punishment, an end to sexual harassment of female students, free textbooks, and qualified teachers.

13. Opening of Parliament (25 January 1985).

14. *Sunday Times* (12 May 1985).

15. Personal communication.

16. *Sunday Times* (6 October 1985).

17. Philip H. Frankel, "Consensus, Consociation and Co-optation in South African Politics," p. 489.

18. Johanna du Preez, *Africana Afrikaner: Master Symbols in South African School Textbooks* (Alberton, 1983). See also SAIRR, *Race Relations Survey* (1984), pp. 655-56.

Conclusion: Prospects for an Evolutionary Transition

1. Contrary to propaganda about "communist terrorists," the ANC's leading theorist officially declares: "The ANC is not a socialist party. It has never pretended to be one, has never said it was, and is not trying to be" (Thabo Mbeki, "The Futton Thesis: A Rejoinder," p. 609).

2. "Sometime, and probably soon," commented right-wing journalist Martin Spring, in *Star Weekly* (12 August 1985), "the authorities will get a grip on the situation, the agitators will all be locked up, the kids will get fed up with being birdshotted and tearsmoked, and things will start to return to normal." The same patriotic author owns a consulting firm that advises how to acquire a foreign passport.

3. *Indicator SA* 3: 1 (Winter 1985): 9.

4. *Los Angeles Times* (23 August 1985): 5.

5. Jonathan Steele, "Apartheid's Crumbling Bastions," *Marxism Today* (September 1985).

6. Human Science Research Council (HSRC), *The South African Society: Realities and Future Prospects* (Pretoria: HSRC, 1985).

7. Robert Rotberg, "Seven Scenarios for South Africa," *CSIS Africa Notes* 48 (29 October 1985): 3.

8. For a comprehensive recent elaboration of these interests see Merle Lipton, *Capitalism and Apartheid* (Aldershot: Gower, 1985).

9. Ken Owen, "Inside South Africa: A Status Report," *CSIS Africa Notes* 44 (30 June 1985): 4.

10. Claus Offe, *Disorganized Capitalism* (Princeton: MIT, 1985).

Bibliography

This select bibliography on the society and politics of South Africa does not include all the sources cited or used in this study. Preference is given to major academic or journalistic work with a focus on recent political events and controversies.

Adam, Heribert. 1971. *Modernizing Racial Domination*. Berkeley and Los Angeles: University of California Press.

———. 1973. "The Rise of Black Consciousness in South Africa." *Race* 15: 2 (October), pp. 149–65.

———. 1975. "Conflict and Change in South Africa." Pp. 211–44 in D. Baker, *Politics of Race*. London: Saxon House.

———. 1975. "Internal Constellations and Potentials for Change." Pp. 303–28 in L. Thompson and J. Butler, *Change in Contemporary South Africa*. Berkeley and Los Angeles: University of California Press.

———. 1976. "Ideologies of Dedication vs. Blueprints of Expedience." *Social Dynamics* 2: 2 (Cape Town), pp. 83–91.

———. 1977. "When the Chips Are Down: Confrontation and Accommodation in South Africa." *Contemporary Crisis* 1 (October), pp. 417–35.

———. 1979. "Three Perspectives of the Future of South Africa." *International Journal of Comparative Sociology* XX: 1/2, pp. 126–36.

———. 1980. "Minority Monopoly in Transition: Recent Policy Shifts of the South African State." *Journal of Modern African Studies* 18: 4, pp. 611–26.

———. 1983. "Outside Influence on South Africa: Afrikanerdom in Disarray." *Journal of Modern African Studies* 21: 2, pp. 235–51.

———. 1984. "Racial Capitalism vs. Capitalist Nonracialism." *Ethnic and Racial Studies* 7: 2 (May).

Adam, Heribert, ed. 1971. *South Africa: Sociological Perspectives*. London: Oxford University Press.

————. 1983. *South Africa: The Limits of Reform Politics*. Leiden: E. J. Brill.

Adam, Heribert, and Hermann Giliomee. 1979. *Ethnic Power Mobilized: Can South Africa Change?* New Haven: Yale University Press.

Alexander, Neville. 1983. "Nation and Ethnicity in South Africa." Paper presented at the National Forum Hammanskraal Conference.

————. 1985. *Sow the Wind*. Johannesburg: Skotaville.

Barnett, Ursula A. 1983. *A Vision of Order: A Study of Black South African Literature in English, 1914–1980*. Amherst: The University of Massachusetts Press.

Beckett, Denis. 1985. *Permanent Peace*. Braam-Fontain: Saga Press.

Bekker, S., and R. Humphries. 1985. *From Control to Confusion: The Changing Role of Administration Boards in South Africa, 1971–1983*. Pietermaritzburg and Johannesburg: Butterworth.

Benson, Mary. 1966. *The Struggle for a Birthright*. Middlesex: Penguin.

Benyon, John A., ed. 1978. *Constitutional Change in South Africa*. Pietermaritzburg: University of Natal Press.

Bissell, Richard E. and Chester A. Crocker, eds. 1979. *South Africa into the 1980s*. Boulder, Colo.: Westview Press.

Boulle, Laurence. 1984. *Constitutional Reform and the Apartheid State*. New York: St. Martin's Press.

Brewer, J. 1981. "The Modern Janus: Inkatha's Role in Black Liberation." Pp. 100–107 in Institute of Commonwealth Studies, The Societies of Southern Africa in the 19th and 20th Centuries 12.

————. 1985. "The Membership of Inkatha in Kwa Mashu." *African Affairs* 87.

Breytenbach, Breyten. 1984. *The True Confessions of an Albino Terrorist*. Emmarentia (South Africa 2029, Box 85218): Taurus.

Brotz, Howard. 1977. *The Politics of South Africa*. London: Oxford University Press.

Buroway, Michael. 1982. "State and Social Revolution in South Africa." *Kapitalistate* 9, pp. 93–122.

Buthelezi Commission Report. 1982. 2 vols. Durban: H. & H. Publications.

Buthelezi, Gatsha. 1979. *Power Is Ours*. New York: Books in Focus.

Butler, Jeffrey, Robert Rotberg, and John Adams. 1977. *The Black Homelands of South Africa*. Berkeley and Los Angeles: University of California Press.

Callaghy, Thomas M., ed. 1983. *South Africa in Southern Africa: The Intensifying Vortex of Violence*. New York: Praeger.

Callinicos, Alex, and John Rogers. 1977. *Southern Africa after Soweto*. London: Pluto Press.

Caportorti, Francesco. 1979. *Study on the Rights of Persons belonging to Ethnic, Religious, and Linguistic Minorities*. New York: United Nations Publications, No. e.78.xiv.1.

Carter, Gwendolen M. 1958. *The Politics of Inequality.* London: Thames and Hudson.

———. 1980. *Which Way Is South Africa Going?* Bloomington: Indiana University Press.

Carter, Gwendolen M., Thomas Karis, and Newell M. Stultz. 1967. *South Africa's Transkei.* Evanston: Northwestern University Press.

Cell, John W. 1982. *The Highest Stage of White Supremacy.* Cambridge, Eng.: Cambridge University Press.

Communist Party of South Africa. N.d. *The Road to South African Freedom.* London: Inkululeko.

———. 1976. "The Enemy Hidden under the Same Colour." *African Communist* 65, pp. 16–40.

Corder, Hugh. 1984. *Justice at Work.* Cape Town: Juta.

Crocker, Chester, 1981. "South Africa: Strategy for Change." *Foreign Affairs* 59, 2 (Winter): 323–51.

Davidson, Basil. 1984. "Apartheid: A System beyond Reform." *Socialist Affairs* (March), pp. 12–17.

Davies, Robert, and Dan O'Meara. 1984. "Total Strategy in Southern Africa: An Analysis of South African Regional Policy since 1978." *Journal of Southern African Studies* 11: 2 (April): 183–211.

de Crespigny, Anthony, and Robert Schrire, eds. 1978. *The Government and Politics of South Africa.* Cape Town: Juta.

de Klerk, Willem. 1984. *The Second (R)evolution: Afrikanerdom and the Crisis of Identity.* Johannesburg: Jonathan Ball.

de Lange, A. Roukens. 1984. "Demographic Tendencies, Technological Development and the Future of Apartheid." Paper presented at University of the Western Cape Conference, Bellville, 8–10 October.

de St. Jorre, John. 1977. *A House Divided.* New York: Carnegie Endowment for International Peace.

Dhlomo, Oscar. 1983. "The Strategy of Inkatha and Its Critics." In Adam, ed., 1983.

Dickie-Clark, Hamish. 1966. *The Marginal Situation.* London: Routledge & Kegan Paul.

———. 1976. "The Study of Conflict in South Africa and Northern Ireland." *Social Dynamics* 2: 1, pp. 53–59.

Dreyer, Peter. 1980. *Martyrs and Fanatics.* New York: Simon and Schuster.

Dugard, John. 1978. *Human Rights and the South African Legal Order.* Princeton: Princeton University Press.

du Toit, André. 1980. "Emerging Strategies for Political Control: Nationalist Afrikanerdom." In Price and Rosberg, eds.

du Toit, André, and Hermann Giliomee. 1983. *Afrikaner Political Thought, 1780–1850.* Cape Town: David Philip.

Ensor, Paula, et al. 1980. *South Africa: The Workers' Movement, SACTU and the ANC—A Struggle for Marxist Policies.* London: Cambridge Heath Press.

Fatton, Robert. 1984. "The African National Congress of South Africa: The Limitations of a Revolutionary Strategy." *Canadian Journal of African Studies* 18: 3, pp. 593–608.

Feit, Edward. 1967. *African Opposition in South Africa.* Stanford: Hoover Institution on War, Revolution and Peace.

Forsyth, Murray. 1984. *Federalism and the Future of South Africa.* Johannesburg: South African Institute of International Affairs.

Foster, Joe. 1982. "The Workers' Struggle—Where Does FOSATU Stand?" Durban: FOSATU Occasional Publication no. 5.

Frankel, Philip H. 1980. "Consensus, Consociation and Co-optation in South African Politics." *Cahiers d'Etudes Africaines* 80: XX/4, pp. 473–94.

———. 1980. "South Africa: The Politics of Police Control." *Comparative Politics* 12: 4 (July), pp. 481–99.

———. 1984. *Pretoria's Praetorians: Civil-Military Relations in South Africa.* Cambridge, Eng.: Cambridge University Press.

Fredrickson, George. 1981. *White Supremacy: A Comparative Study in American and South African History.* New York: Oxford University Press.

Gann, L. H., and Peter Duignan. 1980. *Why South Africa Will Survive.* London: St. Martin's Press.

Gastrow, Shelag. 1985. *Who's Who in South African Politics.* Johannesburg: Raven Press.

Geber, Beryl A., and Stanton P. Newman. 1980. *Soweto's Children.* London: Academic Press.

Geertz, Clifford. 1963. "The Integrative Revolution: Primordial Sentiments and Civil Politics in the New States." In Clifford Geertz, ed., *Old Societies and New States.* New York: The Free Press.

Gerhart, Gail M. 1978. *Black Power in South Africa.* Berkeley and Los Angeles: University of California Press.

Gibson, Richard. 1972. *African Liberation Movements.* London: Oxford University Press.

Giliomee, Hermann. 1981. "The Magic Moment? South Africa between Past and Future." Pp. 177–200 in Alfred O. Hero and John Barratt, eds., *The American People and South Africa.* Lexington, Mass.: D.C. Heath.

———. 1982. *The Parting of the Ways: South African Politics 1976–82.* Cape Town: David Philip.

———. 1984. "Politics: White Supremacy Out, Black Supremacy Contained." *Energos* (Mobil Oil, S.A.), pp. 25–44.

Giliomee, Hermann, and Lawrence Schlemmer, eds. 1985. *Up against the Fences: Poverty, Passes and Privilege in South Africa.* Cape Town: David Philip.

Gordimer, Nadine. 1983. "Living in the Interregnum." *New York Review of Books* (January 20), pp. 21–29.

Greenberg, Stanley. 1976. "Business Enterprise in a Racial Order." *Politics and Society* 6: 2, pp. 213–40.

———. 1980. *Race and State in Capitalist Development*. New Haven: Yale University Press.

———. 1981. "Economic Growth and Political Change: The South African Case." *Journal of Modern African Studies* 19: 4, pp. 667–704.

Grundy, Kenneth W. 1983. *Soldiers without Politics: Blacks in the South African Armed Forces*. Berkeley: University of California Press.

Hachten, William A., and C. Anthony Gifford. 1984. *The Press and Apartheid*. Madison: University of Wisconsin Press.

Hanf, Theodor. 1983. "Lessons Which Are Never Learnt: Minority Rule in Comparative Perspective." In Adam, ed., 1983.

Hanf, Theodor, et al. 1981. *South Africa: The Chances of Peaceful Change*. Bloomington: Indiana University Press.

Hanlon, Joseph. 1985. *Mocambique: The Revolution under Fire*. London: Zed Books.

Harsh, Ernest. 1980. *South Africa: White Rule, Black Revolt*. New York: Monad Press.

Hill, Christopher R. 1983. *Change in South Africa: Blind Alleys or New Directions?* London: Rex Collings.

Hirson, Baruch. 1979. *Year of Fire, Year of Ash*. London: Zed Press.

Hoernlé, R. F. Alfred. 1939. *South African Native Policy and the Liberal Spirit*. Cape Town: University of Cape Town.

Horowitz, Ralph. 1967. *The Political Economy of South Africa*. London: Weidenfeld and Nicolson.

Huntington, Samuel P. 1981. "Reform and Stability in a Modernizing, Multi-Ethnic Society." *Politikon* 8: 2 (December), pp. 8–26.

Innes, Duncan. 1984. *Anglo American and the Rise of Modern South Africa*. New York: Monthly Review Press.

Isaacs, Harold R. 1975. *The Idols of the Tribe*. New York: Harper.

James, Wilmot G. 1983. "The South African State in Transition." Paper presented at the Annual Meeting of the African Studies Association, Boston, 6–10 December.

———. 1984. "Class, Race, and Democracy: Nolutshungu's South Africa." Paper presented at the Conference on Economic Development and Racial Domination, University of the Western Cape, Bellville, 8–10 October.

———. 1984. "State and Race: Revisionism, Inquiry and Bureaucracism." Paper presented at the Conference on Economic Development and Racial Domination, University of the Western Cape, Bellville, 8–10 October.

Jenkins, Simon. 1983. "Destabilization in Southern Africa." *The Economist* (16–22 July), pp. 19–28.

Johnson, R. W. (1977). *How Long Will South Africa Survive?* London: Macmillan Press.

Johnstone, Frederick. 1976. *Class, Race and Gold.* London: Routledge & Kegan Paul.

Kane-Berman, John. 1979. *South Africa: A Method in the Madness.* London: Pluto Press.

———. 1982. "Inkatha: The Paradox of South African Politics." *Optima* 30.

Karis, T. G. 1983/84. "Revolution in the Making: Black Politics in South Africa." *Foreign Affairs* (Winter), pp. 378–406.

Karis, T., and G. M. Carter, eds. 1972. *From Protest to Challenge.* 3 vols. Stanford: Hoover Institution Press.

Kitchen, Helen, and Michael Clough. 1984. *The United States and South Africa: Realities and Red Herrings.* Washington, D.C.: CSIS.

Kuper, Leo. 1957. *Passive Resistance in South Africa.* New Haven: Yale University Press.

———. 1965. *An African Bourgeoisie.* New Haven: Yale University Press.

———. 1974. *Race, Class and Power.* Chicago: Aldine.

———. 1977. *The Pity of It All: Polarization of Racial and Ethnic Relations.* Minneapolis: University of Minnesota Press.

Kuper, Leo, and M. G. Smith, eds. 1969. *Pluralism in Africa.* Berkeley and Los Angeles: University of California Press.

Lambley, Peter. 1980. *The Psychology of Apartheid.* London: Secker and Warburg.

Lawrence, John C. 1979. *Race Propaganda and South Africa.* London: Victor Gollancz.

Lelyveld, Joseph. 1985. *Move Your Shadow: South Africa Black and White.* New York: Time Books/Random House.

Leonard, Richard. 1983. *South Africa at War.* Westport: Lawrence Hill and Company.

Lerumo, A. 1971. *Fifty Fighting Years.* London: Inkululeko.

Lewis, J. 1984. *Industrialization and Trade Union Organization in South Africa.* Cambridge, Eng.: Cambridge University Press.

Lijphart, Arend. 1977. *Democracy in Plural Societies: A Comparative Evaluation.* New Haven and London: Yale University Press.

———. 1986. *Power-Sharing in South Africa.* Berkeley: Institute of International Studies, University of California.

Lijphart, Arend, and Bernard Grofman, eds. 1984. *Choosing an Electoral System: Issues and Alternatives.* New York: Praeger.

Lipton, Merle. 1985. *Capitalism and Apartheid.* Aldershot: Gower.

Lodge, Tom. 1983. *Black Politics in South Africa.* Johannesburg: Raven Press.

Lombard, J.A. 1978. *Freedom, Welfare and Order.* Pretoria: Bembo.

Magubane, Bernard. 1979. *The Political Economy of Race and Class in South Africa.* New York: Monthly Review Press.

Mandela, Nelson. 1977. "In Our Lifetime." Pp. 245–50 in Thomas Karis, Gwendolen Carter, and Gail Gerhart, eds. *From Protest to Challenge*, vol. 3. Stanford: Hoover Institution Press.

———. 1978. *The Struggle Is My Life*. London: International Defense and Aid Fund.

Marcum, John. 1982. *Education, Race and Social Change in South Africa*. Berkeley: California. University of California Press.

———. 1984. "Angola: A Quarter Century of War." *CSIS Africa Notes* 37 (December 21).

Marquard, Leo. 1960. *The Peoples and Policies of South Africa*. Cape Town: Oxford University Press.

———. 1971. *A Federation of Southern Africa*. London: Oxford University Press.

Mathews, A. S. 1971. *Law, Order and Liberty in South Africa*. Cape Town: Juta.

Mayer, Philip. 1975. "Class, Status, and Ethnicity as Perceived by Johannesburg Africans." Pp. 138–67 in L. Thompson and J. Butler, eds., *Change in Contemporary South Africa*. Berkeley and Los Angeles: University of California Press.

Mbeki, Thabo. 1984. "The Futton Thesis: A Rejoinder." *Canadian Journal of African Studies* 18: 3, pp. 609–12.

McGrath, Mike. 1985. "Economic Growth and the Distribution of Racial Incomes in the South African Economy." *South Africa International* (April), pp. 223–32.

Moodie, D. T. 1975. *The Rise of Afrikanerdom: Power, Apartheid and the Afrikaner Civil Religion*. Berkeley and Los Angeles: University of California Press.

Motlhabi, Mokgethi. 1984. *Black Resistance to Apartheid*. Johannesburg: Skotaville.

Munger, Edwin S. 1967. *Afrikaner and African Nationalism*. London: Oxford University Press.

Nasser, Martin. 1984. "Report on Black Employee Attitudes to Capitalism." Pretoria: UNISA School of Business Leadership.

Nolutshungu, Sam C. 1982. *Changing South Africa*. Manchester: Manchester University Press.

North, James. 1985. *Freedom Rising*. New York: Macmillan.

Odendaal, André. 1984. *Vukani Bantu! The Beginning of Black Protest Politics in South Africa to 1912*. Cape Town: David Philip.

O'Dowd, M. 1974. "South Africa in the Light of the Stages of Economic Growth." Pp. 29–44 in A. Leftwich, ed., *South Africa*. London: Allison & Busby.

O'Meara, D. 1983. *Volkskapitalisme*. Cambridge, Eng.: Cambridge University Press.

O'Meara, Patrick. 1981. "South Africa: Mobilization, Revolt and Crisis." *Canadian Journal of African Studies* 15: 3.

Posel, Deborah. 1982. "State Ideology and Legitimation: The Contemporary South African Case." Paper presented at the Conference on South Africa and the Comparative Study of Class, Race and Nationalism, New York (September).

Price, Robert M. and Carl G. Rosberg, eds. 1980. *The Apartheid Regime: Political Power and Racial Domination*. Berkeley: Institute of International Studies.

Prior, Andrew. 1984. "Political Culture and Violence: A Case Study of the African National Congress of South Africa." *Politikon* 11: 2 (December), pp. 12–20.

Rantete, Johannes. 1984. *The Third Day of September: An Eye-Witness Account of the Sebokeng Rebellion of 1984*. Johannesburg: Ravan Press.

Report of the Study Commission on U.S. Policy toward Southern Africa. 1981. *South Africa: Time Running Out*. Berkeley and Los Angeles: University of California Press.

Rhoodie, Nic. 1983. *Intergroup Conflict in Deeply Segmented Societies*. Pretoria: HSRC.

———. 1983. "Value Consensus as a Prerequisite for Consociational Federalism in Southern Africa." In D. J. van Vuuren and D. J. Kriek, eds., *Political Alternatives for Southern Africa*. Durban: Butterworth.

Rhoodie, Nic, ed. 1979. *Intergroup Accommodation in Plural Societies*. London: MacMillan.

Rich, Paul. 1984. *White Power and the Liberal Conscience*. Johannesburg: Ravan.

Rotberg, Robert. 1980. *Suffer the Future: Policy Choices in Southern Africa*. Cambridge, Mass.: Harvard University Press.

Rotberg, Robert I., and John Barratt, eds. 1980. *Conflict and Compromise in South Africa*. Lexington, Mass.: Lexington Books.

Roux, Edward. 1966. *Time Longer than Rope*. Madison: University of Wisconsin Press.

Saul, John, and Stephen Gelb. 1981. *The Crisis in South Africa: Class Defense, Class Revolution*. New York: Monthly Review Press.

Savage, Michael. 1977. "Costs of Enforcing Apartheid and Problems of Change." *African Affairs* 76: 304 (July), pp. 287–302.

———. 1983. "Pass Laws and the Disorganization and Reorganization of the African Population in South Africa." Manuscript.

———. 1985. "An Anatomy of the South African Corporate Economy: Ownership, Control and the Interlocking Directorate." Manuscript, Centre for African Studies, University of Cape Town.

Schlemmer, Lawrence. 1980. "The Stirring Giant: Observations on the Inkatha and Other Black Political Movements in South Africa." In Carl Rosberg and Robert Price, eds., *The Apartheid Regime*. Berkeley and Los Angeles: University of California Press.

————. 1983. "Build-Up to Revolution or Impasse?" In Adam, ed., 1983.

————. 1984. *Black Workers' Attitudes*. Durban: University of Natal.

Schlemmer, Lawrence, and Valerie Möller. 1982. "Migrant Labour in South Africa." Manuscript, Durban, Centre for Applied Social Sciences, University of Natal.

Simkins, Charles. 1984. "Society." *Energos* 10, pp. 108–21.

Sizwe, N. 1976. *One Azania, One Nation: The National Question in South Africa*. London: Zed Press.

Slovo, Joe. 1976. "South Africa—No Middle Road." In B. Davidson, J. Slovo, and A. R. Wilkinson, *Southern Africa: The New Politics of Revolution*. Harmondsworth: Penguin.

Smith, A. B. 1983. "The Hotnot Syndrome: Myth-Making in the South African School Textbooks." *Social Dynamics* 9: 2, pp. 37–49.

South African Institute of Race Relations (SAIRR). 1985. *Race Relations Survey 1984*. Johannesburg: SAIRR.

Southall, R. 1981. "Buthelezi, Inkatha and the Politics of Compromise." *African Affairs* 80, pp. 453–81.

————. 1983. "Consociationalism in South Africa: The Buthelezi Commission and Beyond." *Journal of Modern African Studies* 21.

Stultz, N. M. 1979. *Transkei's Half Loaf.* New Haven: Yale University Press.

Suttner, Raymond. 1985. "The Freedom Charter: The People's Charter in the Nineteen-Eighties." *South Africa International* (April), pp. 233–52.

Tambo, Oliver. 1977. "The Building of a Nation." In ANC, ed., *ANC Speaks: Documents and Statements of the African National Congress, 1955–1976*.

Thompson, Leonard. 1985. *The Mythologies of Apartheid*. New Haven: Yale University Press.

Thompson, L., and A. Prior. 1982. *South African Politics*. New Haven: Yale University Press.

Tötemeyer, Gerhard. 1984. *The African University in a Divided Society*. Manuscript.

Turok, Ben. 1974. "South Africa: The Search for a Strategy." Pp. 341–76 in Ralph Miliband and John Saville, eds., *The Socialist Register 1973*. London: The Merlin Press.

Uhlig, Mark. 1984. "The Coming Struggle for Power in South Africa." *New York Review of Books* (2 February), pp. 27–31.

van den Berghe, Pierre L. (1965). *South Africa: A Study in Conflict*. Middletown: Wesleyan University Press.

————. 1971. "The Benign Quota." *American Sociologist* 6: 3, pp. 40–43.

————. 1981. *The Ethnic Phenomenon*. New York: Elsevier.

van den Berghe, Pierre L., ed. 1979. *The Liberal Dilemma in South Africa*. London: Croom Helm.

van der Merwe, H. W., and Schrire, R. 1980. *Race and Ethnicity*. Cape Town: David Philip.

van Vuuren, D. J., and D. J. Kriek, eds. 1983. *Political Alternatives for Southern Africa*. Durban: Butterworth.

Van Zyl Slabbert, F. 1983. "Sham Reform and Conflict Regulation in a Divided Society." In Adam, ed., 1983.

———. 1985. *The Last White Parliament*. Johannesburg: Jonathan Ball.

Van Zyl Slabbert, F., and David Welsh. 1979. *South Africa's Options*. Cape Town: David Philip.

Van Zyl Slabbert, F., and Jeff Opland, eds. 1980. *South Africa: Dilemmas of Evolutionary Change*. Grahamstown: Institute of Social and Economic Research, Rhodes University.

Villa-Vicencio, Charles, and John de Gruchy, eds. 1985. *Resistance and Hope: South African Essays in Honour of Beyers Naudé*. Cape Town: David Philip.

Walshe, Peter. 1971. *The Rise of African Nationalism in South Africa*. Berkeley and Los Angeles: University of California Press.

Wassenaar, A. D. 1977. *Assault on Private Enterprise*. Cape Town: Tafelberg.

Welsh, David. 1974. "The Political Economy of Afrikaner Nationalism." In A. Leftwich, ed., *South Africa: Economic Growth and Political Change*. London: Allison and Busby.

———. 1984. Review of P. Rich, *White Power and the Liberal Conscience*, *Social Dynamics* 10: 1, pp. 66–82.

Wisner, Frank. 1984. "Southern Africa: An American Perspective Today." *South Africa International* (January).

Woods, Donald. 1979. *Biko*. New York: Vintage.

Wright, Harrison M. 1977. *The Burden of the Present*. Cape Town: David Philip.

Yudelman, David. 1983. *The Emergence of Modern South Africa*. Westport, Conn.: Greenwood.

Index

Abercrombie, Nicholas, 142
  cited, 277
Accommodation, 212, 233,
  238–43, 248, 249, 261
Adam, Heribert, xii–xiii
  cited, 272, 273
Adorno, Theodor W., xii
Affirmative action, 41, 203, 230
Africanization, 203, 205, 221,
  230–33
African National Congress (ANC),
  ix–x, xiv, 93–99 passim, 165,
  195, 213, 250–62 passim
  Botha and, 117–18, 123, 156
  Buthelezi and, 83, 84, 87–88,
    127–28, 193, 258
  Charterists oriented toward, 77
  cited, 274
  on citizenship, 28
  and corporate federation, 219
  migrant laborers and, 178
  in negotiations, 117–28, 206,
    239, 240, 241, 243
  nonracialism of, 54, 196
  and religion, 202
  and revolution, 164
  and socialism, 96, 248, 257, 282
  and township unrest, 110, 116,
    127, 202, 228, 257–58
  and unions, 94, 152, 187, 188,
    189, 193–94, 258
Africans
  in civil service, 143, 203, 230–33
  collaborating, 10, 78–79, 151

constitution and, 69–70, 148,
  277
farms of, 47, 270
income levels of, 171
Indian relations with, 83–85,
  86, 95
in labor hierarchies, 51, 176,
  177
languages of, 48–49, 221
media aimed at, 163
middle class, 151, 163, 250
and nonracialism, 85, 196
Pan African Congress and, 97
property confiscations from,
  223
See also Black nationalism; Zulus
Afrikaanse Handelsinstituut, 24
Afrikaans language, 221, 273
Afrikaans press, 68, 136, 245
Afrikaner nationalism, 28, 43–57,
  61, 64, 65, 165, 248
  and capitalism, 44–45, 46, 56,
    198
  consociational model of, 212
  critical moralists and, 73
  deracialization of, 32
  economic ethnicity of, 30
  and nonracialism, 219–20
  political ethnicity of, 31
  See also National Party
Afrikaners, 252
  in Boer War, 43, 45, 193
  and economic interdependence,
    203

Afrikaners (*continued*)
  farming by, 5, 10, 21, 43–44, 47,
    48, 60, 204, 253–54
  in history textbooks, 233, 247
  income levels of, 273
  politics of (general), 55, 58–76,
    163–64. *See also* Afrikaner
    nationalism; State
  "White Bantustans" for, 228
Afrikaner-Weerstandbeweging
    (AWB), 61
Aggett, Neil, 54, 101
Agricultural societies, partition in,
    39
Agriculture. *See* Farming
Alexander, Neville, 97, 98, 146
  cited, 275, 277
Aliens and Immigration Law
    Amendments Act, 140
Americanization, 153, 158. *See also*
    Consumerism
Amnesty International, cited, 276
Amritsar killings, India, 275
ANC. *See* African National
    Congress
Anglicanism, 199
Anglicization, 47
Anglo-American Corporation, 23,
    117
Angola, 118, 120, 126
Antagonisms
  intra-Black, 83–84, 95, 127–28
  cultural, 52–53
  ethnic, 31, 33–36, 37–38, 40
  Pretoria–KwaZulu, 89–90
  See also Violence
Anti-capitalist forums, 78, 97–103
Anti-racialism, 53
Anti-Semitism, 36
Ardington, Libby, xvi
Ardington, Tony, xvi
Arenstein, Rowley, xvii, 54
Armenians, in Turkey, 37
Armies, 227–28, 279
  South African, 46, 66–67, 109,
    136, 152, 165–66, 228, 253,
    257
  Zulu, 47

Arms supply, 120
Asian independence movements,
    28
Asian settlers, 37, 38, 223. *See also*
    Indians, South African
Austria, 242
Authoritarianism, 12–13, 60, 82,
    164
Autonomy, 29, 220–21, 229, 271
Azania, 99, 256
Azanian Confederation of Trade
    Unions (AZACTU), 192
"Azanian People's Manifesto," 99
Azanian People's Organization
    (AZAPO), 95, 98, 101, 102

Baley, Jim, 158–59
Banton, Michael, 16
  cited, 270, 271, 280
Bantu education, 53, 54, 235
Bantustans. *See* Homelands
Barnett, Ursula, cited, 281
Batman, 158
Bauer, Otto, 28
Beeld, 123
Belgium, 210
Bhengu, M. J., cited, 275
Biko, Steve, 65, 106, 113
Black Christmas, 115
Black Consciousness (BC), 49, 54,
    83, 95, 96, 97–102
  anti-American stance of, 94
  and consumerism, 160
  and National Forum, 77, 98, 99
  and UDF, 77, 93, 98
  and unions, 100–101, 189,
    192–95
Black middle class, 16–17, 95–96,
    174–79, 233, 250
  ANC and, 95–96, 97, 98, 257
  Black Consciousness and, 54,
    97–98, 100, 101
  and capitalism, 45, 95, 97–98,
    147, 174, 176, 257
  collaboration opposed by, 149
  constitutional reforms and, 148,
    150, 151, 277
  education for, 235

Group Areas Act and, 117, 149, 224

media for, 163

Black nationalism, 28, 43–57, 165, 213–14, 220, 248

and capitalism, 44, 45, 51, 56, 147–48, 198, 256

critical moralists and, 73

and secessionism, 217

White liberalism and, 54–55, 202

Blacks, 14–15

in armed forces, 46, 47, 165, 228, 279

businessmen among, 17, 147, 149, 174–75

education of, 17, 113, 114–15, 166, 230, 232, 233–38

in history textbooks, 233, 247

in judiciary system, 231–32

police among, 9, 139, 228, 279

politicized, 55–57, 76, 77–128, 135, 149, 152–53, 189, 194.

See also Black nationalism

violence between, 56, 84–86, 88, 95, 109–17, 255

See also Africans; Coloreds; Indians; Labor; Urban Blacks

Black Sash, 101

Black theology, 49–50, 99–100, 199. *See also* Christians/ Christianity

Bloom, Tony, 123

Boer War, 43, 45, 193

Boesak, Allan, 94, 109, 281

Bonacich, Edna, 33

cited, 271

Booysen, Hercules, 65

Bophuthatswana, 78, 217

Bop-TV, 158

Botha, P. W., 119, 254

and ANC, 117–18, 123, 156

and Buthelezi, 89

and colonialism, 146

constitutional reforms of, 68, 69, 71, 239, 260

economic development under, 20, 21

and military, 66

Tutu on, 280

and Zion Christian Church, 156, 201

Botha-Malan junta, 98–99

Botswana, 107

Bottomore, Tom, cited, 271

Bourgeoisie. *See* Embourgeoisement; Middle class

Boycotts, 79, 80, 154

consumer, 46, 82, 115, 159, 189, 193, 194

UDF and, 94–95, 189, 191, 192

unions and, 94, 189, 191–92, 193, 194

Brass, Paul, 51–52

cited, 273

Brave New World, 168

Brewer, J., 84

cited, 274, 275

Breytenbach, Breyten, 126, 128, 137

cited, 276

Britain

Afrikaner struggle against, 23, 47, 49

ethnic antagonism in, 35

in India, 275

labor relations system of, 180–81

and multiethnic armies, 279

union and anti-apartheid movement in, 188

See also English South Africans

Broederbond, 59, 60, 64

Brown, Bob, xvii

Brown, Peter, 76

Browne, D. R., cited, 278

Bryer, Monte, xvii

Buroway, Michael, 146

cited, 277, 278

Business, 18–19, 22–26, 58, 209, 253–61

Black, 17, 110, 147, 149, 174–75

and decentralization, 20

education sponsored by, 238

English, 10, 44, 45, 55, 68, 70, 243

Business (*continued*)
and labor conflicts, 23–24, 123,
   180–83, 188, 258–60. *See
   also* Unions
law enforcement by, 139–40
and negotiations, 117–18, 123,
   258
See also Free enterprise policies
Buthelezi, M., xiv, 77, 82–92 passim, 165, 239
and ANC, 83, 84, 87–88,
   127–28, 193, 258
business and, 258
cited, 274, 275
and Indians, 83, 84, 277
and power-sharing, 84, 254
See also Inkatha
Buthelezi Commission, xvi, 90,
   172
Bywoners, 47

Calvinism, 47, 49, 50, 72, 199. *See
   also* Christians/Christianity
Camay, Piroshaw, 191
Canada, xi–xii, 33, 44, 210, 223,
   224, 238
Cape, 46–47, 172. *See also* Eastern
   Cape; Western Cape
Cape Action League, 101
Cape Chamber of Industries, 192
Cape Flat squatters, 172
Cape Times, 68
Cape Town, 148
Cape Town Municipal Workers
   Union, 189
Capital. *See* Investment
Capitalism, 5–8, 22–23, 44–45,
   46, 213, 248–49, 255, 263
Black, 21–22, 95, 147–48, 174,
   198, 256, 257
consumer. *See* Consumerism
co-optation and, 51, 56, 146–48
disorganized, 260
and equity issues, 19, 171
forums against, 78, 97–103
and influx control, 25
and Soviet–South Africa rela-
   tions, 120

UDF coalition and, 95
unions and, 25, 46, 188
Capitalists. *See* Business
Caportori, Francesco, cited, 281
Carter, G. M., cited, 273
Caste, 40, 42–43
Catholicism, 199
Censorship, 45–46
Central Business Districts (CBD's),
   175
Centralism, 217
Chamber of Mines, 23, 184
Charterists, 77. *See also* Freedom
   Charter
Chetty, Kasval, xvii
Chinese, in South Asia, 37, 38
Chinese cultural revolution, 115
Christians/Christianity, 50, 125,
   136, 160, 197–202, 281
Black, 49–50, 99–100, 156, 161,
   198–202, 248
White, 47, 49, 50, 63–64, 72,
   156, 198, 248
Christmas, 115, 159
Churches. *See* Christians/
   Christianity
Ciskei, 78–79, 141, 192, 217
Citizenship
South African, 11, 28, 182, 251,
   259, 270
West German, 41, 272
City Press, 123
Civil disobedience, 130
Civil service, 45, 64–65, 209
Africanization of, 203, 230–33
Blacks in, 45, 56, 143–44
Conservative Party members in,
   62
language requirement for, 221
National Party members in, 25
Class
Black Consciousness and, 101
among Christians, 198
convergence with race, 13,
   16–17, 56
defusion of conflict over, 170,
   174, 179, 230
economic ethnicity and, 51

Groups Areas Act/influx control and, 117, 172, 224
Indian divisions in, 277
intra-Black conflict over, 117, 250
parliamentary system and, 18
technocratic liberation and, 249
and UDF appeal, 93
See also Middle class; Poverty/ poor people; Ruling class; Working class
Class analysis, 7, 32, 34, 98, 167. See also Marxism
Class interests, 26, 32, 64, 213
Clerictocracy, 50
Clough, Michael, cited, 276
Coercion, state, 5, 6, 39, 122, 134–42, 167–68, 250, 255
by Nazi fascism, 37
by police brutality, 104
See also Police; Violence
Coetzee, Johan M., 85
cited, 274, 277
Collaborators/collaboration, 10, 78–81, 122, 146, 150–51, 154
among Coloreds and Indians, 10, 49, 79–80, 81, 149
middle class opposed to, 149
unions and, 193, 259
Colonialism, xiii, 130, 146, 159, 229
Colored labor preference policy, 11, 172, 176
Coloreds, 13–14, 62, 107, 246
Black Consciousness and, 97, 101–2
in civil service, 143
co-optation of, 10, 49, 69, 144, 145, 151
educational budget for, 236
and extra-institutional protest/ boycott, 79, 80, 92, 95, 96, 191
and Group Areas Act, 139, 223
income levels of, 171, 176
Labor Party of, 77, 79, 81, 277
labor preference policy for, 11, 172, 176

languages of, 49, 221
media and, 163, 245
nonracialism advocated by, 67, 196
parliamentary rights of, 67, 79–80, 145, 166, 277
voting by, 14, 135, 148, 165–66
Commercial Catering and Allied Workers Union, 189
Communalism, 12, 14, 21, 47, 97, 160
Communism, 119, 198, 257–58
Communist Party of South Africa (CPSA), 96, 121, 125
Community, concept of, 207
Community unions, 191–92
Comparative reference groups, 112
Compensation, for property confiscations, 223
Competition, 31, 36, 38–39, 131, 197
Compliance, 40, 129–69, 179
Compromise, 212. See also Consociationalism
Concessions, 150, 205, 233, 238–239, 251
Confederation, 216
Conflict regulation mechanisms, 39, 71, 167, 169, 181, 238–43. See also Unions
Congress. See African National Congress
Congress of South African Students (COSAS), 114, 282
Congress of South African Trade Unions (COSATU), 193–94
Conservative Party (CP), South African, 60, 61, 62, 67, 69, 248–49
Conservative party (CDU), West German, 41
Consociationalism, 14, 38–39, 206–9, 212, 216, 226, 242–43
Constitution (1983), 67–71, 77, 93, 121, 135, 148–50, 163, 277
business and, 68, 70, 260

Constitution (1983) (*continued*)
  concessions necessary with, 150,
    238
  Inkatha opposed to, 91
  intra-Black conflict intensified
    by, 84, 91, 144–45, 149–50
  National Party and, 70–71, 93,
    135, 168, 261
  Progressive Federal Party and,
    70, 74, 91
Constitutional alternatives, 215–22
Constitutional assembly, 261–62
"Constructive engagement," 93,
  136
Consumer boycotts, 46, 82, 115,
  159, 189, 193, 194
Consumerism, 56, 103, 153,
  158–63, 168, 248
Cooper, Sath, 97
Cooperatives, farming, 173
Co-optation, 45, 51, 135, 144–54,
  167, 168, 205, 250
  of Coloreds, 10, 49, 69, 144,
    145, 151
  by consumerism, 56, 168
  and education, 235, 237
  of Indians, 10, 49, 69, 144–45,
    148, 149, 151
  Inkatha and, 195
  of self-reliant ethnic groups, 38,
    39
  of stigmatized subordinates, 41
  unions and, 179, 195
Coovadia, Jerry, xiv, xvi
Corder, Hugh, 231
Corporate federation, 216, 218–19
Corporatism, 12–13, 60, 164
COSAS, 114, 282
Cottage industries, 20
Council of Unions of South Africa
  (CUSA), 189, 191, 192, 194
Councils
  cultural, 229
  municipal/regional, 225–26
  urban community, 79, 110–12,
    140, 150
Courts, 231–32
  Industrial, 181, 182, 194, 259
Critical moralists, 58, 73–76

Critical theory, xii–xiii, xiv, 2, 3
Crossroads case, 105, 109
Cuba, 119
Cultural autonomy, 29, 220–21,
  229
Cultural councils, 229
Cultural distance, 210
Cultural ethnicity, 29–30, 31, 48,
  220
Cultural federalism, 221
Cultural incompatibility, 52
Cultural lag, 244
Cultural narcissism, 37–38, 40
Cultural pluralism, 51–53, 210–
  11, 212, 213
Cultural revivalism, x, 46, 53, 54
Currency, 18
Curricula, school, 233, 234, 247
Curry, David, 79, 277
Cyprus, 210

Davidson, Basil, 123
  cited, 276
Davies, Robert, 146–47
  cited, 269, 277
Death squads, 61, 65, 107
Decentralization, 18, 19–20, 217,
  218
Defiance Campaign, 94
Degenaar, Johan, xvi, 73
de Gruchy, John, cited, 281
de Klerk, Willem, 31
  cited, 271
de Klerk, Wimpie, 245
de Lange, A. Roukens, 172–73
  cited, 279
de Lange Panel, 237
Delegitimation, 272
Democracy, 71, 148, 166, 196, 212,
  216, 217, 218
  ANC and, 98, 128
  economic, 17–22, 181, 182, 209
  group, 12, 14
  and military, 65–66
  political, 17–22, 181, 182, 209
  proletarian, 160
  social, 95, 98, 171, 261, 263
  Western, 16, 52, 208, 218

Democratic socialism, 23, 217–18,
    251
Denationalization, 11, 13, 20, 39
Denitch, Bogdan, cited, 276
Department of Foreign Affairs, 66
Department of Indian Affairs, 81
Department of Internal Affairs,
    140
Dependency, 135, 142–44, 167,
    169
Depoliticization
    Black, 156–57, 158, 169
    media and, 158, 163
    of technocracy, 12, 250
    Western, 182
Deracialization, 10, 17, 32, 233,
    249, 250, 263
    business and, 209
    civil service affected by, 65
    consumerism and, 153
    as co-optation, 145–46
    and self-identification, 216
    See also Nonracialism
Detainees' Parents Support Com-
    mittee, 136
Deutsche Akademischer Aus-
    tauschdienst, xi
Dhlamini, Chris, 23–24
Dhlamini, Sipho, cited, 269
Dhlomo, Oscar, xv, xvi, 82
Dickie-Clark, Hamish, x, xvii, 131
    cited, 276
Dictatorship, 65, 66
Disinvestment, 87, 88, 152,
    190–91
Disorganized capitalism, 260
Dissent, 103, 156–57
Disunity, 46–47. See also Unity
Doctors' salaries, 149, 166
"Dominant ideology thesis," 142
Driefontain, 270
Drum Magazine, 159
Dugard, John, xvii, 231–32
    cited, 281
du Plessis, Fred, 118
du Preez, Johanna, 247
    cited, 282
Durban, 95, 111, 165
    Inkatha, 82, 91, 165

Moodley in, x, xi
newspapers of, 68, 175
shantytowns of, 172
surveys in, xv
du Toit, André, xvi, 156
    cited, 273, 278
du Toit, Mareta, xvi
Dyer, General, 275

Eastern Cape, 86, 113, 192, 193,
    221
East Germany, 163
East Rand, 178
Economic democracy, 17–22, 181,
    182, 209
Economic ethnicity, 29–30, 31,
    50–52, 220
Economic interdependence, 39,
    203–14, 218, 248
Economics, 6, 33, 45, 229, 230–33,
    252–53, 261, 263
    African-Indian, 84, 86
    ANC on, 95, 257
    of Bantustans, 20–22, 78, 191,
        204, 253
    Black Consciousness and, 97, 98
    of Black nationalism, 44, 45, 46,
        51, 56, 147–48, 198, 256
    Buthelezi and, 88, 89
    in co-optation, 51, 56, 147–48,
        149, 168, 179
    in ethnic states, 6, 155
    immigrant minorities and, 42
    international, 45, 120. See also
        under Investment
    of scapegoat minorities, 37
    of stigmatized subordinates, 40
    UDF on, 95
    See also Capitalism; Funding; In-
        come levels; Labor; Poverty/
        poor people; Recessions;
        Unions; Welfare schemes
Economist, 107, 220
Education, 31, 42, 103, 220–21,
    223, 229
    Bantu, 53, 54, 235
    Black, 17, 113, 114–15, 166,
        230, 232, 233–38
    expenditures on, 170, 234, 236

Education (*continued*)
  White, 63, 170, 234, 236
  See also Reeducation, attitudinal
Elandsrand Mine, xvi
Elections, 14, 73, 84, 135, 148–49,
    262. *See also* Voting
Eloff Commission, 136
Embarrassment, politics of, 80
Embourgeoisement, 170, 174–79,
    187
Emergency, state of, 106, 193
Employer organizations, 23, 24
Employment bureau recruiting,
    184
Employment projections, 171–73.
    See also Labor; Occupation;
    Unemployment
English language, 48, 221, 234,
    273
English press, 68, 152
English South Africans
  in business sector, 10, 44, 45, 55,
    68, 70, 243
  in Conservative Party, 61
  Progressive Federal Party identi-
    fied with, 70, 74
Equality/equity issues, 182, 214,
    230–33, 252, 261
  capitalism and, 19, 171
  economic ethnicity and, 29–30
  in education, 17, 233–34,
    236–37
  re income, 16–17, 149, 166, 171,
    175–76, 236, 273
Equalization payments, 230
Ethnicity, 26, 27, 196, 220, 222,
    229
  Black Consciousness and, 99
  cultural, 29–30, 31, 48, 220
  economic, 29–30, 31, 50–52,
    220
  fragmentation with, 153, 156,
    217
  and free enterprise policies, 213
  immigrant, 42–43
  Inkatha and, 82–83
  partition and, 209
  political/legal, 29, 30–31, 52–53,
    220

politicized, 27–36, 189. *See also*
    Nationalism
  vs. race, 16, 216
  and regionalism, 217
Ethnic Power Mobilized, xiii
Ethnic pride, 32, 43
Ethnic states, 4, 5, 30, 129–34,
    166, 271
  economics in, 6, 155
  media manipulation in, 156,
    163–64
  militarized polity in, 66
Ethnocentrism, occupational, 34,
    35
Europe
  class conflict defused in, 170,
    174, 179, 230
  economic unification of, 210
  franchise in, 209
  immigrants from, 17, 42
  labor in, 34, 41, 170, 179, 188
  metropolitan financing in, 224
  nationalism in, 28
  See also individual countries
Expenditures, government, 24–
    25, 137–38, 170–71, 230
  on education, 170, 234, 236
  See also Subsidies, state
Extra-institutional protest, 78, 79,
    88, 92–97, 103, 148, 193. *See
    also* Boycotts

Farming
  Afrikaner, 5, 10, 21, 43–44, 47,
    48, 60, 204, 253–54
  Black, 20, 21, 47, 173, 177–78,
    270
  subsistence, 19, 20, 21, 47,
    177–78
Federalism, 19, 38–39, 74–76,
    216, 218–19, 221, 251
Federation of South African Trade
    Unions (FOSATU), 23–24,
    185–93 passim
Fernando, Tissa, xvii
Field control, 137–38
Financial Mail (Johannesburg), 68,
    111, 181–82
Fisher, Bram, 54

Food and Canning Workers
Union, 189
Ford Motor Company, 113
Forsyth, Murray, 219
cited, 281
Fort Hare University, 113
FOSATU. *See* Federation of South
African Trade Unions
Foster, Joe, 187, 190
cited, 280
Fragmentation, 144–45, 150, 153,
156, 164, 168, 217, 237
France, 27, 65
Franchise, universal, 170, 182,
208, 209, 211, 251. *See also*
Voting
Frankel, Philip H., cited, 273, 282
Frankfurt School, xi, xii–xiii, xiv
Freedom Charter, 95–96, 98, 99,
102, 210, 213, 221, 257
Free enterprise policies, 171, 213,
261
Black bourgeoisie and, 147
equity issues over, 19, 261
right wing and, 60
unions and, 259, 261
Frelimo, 118
French Revolution, 27
Friedeburg, Ludwig von, xii
Friedrich, C., 218
Functionalism, 167
Funding
international, of unions, 187–88
See also Expenditures, govern-
ment; Investment

Gamson, William A., cited, 277
Gandhian tradition, 85, 94, 125,
159, 160
Gandhi settlement rioting, 84–85
Geertz, Clifford, cited, 271
General Allied Workers' Union
(GAWU), 191
General Motors, 113
General Workers Union, 189
Gerhart, Gail M., cited, 273
Germany, 242, 259. *See also* East
Germany; Nazi Germany;
West Germany

Giliomee, Annette, xvi
Giliomee, Hermann, xiii, xvi, 151,
193, 251
cited, 272, 273, 279
Godsell, Bobby, xvi
Goode, Patrick, cited, 271
Gordimer, Nadine, ix
cited, 269
Government. *See* State
Graig, Gordon, 36
cited, 271
Gramsci, Antonio, 276
Gramscian tradition, 5–6
Greenberg, Stanley, 6, 171–72, 271
cited, 269, 276, 279
Grice, Dushane, xvi
Group Areas Act, 12, 117, 149,
222–27, 252
business affected by, 175
Moodley family affected by, x, xi
private policing for, 139
Group boundaries, racial, 13, 15–
16, 53, 206, 210–11. *See also*
Ethnicity
Group democracy, 12, 14
Group formation, 33, 208, 218–19
Afrikaner, 31–32, 44
imposed, 13–15, 53–54, 229,
252
See also Identity, group
Grundy, Kenneth W., 165, 279
cited, 273
Guestworkers, 41. *See also* Migrant
labor
Gulf state Palestinians, 37–38
Gumede, A. J., cited, 275
Gun licenses, 81
Gurr, Ted R., 166–67
cited, 279
Guterman, N., cited, 271

Habermas, Jürgen, xii, 272
cited, 279
Halperin, Maurice, xvii
Hammanskraal Manifesto, 97
Hanf, Theodor, xvii, 83, 162
cited, 273, 274, 278, 281
Heard, Tony, xvi

Hechter, Michael, 33
    cited, 271
Hegemony, 5, 10, 179, 259, 276
Herstigte Nasionale Party (HNP),
    58, 60, 61, 67, 254
Hertzog, Albert, 60
Hervormde Kerk, 63
Heunis, Chris, 63
Hindus/Hinduism, 49, 50, 99, 197,
    277
History textbooks, 233, 247
HNP. See Herstigte Nasionale
    Party
Holiday observance, 229
Homelands (Bantustans), 20–21,
    39, 78–79, 86, 91, 140, 156,
    270
    bureaucracies of, 20, 56, 150–
        51, 217
    finances for, 21–22, 78, 191, 204
    labor in, 21–22, 172, 184, 205,
        253
    law enforcement in, 141
    in power-sharing arrangements,
        216–17, 218
Hope, Marjorie, cited, 281
Horkheimer, Max, xii, 36
Horowitz, Donald L., cited, 280
Horowitz, I. L., cited, 276
Hostility. See Antagonisms
Housing, 137, 173, 204, 230, 232.
    See also Rent collection
Human Science Research Council
    (HSRC), 123, 245, 246, 252
    cited, 282
Huntington, Samuel P., 15, 211
    cited, 270, 281
Huxley, Aldous, 168

Ideal interests, 7, 32
Identity, group, 7, 13, 14, 16, 31
    ethnic, 16, 30, 43, 44, 53, 131–
        32, 133, 165, 196
    occupational, 34, 35
    violence and, 106–7
    See also Group boundaries, racial
Ideology, 130–33, 211, 248, 252
    manipulative, 46–47, 103, 130,
        155–68 passim

    See also Politics/politicization;
        Reeducation, attitudinal
Illegitimacy. See Legitimacy
Immigrants, 17, 33, 36, 41–43. See
    also Migrant labor
Inanda riots, 84–85
Income levels, 16–17, 171, 172,
    175–76, 232, 273
    civil servants', 16–17, 25
    professionals', 16, 149, 166, 236
    working class, 172, 176, 254,
        259
Independence, of homelands, 39,
    78–79
Independence movements, 28
India, 40, 275
Indians, South African, ix–xi, 37–
    38, 62, 161, 246
    Black Consciousness and, 97,
        101–2
    in civil service, 143
    collaborators among, 10, 49, 79,
        80, 81, 149
    and co-optation, 10, 49, 69,
        144–45, 148, 149, 151
    educational budget for, 236
    and extra-institutional protest/
        boycotts, 79, 80, 92, 95, 96
    and Group Areas Act, x, 139
    income levels of, 171, 176
    and intra-Black conflicts, 83,
        84–85, 86, 95
    in labor hierarchies, 176, 177
    languages of, 49, 221
    media and, 163
    nonracialism advocated by, 67,
        196
    parliamentary rights of, 67, 79–
        80, 145, 166, 277
    religions of, 50, 277
    voting by, 14, 84, 135, 148, 165–
        66, 277
Indian Teachers' Federation, 278
Individualism, 196–97
Industrial Court, 181, 182, 194,
    259
Industrialization, 22, 39, 242–43
Industrial relations, 208. See also
    Labor; Unions

Inequality/inequity. *See* Equality/
  equity issues
Inflation, 25
Influx control, 17, 172, 204–5, 253
  co-optation and, 144, 153
  and housing, 137, 173, 204
  orderly urbanization policy and,
    11, 25, 153, 204
  private assistance in, 140
Informal contacts, 239, 241
Ingvavuma land deal, 90
Inkatha, 82–95 passim, 113, 165,
    185, 193, 194–95, 239, 248
  and ANC, 83, 84, 87–88, 127–
    28, 193, 258
  Arenstein championing, xvii
  business and, 258
  cultural revivalism of, 46
Insiders, 30
Institute for Black Research, cited,
  278
Institute of Social Research, xii
Institutional analysis, 1–2, 7. *See
  also* Extra-institutional protest
Institutional guerrilla warfare, 103
Intellectuals, 97, 102, 277–78
Internalization, of security, 137,
    141–42
International Confederation of
  Free Trade Unions (ICFTU),
  190
International investment. *See under*
  Investment
International law, 13
Investment
  in Bantustans, 20–22
  foreign, 20–22, 68, 152, 191
  See also Disinvestment
Ireland, 131, 203, 210
Isaacs, Harold R., cited, 271
Isibonelo High School, xv
Isithebe, 22
Islam/Muslims, 49, 50, 99, 197,
    277
Israel, 30, 66, 133, 257, 279

James, Wilmot G., xvi, 151
  cited, 270, 278
Jameson Raid, 193

Japan, 180
Japanese-Canadians, 223
Jews
  in Nazi Germany, 36–37
  See also Israel
Johannesburg
  newspapers of, 68, 107, 111,
    181–82
  surveys in, xv
Johnson, Chalmers, 166–67
  cited, 279
Johnstone, Frederick, 7
  cited, 270
Jooste, C. P., x
Jordan, Jean, xviii
Joseph, Helen, 54
Judaism, 99, 197
Judiciary system, 231–32. *See also*
  Industrial Court; Legality
Just war, 200

Kairos theologians, 200
Kane-Berman, John, xvii
  cited, 274, 277
Kannemeyer, Donald, 104, 106
Karis, T., cited, 273
Kaunda, Kenneth, 117, 124–25
  cited, 280
Kennan, George F., 133
  cited, 276
Kennedy, Edward, 24, 94
Kent State University killings, 275
Khayelitsha, 172
Kiernan, James, 201
  cited, 280
Kinship ties, 32–33, 47
Kitchen, Helen, cited, 276
Kruger, Jimmy, 106
Kundera, Milan, 213
  cited, 281
Kuper, Leo, x
  cited, 273
Kwa Mashu, 84, 91
Kwa-Ngema, 270
KwaZulu, 83, 87, 89–90, 92,
    101–2, 111

Labor, 5, 6, 33–34, 47, 102, 133,
    256

Labor (*continued*)
  agricultural, 5, 21, 47, 204, 253, 254
  ANC, 94, 96, 178, 187, 188, 193, 258
  Black Consciousness and, 97, 100, 101, 189, 192–95
  after Boer War, 43
  co-optation and, 41, 51, 151–52, 179, 194–95
  dependency of state on, 169
  in Eastern Cape, 86, 113, 192, 193
  embourgeoisement of, 174–79, 187
  in homelands, 21–22, 172, 184, 205, 253
  immigrant, 17, 33, 36, 41–42. *See also* Migrant labor
  manufacturing, 113, 254
  mining, 5, 184–85, 254
  in Natal, 86, 172, 176–77, 277
  preference policies re, 11, 151, 172, 176
  on Rand, 86, 172, 178, 186, 191, 254, 259
  recessions and, 33, 45, 60, 113, 184, 193
  sexual division of, 145
  stigmatized ethnic group, 41
  White, 5, 34, 47, 58–61, 203, 254
  See also Unemployment; Unions
Labor aristocracy, 177
Labor control. *See* Influx control
Labor hierarchy, 51, 176–79
Labor Party, 77, 79, 81, 277
Labor racists, 33–34, 58–61
Laclau, E., cited, 271
Lambley, Peter, cited, 273
Lamontville, 91
Land Act, 270
Land consolidation policy, 254
Land deal, Ingvavuma, 90
Landownership, 11, 270
  AZAPO and, 102
  See also Group Areas Act
Langa shootings, 9, 104, 106

Languages, 29, 31, 49, 197, 198, 220–22, 229, 273
  in Afrikaner nationalism, 44, 48
  Black nationalism and, 48–49
  in schools, 31, 221, 234
Latin America, 50, 60, 61, 65, 66
Law
  international, 13
  See also Legality
Law enforcement, 137–42. *See also* Coercion; Police
Lawrence, John C., cited, 278
Leaders, 207
Lebanese, in West Africa, 37
Lebanon, 203, 210, 227
Legal ethnicity, 29, 30–31, 52–53, 220
Legality
  in group boundaries, 13, 15–16, 53
  in labor disputes, 182. *See also* Industrial Court
  vs. legitimacy, 129–30
Legal system, 231–32. *See also* Industrial Court
Legitimacy, 6, 13–17, 129–31, 182, 256, 272, 276
  affirmative action enhancing, 41
  and coercion, 6, 65, 136, 137, 141–42, 167–68
  of collaborators, 81
  compliance and, 135, 136, 137, 141–42, 154–57, 166–69
  constitution and, 135, 148, 168, 261
  of educational policy, 237
  internal vs. external, 155
  in multination states, 39
  negotiations and, 239
  of unions, 259
  White politics and, 61, 72, 73, 157
Legitimation, 162, 272, 276
Legitimation crisis, 72, 129–30, 168, 181, 272
Leiss, William, cited, 278
Lekganyane, Bishop, 201
Lelyveld, Joseph, cited, 269

Lenin, V. I., 188, 217–18
le Roux, Pieter, xvi
Lesotho, 118
Liberalism, 8, 54–55, 202, 210,
    220
  Black Consciousness and, 97,
    101, 102
  Liberal Party, 76
Liberation, 4, 110, 165, 249
  ANC theory of, 96
  psychological, 54, 83, 97
  technocratic, 11, 103, 162, 249
Liberation theology, 50, 199. *See
    also* Black theology
Lijphart, Arend, xvii, 208, 213
  cited, 271, 281
Lipset, S. M., 272
Lipton, Merle, 26
  cited, 271, 279, 282
Lodge, Tom, cited, 273
Loewenthal, Leo, xii
Lombard, Jan, 18
  cited, 270
London *Sunday Times*, 152
Lovedale High School, 113
Lowenthal, L., cited, 271
Luangwa National Park meeting,
    117–18
Lumpenproletarians, 178, 250
Lusaka Manifesto, 133–34
Lustick, Ian, 279
Lutheranism, 199

Maasdorp, Gavin, xvi
Mabaso, Lyban, cited, 275
McGrath, M., cited, 176
Machel, Samora, 124–25
MacLennan, John, cited, 275
Magoma, Lent, 192
Maharaj, Mac, 84
Mahoney, Anita, xvii
Mahuilili, Nathaniel, cited, 280
Majoritarianism, 212
Malaya, 31
Malaysia, 37
Malcomess, John, 106
Management positions, Black, 86,
    176, 183, 230

Management techniques, 123, 183,
    237. *See also* Technocracy/
    technocrats
Mandela, Nelson, 92, 95, 120, 127,
    243, 276
  cited, 275
Mangope, Lucas, 78
Manipulation, state, 7, 27, 45, 77,
    130, 155–69 passim, 232,
    250–51
  in Black Consciousness, 101
  through consumerism, 103,
    158–62, 168
  by co-optation, 144, 167, 168,
    237
  of educational institutions, 103,
    237
  by fragmentation, 144, 156, 164,
    168, 237
  of Indians, 144, 277
  through media, 103, 156, 157–
    59, 161–64
  of White reeducation, 244
Manpower Department, 181–82
Mantanzima, Kaiser, 77
Manufacturing, 113, 254
Mao Tse-tung, 115
Marais, Jaap, 61
Marcuse, Herbert, xii
Markinor study, 152
Marriages, 12, 42
Marx, Karl, 65, 142, 147
Marxism, 5, 6, 64, 198, 212–13,
    255, 276
  ANC and, 96
  dominant ideology thesis of, 142
  on ethnic pride, 32
  German, xiii
  on revolution, 160, 167
  UDF accused of, 93
  on working-class solidarity, 34
  See also Neo-Marxism
Material interests, 7, 32. *See also*
    Economics
Mathews, Tony, xvi
Mbeki, Govan, 127
Mbeki, Thabo, 96, 219
  cited, 275, 282

Media, 68, 103, 156, 157–59, 161–
64, 245. *See also* Press; South
African Broadcasting Corpo-
ration; Television
Meer, Fatima, x, xvi, 80, 84
cited, 274, 278
Membership reference group, 112
Menzi High, xv
Meritocracy, 196
Metro Cash and Carry, 158
Middle class
ethnic hostility of, 34–36
White, 25, 44, 51, 62
See also Black middle class
Middlemen minorities, 37–38,
39–40
Migrant labor, 33–34, 36
in South Africa, 5, 33–34, 86,
100, 151, 172, 177–79, 184,
204–5, 221, 254
in the United States, 33
in West Germany, 33, 41–42
Military, 39, 227–28, 250
ANC and, 119–20, 124, 125–26
South African, 46, 47, 65–67,
228
See also Armies
Miners/mining companies, xvi, 5,
184–85, 254
Mineworkers Union, 59, 184, 189,
190, 254
Ministers of Manpower, 181–82,
192
Mission in Exile. *See* African Na-
tional Congress
Mkhize, Saul, 270
Modernizing Racial Domination, xiii
Molefe, Themba, 110
Möller, Valerie, 178–79
cited, 279
Moodie, D. T., cited, 273, 276
Moodley, Amarthan, xviii
Moodley, Kogila, ix–xi
cited, 272
Moodley, Percy, xviii
Moore, Barrington, 115, 142
cited, 275, 277
Moral indifference, 3
Moralists, critical, 58, 73–76

Moral legitimacy, 39, 142, 168
Motanyane, Maud, 114
Mothobi, Don, xvii
Motlana, N., xiv
Motor industry, 113
Mozambique, 118, 119, 120, 124,
269
Mphahlele, E., 201–2
cited, 281
Mugabe, Robert, 118
Multiculturalism, 216–21, 229
Multilingualism, 38, 221
Multiracialism, 76, 80
in consociational model, 212
consumerism and, 168
democracies and, 16
and KwaZulu/Inkatha/Buthe-
lezi, 90, 254, 258
and security loyalty, 279
Muslims. *See* Islam/Muslims
Muzorewa, Abel, 89

Naicker, Monty, x
Namibia, 230
Narcissism, cultural, 37–38, 40
Nasionale Pers, 123
Nasser, Martin, 278
Natal, xvi, 172, 277
African-Indian relations in,
83–84
business in, 258
farmers of, 254
Inkatha in, 84, 85, 86, 113
labor hierarchies in, 176–77
languages in, 221
Natal Indian Congress (NIC), 99,
278
Natal University Medical School,
xv–xvi, 95
Nation, defined, 28
National convention strategy, 98–
99, 206, 262. *See also*
Consociationalism
National Forum, 77, 98, 99
Nationalism, 11, 26, 27–29, 164–
66, 233
Quebec, 44, 210
and secessionism, 217

See also Afrikaner nationalism;
Black nationalism
Nationalization, of industries, 95,
257
National Party (NP), 10, 30, 168,
196, 241, 245, 276
civil servants in, 25
and constitutional reforms, 70–
71, 93, 135, 168, 261
and co-optation, 145, 168
de-ethnicization of, 207
and HNP, 58, 60, 61, 254
Indians in, 277
Inkatha and, 89
relationship with military, 66,
253
1982 split in, 10, 64, 73, 77, 254
1948 victory of, 46
police of, 253
poster slogan of, 61
press outlets of, 123, 245
and Progressive Federal Party,
74
regionalism advocated by, 19
UDF and, 92, 93, 135
National Union of Mineworkers
(NUM), 59, 184, 189, 190,
254
National Union of South African
Students (NUSAS), x, 101
Native Americans, 229
Naudé, Beyers, 54, 136, 280
Nazi Germany, xii, 36–37, 223,
272
Nederduitse Gereformeerde Kerk,
63
Negotiations
government-Black, 11–12, 117–
28, 153, 206, 239–43, 251,
252, 258, 261, 262
union, 10, 194
Neoapartheid, 11, 20, 168, 204
Neo-Marxism, 7, 33
Netherlands, 242
Newspapers, 123, 163. *See also*
Press; *individual papers*
Ngema, Stuurman, 270
Nigel, Mark, xvi
Nigeria, 210

1984 (Orwell), 155, 160, 162, 164,
168
Nkomati accord, 118, 119, 125,
250
Nkomo, William F., 89, 118
Nobel Peace Prize, 152
Nolutshungu, Sam C., 146, 151
cited, 273, 277
Nonracialism, 5, 53, 67, 196, 210,
214, 263
and African-Indian antagonism,
85
Afrikaner nationalism and,
219–20
of ANC, 54, 196
and capitalism, 146
and democracy, 16, 52, 212,
218, 219–20, 263
Inkatha and, 85, 92
power-sharing and, 212, 216,
261–62
UDF and, 85, 92
unions and, 192, 195
Whites affected by, 204
Normative reference group, 112
North America, xviii
embourgeoisement in, 174
franchise in, 209
immigration to, 42
Native American self-government in, 229
See also Canada; United States
Norton, Robert, cited, 271
Nthembu, Pat, xv–xvi
Ntuzuma College of Education, xv
NUSAS, x, 101

Occupation
and risk, 103
See also Civil service; Manage-
ment positions, Black;
Professionals; Working class
Occupational ethnocentrism, 34,
35
Offe, Claus, cited, 282
Ogbu, John, 271
Oligarchy, xiii, 12–13
O'Meara, Dan, 147
cited, 269, 272, 277

Oppenheimer thesis, 171
Orange Free State, 221
Orderly Movement and Settlement
  of Black Persons Bill, 140
Orderly urbanization, 11, 25, 153,
  204
Organization of African Unity
  (OAU), 125
Orkin, Mark, cited, 278
Orthodox ideologues, 58, 62–67
Orwell, George, 155, 160, 162,
  164, 168
Outsiders, 30, 31
Overthrow of dominant group,
  38–39
Owen, Ken, 258–59
  cited, 282

Palestinians, 37–38
Pan African Congress (PAC), 97
Parliaments, 18, 55, 259, 277
  Colored and Indian, 67, 79–80,
    145, 166, 277
  police brutality affidavits in, 106
Partition/secession, 38, 39, 208–9,
  217, 218
Pass laws, 137, 140, 144
Paternalism, 40–41, 239. See also
  Patronage-client alliances
Paton, Alan, 280
Patronage-client alliances, 78–81.
  See also Collaborators/
  collaboration
Pension funds, 182–83
Peretz, Don, cited, 279
Peterson, William, cited, 270
"Picannins," 184
Pluralism, 51–53, 210–11, 212,
  213
Poland, 198–99
Police, 9, 104–6, 107, 108–9, 134,
  136, 227–28, 233
  Black, 9, 139, 228, 279
  Buthelezi and, 82
  and intra-Black violence, 110
  and labor, 141, 193
  political party support among,
    67, 253
  private, 139

Political democracy, 17–22, 181,
  182, 209
Political ethnicity, 29, 30–31, 52–
  53, 220
Political Interference Act, 76, 163,
  207
Political Mythology of Apartheid, 247
Political participation
  on assigned group basis, 14
  by collaborators, 79–80
  in Western societies, 182
  See also Voting
Political parties, 12, 244, 251
  Communist, 96, 121, 125
  Conservative, 60, 61, 62, 67, 69,
    248–49
  German, 41
  Herstigte Nasionale, 58, 60, 61,
    67, 254
  Labor, 77, 79, 81, 277
  Liberal, 76
  See also National Party; Progres-
    sive Federal Party
Political prisoners, 243
Political representation, 14, 224–
  26, 251, 261–62, 277. See also
  Parliaments
Politicized ethnicity, 27–36, 189.
  See also Nationalism
Politics/politicization, xiv, 1–2, 4,
  17–22, 229, 230, 242, 249–51
  Black (general), 55–57, 76, 77–
    128, 135, 149, 152–53, 189,
    194. See also Black
    nationalism
  business and, 10, 18–19, 22–25,
    55, 68, 70, 117–18, 123,
    256, 257–58, 260
  of stigmatized subordinates, 40
  unions and, 51, 82, 94, 126, 152,
    185–87, 190, 209, 250, 258
  West German immigrants and,
    41, 42
  White (general), 55, 58–76,
    163–64. See also Afrikaner
    nationalism; State
  Zionists avoiding, 201
  See also Constitution; Depolitici-
    zation; Negotiations;
    Power-sharing

Poovalingham, Pat, xvi
Port Elizabeth, 191
Posel, Deborah, cited, 276
Posters, party, 61
Poulantzan tradition, 5
Poverty/poor people
    Black, 16, 17, 200, 233
    and consumerism, 160
    rural, 21, 100, 144, 172, 178,
        205, 230
    urban, 100
    White, 46–47, 51, 55, 203
Power-sharing, 10, 145–46, 211–
        12, 216–18, 241, 252
    business and, 123, 254, 258
    Buthelezi and, 84, 254
    Conservative Party and, 62
    consociationalism and, 206, 208,
        216
    constitution of 1983 and, 67, 69,
        70, 71, 150
    in constitutional assembly, 261
Power transfer, 206
Pragmatic institutional opposition,
        78, 81–92
Pragmatic (verligte) outlook, 58
Presentism, 1
Press, 42
    Afrikaans, 68, 136, 245
    Black, 123
    English, 68, 152
    See also individual newspapers
Pretoria, languages in, 221
Pretoria government. See State
Pride, ethnic, 32, 43
Primordialism, 31–32
Prior, Andrew, cited, 269
Prisoners, political, 243
Privatization
    in education, 238
    of industrial labor relations,
        141, 180
    of policing, 139–41
Professionals
    Black, 16, 56, 92, 149, 166, 176,
        236
    collaboration opposed by, 149
    and ethnic hostility, 34–35
    income levels of, 16, 149, 166,
        236

in UDF, 92
    See also Teachers
Progressive Federal Party (PFP),
        60, 73–76, 170
    and constitution, 70, 74, 91
    cultural councils proposed by,
        229
    military and, 67
    regionalism advocated by, 19
Property confiscations, xi, 223–24
Pross, Helge, xii
Protestants, 198, 199. See also
        Calvinism
Psychological factors
    in economic integration, 34–35
    in rebellion, 115–16
    in stigmatization, 40
Psychological liberation, of Black
        Consciousness, 54, 83, 97

Quebec nationalism, 44, 210
Quota system, in surveys, 278

Race
    capitalism and, 5, 23, 97–98,
        147, 171, 213
    class convergence with, 13, 16–
        17, 56
    vs. ethnicity, 16, 216
    stratification by. See Group
        boundaries, racial
    See also Deracialization; Ethnic-
        ity; Multiracialism; Nonra-
        cialism; individual racial
        groups
Radio, 68, 161, 163
Radio South Africa, 161–62
Rajab, Devi, xvi
Rajab, Mahmoud, xiv, xvi
Rajbansi, A., cited, 274
Ramaphosa, Cyril, 190
Rand area, 86, 172
    television in, 158
    unions in, 178, 186, 191, 254,
        259
Random sampling, 278
Rantete, Johannes, cited, 275, 281
Rapes, 232
Rapport, 245
Raspberry, William, cited, 275

Reactionary (*verkrampte*) outlook, 58
Reagan administration, 120, 136
Recessions, 45
  and business-government relations, 123
  ethnic hostility during, 33
  and government spending, 230
  HNP support and, 60
  motor industry affected by, 113
  union activity and, 184, 193
Recognition arrangements, union, 181, 191
Reddy, Jairam N., xvi, 79
Reductionism, 5, 6
Reeducation, attitudinal
  of Blacks, 159–60
  of Whites, 209, 244–47
Reference group theory, 112
Reformist unions, 189–91, 258–59
Regionalism, 18, 19–20, 29, 89, 217, 226–27
Religion, 29, 197–203, 220–21
  in Afrikaner nationalism, 44, 48
  Black Consciousness and, 99–100
  in Black nationalism, 49–50, 198
  of Indians, 50, 277
  See also Christians/Christianity
Relly, Gavin, cited, 270
Relocations, 11. *See also* Group Areas Act
Renner, Karl, 28
Rent collection, 79, 110, 111, 140, 150
Report of the Commission of Inquiry into Labor Legislation, 181
Republic of South Africa (RSA), 77
Resistance, 3, 40, 41, 135, 165, 255
  coercion increasing, 136
  dependency weakening, 143
  depoliticization and, 156–57
  Gandhian, 159
  Radio South Africa on, 161–62
  religion and, 198, 200
  See also African National Congress; Black Consciousness; Extra-institutional protest

Retirement, status insecurity in, 35. *See also* Pension funds
Revenue sharing, 230
Revisionists, 5, 171
Revolution, 160, 164, 167, 259
"Revolution from above," 11
Rhodesia, 61
Rich, Paul, cited, 281
Riekert Commission, 140, 204
Riots, 84–85, 106–7. *See also* Violence
Road Transportation Amendment Bill, 175
Roos, Jack, 192
Rotberg, Robert, cited, 281, 282
Rothschild, Joseph, cited, 278
Royce, Anya Peterson, cited, 272
Ruling class, 9, 10, 18, 58, 67–72, 98. *See also* Technocracy/technocrats
Runciman, W. G., cited, 275
Rupert, Anton, 118
Rural population, 22, 216
  Black Consciousness and, 100
  influx control and, 144, 153, 205
  poor, 21, 100, 144, 172, 178, 205, 230
  See also Farming; Homelands; Migrant labor
Rustomjees, xvi

SABC. *See* South African Broadcasting Corporation
Salaries. *See* Income levels
Samuels, Pat, xv
Sanctions, international, 120
SASO, 65, 101
Saunders, Chris, xvi
Saunders, Pam, xvi
Savage, Michael, xvi
  cited, 273
Scapegoat minorities, 36–38, 39–40
Schlemmer, Lawrence, xvi, 151–52, 176, 178–79
  cited, 271, 274, 275, 278, 279
Scholarships, 238
Schools. *See* Education
Schreiner, Dennys, xvi
Scott, Jay, cited, 279

Sebokeng searches, 116
Secession/partition, 38, 39, 208–9, 217, 218
Secret dialogue, 241, 242
Security, 164, 227–28. *See also* Military; Police
Security agencies, private, 139
Security loyalty, 279
Selective targeting, 137, 138–39
Self-denigration, 42
Self-determination, 27, 28, 29, 53, 78, 228–29
Self-education, political, 115
Self-racism, 97
Self-reliant ethnic groups, 36, 38–39, 40, 271
Serfontein, Henni, xvii
Sex, interethnic, 12, 42
Sexual division of labor, 145
Shantytowns, 172
Sharpeville, 104, 249
Silber, Gus, cited, 278
Simkins, Charles, 171, 236
    cited, 279
Singh, Dharam, 278
Sisulu, Walter, 127
Sizwe, N., cited, 275
Skocpol, Theda, 167
    cited, 279
Slovo, Joe, 187
    cited, 275
Smith, M. G., 52
    cited, 273
Smith, Winston, 164
Smooha, Sammy, 279
Social contact, 223, 241
Social democracy, 95, 98, 171, 261, 263
Social distance, 210
Social engineering, 22, 237, 249. *See also* Management techniques
Socialism, 5, 255, 278
    ANC and, 96, 248, 257, 282
    Black Consciousness and, 100, 189
    democratic, 23, 217–18, 251
    Inkatha and, 248
Social Science Research Council of Canada, xviii

"Solidarity," 277
Sotho language, 48, 221
South African Allied Workers Union (SAAWU), 191
South African Appeals Court, 231
South African Broadcasting Corporation (SABC), xiv, 14, 119, 162
    cited, 270, 276
South African Confederation of Labour, 59
South African Council of Churches, 136, 281
South African Council of Trade Unions (SACTU), 96, 188, 193
South African Defence Force (SADF), 66
South African Indian Council (SAIC), 80, 81
South African Institute of Race Relations (SAIRR), cited, 171, 274, 280, 281, 282
South African Native National Congress, 113
South African Students' Organization (SASO), 65, 101
South Africa: Sociology of a Race Society, xiii
Southall, R., 91
    cited, 274, 275
South Asia, Chinese in, 37, 38
Southern African Development Bank, 21, 138
South-West African People's Organization (SWAPO), 120, 125
Soviet Union, 119–20, 218
Soweto, 112, 178, 202
Sparks, Allister, 198
Spiderman, 158
Spring, Martin, 282
Squatter camps/squatters, 21, 172, 173, 178–79, 204
Sri Lanka, 210
Stability, 39, 151, 251
    business and, 256, 258
    orderly urbanization and, 25
    with welfare schemes, 19, 230
Stalin, J., 217–18
State, 3–4, 5–6, 9–22, 102, 252–53

State (*continued*)
  and business, 18–19, 20, 22–25,
    55, 117–18, 123, 139–40,
    258, 259
  and Buthelezi/KwaZulu, 89–90
  and constitutional assembly, 262
  ethnic dominance by (general),
    36–43
  land policies of, 11, 254, 270. *See
    also* Group Areas Act; Ur-
    banization policy
  negotiations with Blacks by, 11–
    12, 117–28, 153, 206, 239–
    43, 251, 252, 258, 261, 262
  paternalistic, 40–41, 239. *See
    also* Patronage-client
    alliances
  privatization of policing by,
    139–41
  security of, 164, 227–28. *See also*
    Military; Police
  violence of, 9, 36–38, 42, 103–9,
    136, 203, 275
  See also Afrikaner nationalism;
    Botha, P. W.; Coercion,
    state; Constitution; Co-op-
    tation; Deracialization; Eth-
    nic states; Expenditures,
    government; Legitimacy;
    Manipulation, state; Na-
    tional Party; Technocracy/
    technocrats
State Security Council, 66, 121
Status insecurity, 35
Status needs, 35
Status reduction, 34, 204
Steele, Jonathan, cited, 282
Stellenbosch, 252
Steyn, Jan, cited, 279
Stigmatized subordinates, 36, 39–
  41, 42, 48
Strikes, 24, 182, 184, 185, 186,
  193, 194, 254
Student representative councils
  (SRC's), 282
Students
  expenditures on, 236
  intra-Black violence among, 95
  militant, 114, 250, 252, 282
  See also Education

*Study on the Rights of Persons Belong-
  ing to Ethnic, Religious, and Lin-
  guistic Minorities*, 229
Subcontracting, 137, 139–41
Subsidies, state, 60
  for Bantustans, 21–22
  to KwaZulu, 89
  for stigmatized minorities, 41
  See also Welfare schemes
Subsistence farming, 19, 20, 21,
  47, 177–78
Sudan, 210
Suid-Afrikaan, 252
Sun Cities, 72
Sunday Times (Johannesburg), 68,
  107
Sunday Tribune (Durban), 68, 175
Superman, 158
Suzman, Helen, 54, 74
Swaziland, 90, 118, 141
Switzerland, 242
Symbiotic relationship, between
  state and business, 5, 23
Symbolic ethnicity, 42–43

Tambo, Oliver, 83, 98, 124
  cited, 281
Taxation, 18, 25, 60, 139–40,
  223–24
Taxi business, Black, 110, 174–75
Teachers, 63, 114, 236, 238, 247
  salaries of, 149, 166, 236
Technocracy/technocrats, xiii, 12,
  58, 67–72, 162, 205, 248–51
  and deracialization, 17, 146,
    249, 250
  and economic issues, 18, 232,
    261
  and reeducation of Whites, 244
  regionalism advocated by, 19
  and multiracialism, 80, 168
  and negotiations (ANC-govern-
    ment), 123
Technocratic liberation, 11, 103,
  162, 249
Television, 45, 68, 158, 162, 163,
  229, 245–47
Tenancy, 5, 253. *See also* Rent
  collection

Terreblanche, Sampie, 18
    cited, 270
Terrorism, 121, 143. *See also*
    Violence
Teschner, Manfred, xii
Textbooks, 233, 247
The Employment Bureau of Africa (TEBA), 184
Theology, Black, 49–50, 99–100, 199. *See also* Christians/Christianity
Thompson, Leonard, 247
    cited, 269, 281
Tolerance, 157
Totalitarianism, 213, 214
Townships, 11, 172, 224, 270
    business in, 110, 113, 175, 257–58
    councils in, 79, 110–12, 140, 150
    languages in, 221
    lumpenproletarians in, 178
    media in, 162
    and police, 110, 136, 228
    and religion, 202
    unrest in, 110–17, 127, 135–36, 140, 202, 249, 257
Transkei, 77, 78, 217
Transvaal
    and Afrikaner disunity, 46–47
    and constitutional referendum, 68
    farmers in, 253–54
    Hanf survey in, 162
    Indians in, 86, 99, 277
    intra-Black antagonism in, 86
    languages in, 221
    student-initiated stay-away in, 114
    teachers in, 63
Transvaal and Natal Indian Congress, 99
Transvaal Teachers' Organization, 63
Transvaal Onderwysersvereeniging, 63
Treason trial, x
Treurnicht, Andries P., 60, 61, 62, 63, 65
"Tribal academia," xi
Tribalism, 217

Tribal Labour Bureaus, 205
Tshabalala, Ephraim, 112
Turk, Austin T., 137, 169
    cited, 276, 277, 279
Turkey, 37
Tutu, Desmond M., 88, 94, 95, 152, 280
    cited, 281
TV2, 158

UDF. *See* United Democratic Front
Umbumbulo College of Education, xv
Unemployment, 21, 173, 184, 230
    and disinvestment, 152
    among stigmatized minorities, 41
    structural, 19, 45, 171–72
Unions, 10, 23–24, 60, 117, 123, 179–95, 261
    Black Consciousness and, 100–101, 189, 192–95
    business support for, 258–60
    consumer boycotts by, 46, 82, 189, 193, 194
    European, 170, 179, 188
    migrants and, 178, 184
    mineworkers', 59, 184, 189, 190, 254
    and orderly urbanization, 25
    and politics, 51, 82, 94, 126, 152, 185–87, 190, 209, 250, 258
    privatization of disputes of, 141, 180
    White, 10, 51, 58–60
    women in, 145
United Democratic Front (UDF), xiv, 110, 121, 122
    and Black Consciousness, 77, 93, 98
    and Buthelezi, 84, 85, 91–92, 127–28, 258
    cited, 275
    and elections, 135, 148
    emergence of, 77
    extra-institutional protest by, 87–88, 92–95, 97, 193
    in media, 245

United Democratic Front
  (*continued*)
  unions and, 189, 191, 192, 193,
    258
United Nations, 128, 228–29
United States, xviii, 218
  "constructive engagement" of,
    93, 136
  education in, 238
  ethnic pride in, 43
  Kent State killings in, 275
  labor in, 33, 180, 181, 188
  municipal finance in, 224
  and Soviet threat, 120
  UDF and, 93–94
Unity
  Afrikaner and Black nationalism
    both lacking, 46–47
  Black Consciousness and,
    99–101
  union, 189, 192–95
University of Natal, x
University of South Africa
  (UNISA), 139, 171
University of Zululand, 95
Upper class, 34–35
Urban Blacks, 21, 103, 168, 173–
  74. *See also* Black middle class;
  Labor; Townships
Urban Foundation, 123, 173–74,
  233
Urbanization policy, 21, 22, 144,
  173–74, 216
  "orderly," 11, 25, 153, 204
  See also Influx control
Uys, Stanley, xvii

Vaal, 84, 221
Value socialization, 159. *See also*
  Ideology
Vancouver, xi–xii
van den Berghe, Pierre L., x, xvii,
  32
  cited, 271, 280
van der Merwe, H. W., xvi
Van Zyl Slabbert, F., xiv, xvi, 70,
  74, 239
  cited, 274
Van Zyl Slabbert, Jane, xvi

Venda, 78, 217
Verwoerd, Hendrik, 9, 20, 205,
  222, 245
Vietnam, 37
Vilakazi, Absolom L., 102
  cited, 275
Vilakazi, Herbert W., 102
  cited, 275
Viljoen, Gerrit, 63, 270
Villa-Vicencio, Charles, cited, 281
Violence, 38, 88, 103–17, 203,
  230, 249–60 passim
  ANC and, 88, 116, 121, 165,
    243, 250, 255
  intra-Black, 56, 84–86, 88, 95,
    109–17, 255
  state, 9, 36–38, 42, 103–9, 136,
    203, 275
  See also Death squads; Military;
    Police
Volkswagen, 113
Vorster, B. J., 20, 58, 60, 77
Vosloo, Ton, 123
Voting, 14, 81, 195, 211, 225–26,
  261–62
  by Coloreds and Indians, 14, 84,
    135, 148, 165–66, 277
  German migrants denied, 41
  Progressive Federal Party, 73, 74
  and UDF arrests, 135, 148–49
  universal franchise for, 170,
    182, 208, 209, 211, 251

Wages. *See* Income levels
Ward system, 225–26
Washington Post, 134
Wealth, 16, 18. *See also* Income
  levels
Weber, Max, xi, 2, 276
Welfare schemes, 18, 19–20, 42,
  47, 170–74
Welsh, David, xvi, 150
  cited, 272
Welsh, Virginia, xvi
Western Cape, 172, 221
West Germany, xi
  co-determination policy of, 180
  foreigners in, 33, 35, 41–42, 272
  media in, 163

Nazi victims compensated by,
    223
"What Is to Be Done?", 188
Whites, 133–34, 263
    in Black unions, 189, 194
    education of, 63, 170, 234, 236
    Group Areas Act benefits for,
        223–24
    income levels of, 149, 166, 171,
        176, 273
    languages of, 44, 48, 221, 234,
        273
    liberalism among, 54–55, 97,
        101, 102, 202
    middle class, 25, 44, 51, 62
    politics of (general), 55, 58–76,
        163–64. See also Afrikaner
        nationalism; State
    poor, 46–47, 51, 55, 203
    reeducation of, 209, 244–47
    unions of, 10, 51, 58–60
    working class, 5, 34, 47, 58–61,
        203, 254
    See also Afrikaners; English
        South Africans
Wiechers, Marinus, cited, 273
Wiehan Commission, 179, 180,
    181
Wilson, Francis, xvi, 105
    cited, 275
Wisner, Frank, 120
    cited, 276
Witwatersrand, 221
Women, Black, 139, 145
Wong, Yuwa, xvii
Working class, 51, 96, 151, 170,
    187, 277

Black Consciousness and, 97,
    100, 101
embourgeoisement of, 170,
    174–79, 187
ethnic hostility among, 33–34
income levels of, 172, 176, 254,
    259
White, 5, 34, 47, 58–61, 203,
    254
See also Labor
World Alliance of Reformed
    Churches, 63
Writers, Black, 221

Xhosa, 48, 79, 113, 221

Young, James, cited, 281
Youth leadership camps, 238
Yudelman, David, cited, 269, 270
Yugoslavs, 219

ZAPU, 89
Zimbabwe, 61, 89, 124, 206
    and ANC, 118
    army in, 227
    farming in, 204
    Radio South Africa on, 161
Zionist Christian Church, 49, 156,
    160, 200–202
Zulu-factor, 277
Zululand, 22
Zulus, 46, 82–92 passim, 258
    armies of, 47
    language of, 48–49, 221
    See also Inkatha; KwaZulu

About the Authors

HERIBERT ADAM is Professor of Sociology at Simon Fraser University in Vancouver, B.C. He is the author of *Modernizing Racial Domination* (University of California Press) and *Ethnic Power Mobilized* with H. Giliomee (Yale University Press). He has edited and co-authored *South Africa: Sociological Perspectives* (Oxford University Press) and *South Africa: The Limits of Reform Politics* (E. J. Brill).

KOGILA MOODLEY is director of the Multicultural Program in the Faculty of Education at the University of British Columbia, Vancouver, B.C. A born South African from the Indian community, she wrote her Ph.D. dissertation, "Resistance and Accommodation in a Racial Polity," on the political behavior of South African Indians and has published several articles on the subject in addition to various publications on comparative ethnicity and educational policies, among them *Race Relations and Multicultural Education* (U.B.C. Centre for Curriculum Studies and Instruction).

Compositor:	Wilsted & Taylor
Printer:	Vail-Ballou Press
Binder:	Vail-Ballou Press
Text:	Baskerville
Display:	Janson